CHAMPAGNE, UNCORKED

CHAMPAGNE, UNCORKED

THE HOUSE *of* KRUG
and the TIMELESS ALLURE
of the WORLD'S MOST
CELEBRATED DRINK

ALAN TARDI

PUBLICAFFAIRS

New York

PublicAffairs books are available at special discounts for bulk purchases
in the U.S. by corporations, institutions, and other organizations.
For more information, please contact the Special Markets Department
at the Perseus Books Group, 2300 Chestnut Street, Suite 200,
Philadelphia, PA 19103, call (800) 810-4145, ext. 5000,
or e-mail special.markets@perseusbooks.com.

Set in 11.5-point Goudy Oldstyle STD

Library of Congress Cataloging-in-Publication Data

Names: Tardi, Alan, 1956– author.
Title: Champagne, uncorked : the house of Krug and the timeless allure
    of the world's most celebrated drink / Alan Tardi.
Description: First edition. | New York : PublicAffairs, [2016] | Includes
    bibliographical references.
Identifiers: LCCN 2016007400| ISBN 9781610396882 (hardcover) |
    ISBN 9781610396899 (ebook)
Subjects: LCSH: Champagne (Wine)
Classification: LCC TP555 .T37 2016 | DDC 641.2/224—dc23
LC record available at http://lccn.loc.gov/2016007400

First Edition

10 9 8 7 6 5 4 3 2 1

To all the people of Champagne, past, present, and future, who through their limitless passion, consummate skill, and unshakeable commitment make Champagne the superlative libation that it is.

And to Fernanda and Lucia, who put the sparkle into my life.

AUTHOR'S NOTE

THIS is a work of nonfiction, although I have taken the liberty to interpret events and motives, and some of the names of people I encountered on my visits to Champagne have been changed. Information deemed confidential or proprietary by Krug has been omitted.

CONTENTS

PART III: MATURITY: *THE POSTMODERN ERA AND THE REBIRTH OF CHAMPAGNE*

PROLOGUE

GENIE IN THE BOTTLE

WINE exists on two different levels. One is earthly: a comestible beverage, a source of calories, an everyday ritual, a commodity, and, for some, a means of income. The other is extra-terrestrial: an agent of transformation, a mysterious elixir that can stimulate profound sensory experiences, stretching our capacities to smell, taste, see, and even touch; a potion that can magically lift us out of the daily routine and transport us to other times and places, nearby or far away, real or imagined, while at the same time locking us even deeper into a moment; a libation that can bring us from the earthly banal to higher realms of the poetic and even the divine.

These second-level transformational experiences don't have to be earth-shattering events announced by the sounding of celestial trumpets. They are often quite subtle and very brief, and their occurrence is unpredictable and impossible to induce. But anyone who truly loves wine will remember having had experiences like this.

There is also, perhaps, a third level on which wine exists: non-existence. Some people don't drink wine for medical reasons, some just don't like it, and others have either never had it or not yet developed a taste for it. And that's where I was for the first twenty years of my life.

I was born in Chicago and grew up in a suburb adjacent to the city that was "dry." Illinois was not (and probably never will be) a wine-producing region, and wine was not a fixture on our table. Even on the rare occasions when it was there, such as Christmas dinner with the entire extended second-generation Italian family, the sour stuff was of no interest to me whatsoever. I much preferred the syrupy sweet carbonated beverage that midwesterners call *pop*.

Many years and two colleges later, I found myself in New York City and, with nearly two years of accumulated credits, decided to make a now-or-never push to finish my undergraduate degree in the facile, if not necessarily career-oriented, field of liberal arts. I enrolled in the undergraduate division of an alternative institution called the New School for Social Research and set about looking for a job to help finance my educational objective.

I got lucky: I walked into a restaurant and immediately got a job washing dishes (*hey, a job is a job,* I thought). Despite my lack of experience I did pretty well; I quickly got promoted to busboy, then waiter. Eventually I wandered into the open kitchen, and that's where I stayed.

Before that, the idea of cooking had never crossed my mind, but I liked the work, the schedule was flexible, and the money wasn't bad either. In addition to the exotic thrill of preparing food for paying customers, I also got the opportunity (thanks to the open kitchen) to watch them eat it, and much to my surprise, they seemed to enjoy it. I also noticed that many of them were drinking wine with their meal, and they seemed to be enjoying that too. I didn't really understand what the fuss was about; I had no notion of the concept of wine-food pairing and no firsthand experience of what wine could bring to the table. But watching people night after night eating and drinking and having a good time, it wasn't long before I became curious and wanted to try it for myself.

Not far from my school in the West Village was a tiny sliver of a restaurant called Chez Brigitte that consisted of a six-seat Formica counter and three tiny two-tops shoved up against the wall. Here, in the narrow kitchen behind the counter, Brigitte, with the help of a young French assistant, whipped up simple, inexpensive yet tasty food. In addition to the small printed menu, each day of the week featured a special dish such as coq au vin (Monday), gigot d'agneau (Wednesday), or boeuf bourguignon (Thursday). I soon became a regular. I would go two or three times a week after classes, take a seat at the counter, and practice my French with Brigitte and her assistant while I ate.

On my well-trodden path from school to Chez Brigitte I regularly passed by a wine shop, and one evening I decided to pick up a half-bottle to bring with me. The selection of half bottles was limited, but it was a fine place to start. I tried whatever they had and soon began selecting the wine according to the daily special I knew would be on offer that evening: bordeaux with lamb, beaujolais with chicken, gigondas with duck. The French women seemed to get a kick out of it. I began offering them a taste of whatever I had, which they graciously accepted, eliciting comments such as "Ah oui, c'est très bon!" or "C'est pas mal, pas mal de tout."

I don't remember any of the wines—indeed, while perfectly acceptable, they were all remarkably unremarkable—but having them was fun: the rough wine complemented the homey food nicely, and opening the little bottle contributed a festive air to what had already become something of a ritual.

Then it happened.

One night, while heading home to write a paper about George Sand that was due the next day, I happened to pass by a different wine shop. Just for the heck of it, I went inside. Amidst the multitude of dusty bottles on the shelves and counters, my eye fell upon a thick, bulbous bottle with a handwritten label and an unfamiliar but intriguing name: Amarone.

When I got home, I lifted the bottle out of its crumpled brown paper bag, figured out how to chip the shiny red wax off the top, and carefully twisted the screw into the tight yet porous cork, thinking to have half a glass before attacking my homework.

The moment I eased the cork out, a powerful aroma leapt out of the bottle and filled the room like the swirling smoke of a genie that then settled itself into the glass in front of me. An enticingly dark red-black liquid seemed to absorb and reflect all the light around it. Scents of black cherries, licorice, chocolate, soft rubber, rubbing alcohol, and fruitcake (which I had never actually eaten but had smelled on occasion) filled the air. And when I tasted it, flavors of extra-ripe cherries, dried cranberries, black plums, dried figs, and something like fresh tobacco exploded in my mouth and stretched all the way down my throat with a glycerin-like intensity that left a slight burn of bitter almond in its wake.

What's more, the playful genie kept changing. Each time I went back for another sip the wine was different, and it just kept getting better and better. Until it was all gone.

I can't remember what I ate that night, much less the paper I was supposed to write, but the wine left me enthralled (not to mention a bit tipsy). I had never tasted anything like it before, and it felt as if my senses had been shaken awake for the first time.

That experience left an impression long after the wine was finished. It was a sort of turning point. After that, I began to take my part-time job in the restaurant a bit more seriously and even gained a new appreciation for the simple pleasures of Chez Brigitte. And, once I finally had my bachelor's degree, I decided to pursue a career in the kitchen.

I got lucky yet again. I worked in a few superlative restaurants with great chefs (including the legendary Chanterelle with chef/co-owner David Waltuck, in a just-about-to-become-hot area of New York called SoHo, and the game-changing Lafayette with Jean-Georges Vongerichten) and formidable wine lists that helped broaden my vinous (not to mention culinary) horizons. This was not so much a conscious attempt to expand my knowledge as a spontaneous invitation to discover a whole new world that presented itself simply because I happened to be in places where wine was viewed as an essential part of the dining experience and, by extension, of life. Occasionally, bottles with a little leftover wine would make their way back to the kitchen, and each one brought with it a slight thrill of discovery. In this way I became acquainted with many different types of wine, such as vintage port, grand cru burgundy, and first growth bordeaux. This was intriguing and educational, but the genies were far and few between (as genies, I would later learn, usually are). I tried many Champagnes too, some of them quite fancy and expensive, but most of them left me underwhelmed.

Then I tasted Krug. I don't remember which restaurant kitchen I was in or what the circumstances surrounding it were, but I have never forgotten the wine.

When the bottle made the rounds, the first thing I noticed was the name. It didn't sound French, like the other Champagnes I had encountered, and the label featured four stubby letters instead of the usual elegantly italicized script. When someone passed me a glass, I saw a delicate double helix of bubbles slowly circling its way to the surface, and a sniff inside revealed a tightly knit collection of aromas that was subtle yet pungent: crunchy pear, creamy caramel, fragrant lemon, buttery brioche, dried spice, and chalky phosphate.

I took a sip.

Like the amarone's beautiful, softer yet nonetheless potent little sister, the wine expanded on the palate and was full of apparent contradictions—it had grip and body but was elegantly sylphlike and gently effervescent at the same time; there was ripe fruit and tight lemon-rind acidity, rich caramel and flinty mineral. Even more compelling was that these contrasting elements all fit together into a beautifully balanced, cohesive whole that kept evolving on the palate up to a crescendo, then down to a long graceful fade.

I only got one sip: the wine, passed from cook to cook, quickly disappeared. But I took another look at the empty bottle; there was no vintage, which only increased the wine's allure. Beneath the name, whose initial Teutonic gruffness was already beginning to take on an aura of exotic beauty for me, were the words *Grande Cuvée*.[1]

I had never tasted anything quite like it. It had the character, depth, complexity, and finesse that set truly great wines apart from the rest. And the delicate effervescence added a whole other dimension. I was smitten.

I went on to become a chef and restaurateur, and started writing about wine and food. At a certain point early on in my cooking career, before I had my own restaurant, I took a wine class. It was a basic introduction to wine, and the specimens themselves weren't particularly exceptional. But it gave me three fundamental tools: it exposed me to the basic process of critically evaluating a glass of wine (look, smell, taste, spit, reflect, taste again); it forced me to try to describe my impressions of what I tasted, and then share and compare them with other class members' impressions; and in doing so, while thrusting me face to face with the fundamental impossibility of precisely articulating in words something as elusive as a smell or a flavor (much less a particular combination of many), it helped me gradually develop a language to at least roughly indicate with some accuracy what I was experiencing.

As my food and wine career developed, I tasted many, many wines, as well as many Champagnes. Some of them were very good. But few could compare with my Krug experience.

I was not alone. Krug, I learned after that first encounter, holds a special place in the hearts and palates of wine aficionados and Champagne geeks; the name is whispered with reverence, and the unostentatious house routinely receives the very highest scores and accolades. It is the smallest of the so-called *grande marques*, a group of mostly large, well-established Champagne brands, and is quirkily unique and quintessentially classic at the same time.

In the spring of 2012, some twenty years after my initial encounter with the bubbly genie, I happened to receive an invitation to visit Krug in Reims and take part in a tour and blending seminar for journalists, and I jumped at the opportunity.

This was my first visit to the region, and whatever I might have been expecting, it was not what I found. Champagne was very different from any of the other wine areas I had visited, and much harder to get a handle on.

As I traveled by car from Charles de Gaulle Airport, the concentrated morass of urban industry dissolved into a wide expanse of flat fields, out of which vineyards began to emerge only as we neared Reims. Even then, the vine-growing area was less dramatic and less hilly than I'd thought it was going to be. It appeared to be oddly superficial and tightly controlled rather than spontaneous and natural, as if someone had attentively decorated his extensive backyard with well-placed accents of vineyard topiaries. In Reims, many of the famous Champagne houses we passed looked more like palaces than wineries, and outside the city the landscape was both concentrated and distended, with two distinct facets: some places were packed with short rows of perfectly spaced, closely cropped vines extending out as far as the eye could see, while others, completely devoid of vines, were given over to fields or woods or sleepy little villages.

I sensed something strangely mysterious, almost sinister, about the place, as if the placid surroundings of ordered vine rows and gently sloping vineyards were hiding some magical secret deep beneath them.

On the morning of the first day we gathered in the tiny walled estate of Clos du Mesnil, where our host, Olivier Krug, went around pouring amber-yellow liquid from a label-less magnum. After a formal welcome, we raised our glasses, made a toast, and had a taste. While you could tell right away by the color that this was not a young wine, the aroma was invitingly fresh and vivacious, and what had seemed barely bubbly in the glass turned into a persistent tingle on the palate. The first flavor sensation of crème caramel was followed by toasted hazelnuts, lively citric acidity, and a racy mineral finish. "Any guesses on the vintage?" Olivier asked offhandedly, with the slightest hint of mischievousness in his raised eyebrows. Silence. I am no expert on Champagne vintages, especially old ones, but 1996 first crossed my mind. Then I took another look at the color and remembered where I was. 1985 perhaps? Or maybe even 1979? Wrong on all counts: this wine, Olivier said, was vintage 1961. I was dumbfounded! Over fifty years old, still bright and fresh as a spring blossom after a shower, and showing no signs of fading any time soon. In an instant, standing in the gravel court of Clos du Mesnil on a crisp morning in early spring, time seemed to warp, to expand and contract simultaneously; time seemed to have become, well, timeless.

The next day, back in Reims, we had a tasting of still wines from the recent vintage along with a handful of older reserve wines, then broke into small groups and, seated at large round tables, got to play with a dozen different samples to try to come up with our own Grande Cuvée blend. It was a tough but fascinating exercise and we got to taste and critique all of our entries. Then we tasted theirs . . .

These experiences were stimulating and engaging but, like a good book or charming company, they left me wanting more. This first foray into the peculiar world of Champagne raised many more questions than it answered: How could a wine of such advanced age still seem so fresh and alive, being both a well-preserved relic of time gone by and yet somehow timeless? How is it that numerous different wines from different grape varieties, different places, and even different vintages can be blended together into a seamless whole that is much more than the sum of its parts, a whole in which each of the numerous constituents makes its own special contribution without sacrificing its individual identity? What was the mysterious secret that seemed to be lurking beneath the cool Gallic surface? And where did the genie that appeared late one night in a New York restaurant kitchen and left an indelible impression in my sensory data bank for over two decades actually come from?

These questions lingered long after I got home and persisted despite my best attempts to ignore or dispel them. Though I didn't quite

know how, the house of Krug seemed the portal to finding the an-
swers and the Grande Cuvée, this strange composite of time and
place, seemed the key. My nagging curiosity grew into an obsession: I
had to somehow unlock that door and see what was behind it.

Not knowing what else to do, I wrote to Olivier Krug, director
and sixth-generation descendant of the founder of the company, and
Margareth Henríquez, its president and chief executive officer. A
few weeks later Henríquez, much to my surprise, wrote back. Champagne houses have a reputation for being guardedly secretive, and
part of me had expected to be flatly dismissed or politely ignored.
Even more surprising, her response was not an outright refusal. Henríquez said she was intrigued but needed more information about exactly what I wanted to do.

We corresponded back and forth for nearly a year. Gradually,
things began to take shape, though much still remained unavoidably
blurry. It was hard to precisely articulate what I wanted to do because
so much was unknown to me. But, like an archaeologist setting out
to discover some lost civilization, I knew I wanted to trace each and
every step in the process of creating Krug Grande Cuvée to better
understand Champagne, as well as the method of making it and the
place it comes from. In order to do this I would need complete and
unfettered access to everyone and everything involved, including
the sacred sanctuary of the tasting room. And in order to make any
sense out of what I might find, I also knew I would have to learn
much, much more about the Champagne region and the history and
evolution of the wine.

Finally, after getting the approval of the *chef de cave*, Margareth
said yes.

And the following spring I embarked on a new journey.

RUE COQUEBERT

IT'S a typical late-autumn day in Champagne. Dampness hangs heavy in the sky, as if it can't decide whether to rain or snow or just sit there, while the pallid sun makes a halfhearted attempt to break through the haze but quickly gives up and crawls back under cover.

The vineyards that were green and vibrant and crawling with people just a few weeks ago are now mostly deserted, punctuated by the occasional *vigneron* (winegrower) on a low portable stool getting a jump-start on pruning, while the gnarly bare vines complacently slip into lethargy.

In the center of Reims, *pâtisseries* stock showcases with shiny tarts and creamy meringues while boutiques dismantle their now outdated window displays in anticipation of the coming holiday season. Industrious Rémois charge through their daily routines while stragglers linger inside cafés on the mostly deserted Place Drouet-d'Erlon, and tourists mill about the imposing Gothic cathedral that sits in stony silence, keeping to itself the multitude of glorious and infamous events it has witnessed over the centuries. Cars zip back and forth on the boulevards and mostly empty trams crawl along their rails, bells ringing hollowly, until the time comes to bring their patrons back home from work.

There's an odd quiet, a pervasive feeling of suspension.

A pall has fallen over Champagne like a thick down blanket—well, over most of it.

Walk up boulevard Lundy, away from the cathedral and the center of town, past well-kept apartment buildings, the Anglican church, and several sedately ornate, elegant châteaux that are the palatial headquarters of some of the most famous Champagne firms. Before you get to the post office on the left and the airplane hangar–like Boulingrin market, turn right onto a narrow side street called rue Coquebert.

Several meters in on the left you come to a maroon gate, opening (if it happens to be open) onto a large rectangular courtyard bordered by a three-sided conglomeration of two-story neoclassical buildings. Each section looks a bit different, as if constructed at different times or designed by different people, though they are stylistically similar and fit together into a pleasant if decidedly archaic whole. Peaked eaves project above the upper edge of the second floor and the windows have decorative burnt sienna–colored brickwork over the top, which makes them resemble heavily mascaraed eyes.

A chain across the entryway keeps trespassers out, and a guard behind a glass door attentively monitors comings and goings. Inside, blue-jumpsuited workers roll old barrels from one side of the courtyard into an opening on the other, moving slowly and methodically, as if thinking of lunch or the weekend or the holidays ahead.

Built into the center of the concrete façade under an eave at the far end of the courtyard is a large clock—the time is 10:54—and on the second floor, directly under the clock, is a room that looks out onto the courtyard.

The space inside the room is simple and functional, even a bit bare. The walls and ceiling are a neutral creamy white. A glass wall separates this room from the one on the other side, which is full of cluttered desks and a long counter covered with laboratory beakers; a refrigerator sits in the corner, and slatted blinds cover the windows.

In the center of the room is a large smooth-topped kidney-shaped table with five round sinks built into it, each with its own faucet, waterspout, and drain. A cluster of tall, tapered, clear glass bottles sits in the center of the table. The liquid inside them varies from transparent beige to pale yellow, and each bottle sports a small hand-written label displaying a few letters and numbers.

The table is surrounded by five tall swivel chairs, three of which are occupied: Julie, assistant winemaker, supervises the harvest and vinification at Clos du Mesnil, one of the winery's most prestigious estates; Laurent is in charge of overall vinification; and twenty-three-year-old Jérôme is the youngest member of the enology team and most recent arrival.

This day began like any other: as each arrived at Rue Coquebert and traversed the courtyard to their workplaces in the rear, there was the usual flurry of air kisses, handshakes, and "*Salut, ça va!*" with jump-suited workers and colleagues. At around nine o'clock the enology crew congregated in the coffee closet, as they do most every day, to chat and gossip over an espresso, then each went on about his or her business. But it wouldn't be business as usual for long because, despite outward appearances, today is not just any day.

Today is the first tasting of the wines from the most recent harvest of 2013, the beginning of an exhaustive process that will last for months and result in critical decisions that will resonate for many years to come. And the young enologists, while they might try to feign otherwise, are well aware of it.

There's a pervasive, barely contained sense of tension and antici-pation in the air. All of them have done this before (except Jérôme, perhaps, who makes a noble effort to contain his excitement). But it happens only once a year, each year is different, and you never know exactly what's going to happen. Even the most seasoned veterans cannot help feeling a bit curious and excited, even a little nervous, as if they've been dealt a hand of cards in a high-stakes game of poker and can't wait to see what they've got.

But they can't look yet.

So they sit in silence, swiveling back and forth or staring off into space, each in their own world. Their minds drift: they think back over the growing season, the harvest, and the fermentation, wondering whether they got it right, hoping they made the right decisions, wondering how this vintage will turn out.

The recent harvest was not an easy one—it rarely is—but it got done: the grapes were picked and crushed, the juice was fermented, the wines made. And now samples of fifteen of them, the first ones, siphoned out from the barrels, are sitting in the clear glass bottles on the table.

The clock ticks steadily on. These quiet minutes are a fulcrum, a luxurious moment of reflection and anticipation, a brief pause at a bend in the long road that lies ahead. In a way, their work is done. In another way, it is just beginning.

As the big hand inches straight up to twelve and the smaller hand settles squarely in front of eleven, the door opens and Chef de Cave Eric Lebel bounces briskly into the room in a black suit with open-collared white shirt, clutching a big black notebook. He says *bonjour* to no one in particular, slips into his seat, and pauses a moment to look up and around at the three individuals who have suddenly sat up to attention. As he opens the notebook and takes a pen out of his jacket pocket, the corners of his mouth crinkle into the slightest hint of a smile, black pen poised in readiness before the blank page. "So, shall we begin?"

PART I

IN THE BEGINNING
THE BIRTH OF CHAMPAGNE

CHAPTER 1

❧ ❦

WHAT LIES BENEATH–
LA CHAMPAGNE VITICOLE

CHAMPAGNE is not like other wine regions. It's not as dramatic or picturesque as many of the other famous wine areas, and it's much more spread out and disjointed. You can get an idea of this just by looking at the map: where most other wine regions appear as a contiguous blob or swath, Champagne looks as if someone splattered paint on a canvas, creating a hodgepodge of small irregular splotches over a wide-open space, more concentrated in some parts and sparser in others.

And that's basically how it is: the splotches represent the official Champagne growing region (known as *la Champagne viticole*) and that's where the vines are; no splotches means it's not part of the appellation, which partly explains why it's possible to find dense forests or fields of sugar beets right next to prestigious grand cru vineyards.

Now, if Jackson Pollock had designed it, this might be pure artistic fancy. But this map was essentially created by nature and articulated by farmers and winemakers over a long period of time. (See the map of the Champagne area on page 1 of the glossy insert.) The vines are where they are mostly because those particular places have been proven, by trial and error over hundreds of years, to be good

7

places to grow grapes.[1] And while many of the common factors of *terroir*, such as altitude and exposition, do have an impact, in Champagne what really makes these places good—and significantly different from the vineless ones right next to them—has much to do with what lies beneath the surface.[2]

The principal section of the Champagne zone, in the northern department of the Marne, lies on the eastern side of a geologic formation called the Paris Basin, a large indentation in the earth that extends from present-day Alsace in the east to coastal Normandy in the west, with Paris roughly in the middle. The dip was originally formed in the Triassic period about 250 million years ago and partially filled in during the subsequent Jurassic. Most of the critical activity, however, occurred during the turbulent Cretaceous period, when the earth was lifted by seismic activity, causing the water that covered it to retreat and leave behind a thick sludge of marine material, including huge deposits of a now extinct type of squid known as a belemnite and an ancient type of sea urchin called a micraster. Left high and dry, the stuff decayed, dried out, and, over millions of years, turned into a compressed layer of chalk.

Finally, during the Tertiary period (about 68 to 1.8 million years ago), a series of geologic events lifted some portions of the chalk into cliffs and displaced others, covering just about everything with a sedimentary layer of varying thickness consisting of various combinations of limestone, clay, sand, and marl.

In some places the chalk is hundreds of feet thick and vine roots are forced to grow deep down into fissures to find moisture, while in others the chalk layer is thinner or broken up and mixed with other types of matter, all of which makes a big difference to the grapes that are grown in it. Most of the belemnite chalk is found on higher elevations, while the micraster is usually present on lower slopes and valleys. But even more important than the type of chalk is how it was displaced and reshaped by geologic upheaval. The Vallée de la Marne, for example, is a flatter valley with more soil on top of the chalk and alluvial deposits left by the river that cuts through it, while certain areas of the Montagne de Reims and Côte des Blancs consist of very deep veins of chalk with a shallow layer of topsoil.

"Champagne owes its greatness as a wine province to the chalk of the Upper Cretaceous," says geologist James E. Wilson. "Champagne's vines have their heads in the Tertiary and their feet in the Cretaceous. . . . The trunks and branches of the vineplants, the 'heads,' grow upward from the soils of the Tertiary slope wash, while the roots, the 'feet,' explore the underlying, fractured Cretaceous chalk."[3]

So what's so great about chalk?

Chalk is softer and more porous than limestone and less dense than clay. This means it offers excellent drainage, which is important for avoiding root rot, but also acts like a sponge to retain water and release it to the roots of the vines when they need it. Deposits of chalk under a thin layer of topsoil absorb heat from the sun during the day and release it at night, helping to protect the vines from cold temperatures, which helps explain why vines in Champagne are densely planted and trained low to the ground. Finally, the organic composition of chalk gives the wines made from grapes grown in it distinct mineral flavors, crisp acidity, a lighter, more elegant body, and even a natural tendency towards a slight fizz (known as *pétillance* in French), all of which helps increase the wine's potential for longevity.

But geology is just the tip of the iceberg.

Besides soil, the other critical factor in understanding *la Champagne viticole* is the climate.

The region is located in northeastern France near the 49th parallel north, the invisible boundary beyond which it becomes too cold for grapevines to grow.[4] Days of sunlight are relatively few and annual rainfall is moderate.[5] While oceanic influences help mitigate extreme temperatures in both winter and summer, the continental effects of an inland location often get the upper hand, resulting in devastating spring frosts and sporadic hailstorms during summer and early autumn.

The combination of a northern climate and complex geology makes for a unique, extremely fragmented, and particularly challenging environment in which to grow wine grapes. Were it not for the stubbornness, stoicism, and ingenuity of its inhabitants (as well as, perhaps, their determination not to let their southern neighbors in Burgundy get the upper hand), winemaking in this area would probably have been abandoned long before the name *Champagne* became familiar throughout the world.

La Champagne viticole covers a vast surface area comprising five *départements* (the French equivalent of a county) in three different regions: Marne, Haute-Marne, and Aube in the region of Champagne-Ardenne; Seine-et-Marne in the region of Île de France; and Aisne in the region of Picardy.[6] It contains 320 towns and thousands of named vineyard sites (known as *lieux-dits*) extending over a huge surface area of over a hundred miles from north to south and over sixty miles from east to west. But of this extensive area, only 33,500 hectares (nearly 83,000 acres) under vine (represented by the splotches all over the map) comprise the Champagne AOC appellation.[7]

There are four main growing areas. In the north, the Marne, with its two commercial and administrative capitals of Reims and Épernay, is divided into three main sections: the Montagne de Reims, the Vallée de la Marne (also known as the Rivière), and the Côte des Blancs. The fourth main area, the Côte des Bar in the department of the Aube, consists of two parts, the Bar-sur-Aube and Bar-sur-Seine. Besides these four main sections, there are a number of satellite areas, including the Vallée de la Vesle, Vallée de l'Ardre, and the Massif de Saint-Thierry to the northwest of Reims; the Côte de Sézanne just south of the Côte des Blancs; Vitry-le-François off by itself to the southeast; and the towns of Les Riceys and Montgueux in the Aube.

While each area, each town, and indeed each vineyard has its own unique features, there are major differences between the north and the south: the Aube has a different geologic composition than the Marne, with significantly less chalk and more limestone and clay.[8]

Adding to the complexity of terroir is the fact that there are a number of different grape varieties.

Seven different grape varieties may legally be used to make Champagne; three of them—the white chardonnay, red meunier, and pinot noir[9]—are by far the most important and most widely planted. The four other permitted grapes, the so-called lost varieties—arbane, petit meslier, pinot blanc, and pinot gris—are quite obscure and today make up less than 0.3 percent of the vines planted.[10]

Over time certain areas have demonstrated themselves to be particularly well suited for certain grape varieties. The Montagne de Reims is most renowned for its pinot noir, the valley along the Marne River is ideal for meunier, and, as its name suggests, the Côte des Blancs is almost entirely devoted to white grapes, principally chardonnay.[11] The Aube grows pinot noir and chardonnay as well as its local specialty, pinot blanc, though with its more southern position and limestone-clay soil, the character of the grapes is distinctly different from those of the Marne—riper, rounder, and darker in color, with a bit less mineral finesse.

In most areas, winemaking is a fairly straightforward process: grow the grapes, pick them when they're ripe, crush, ferment (red grapes are typically macerated with the skins to extract color), and *voilà!*— wine. Not so in Champagne.

Ripening is not always easy in the volatile northern climate, and due to the diversity and expanse of the growing area, some subzones and some grape varieties do significantly better in some years than others.

Over centuries of grappling with the unpredictable forces of nature only to have the fruit of their labors destroyed by a flash hailstorm or other devastating act of God, winemakers in Champagne, unable to change the weather and unwilling to go anywhere else, eventually realized that the best, if not only, way to hedge their bets was to source different grape varieties from different areas throughout the zone.

Besides helping to ensure they would have something to make wine with, the superior qualities of one grape variety from a particular area in a given year helped compensate for the shortcomings of another. Given the great variations in quality and quantity from one year to the next, winemakers began to set aside some wine in excellent bountiful years to help make up for shortfalls in the inevitable poor ones.[12] Thus, blending—an essential and fundamental aspect of the wine that developed into what we now know as Champagne—was born.

CHAPTER 2

INTO THE VINEYARDS– VINTAGE 2013

"*C'EST pas gagné cette année, non, pas du tout.*" We haven't won this year yet,[1] says Eric in response to my casual question about how the vintage is shaping up. His low, scowling voice suggests a French version of Clint Eastwood on his way to a shoot-out.

We're sitting in his Audi, which has been decked out like a mobile command post with his smartphone hooked into the car's audio and digital display, radar detection device, and GPS navigation, crawling through morning traffic out of Reims, on our way to visit some of Krug's suppliers and their vineyards. Eric's been doing this for nearly a month now and has already logged over a thousand miles on his odometer.

"It's mid-September," he says. "Usually harvest is starting to wind down about now. This year we haven't even started yet."

Without taking his eyes off the road, he takes a square piece of chewing gum from the plastic receptacle in the cup holder and, popping it in his mouth, gives me a snapshot of the growing season thus far.

Heavy snows along with frequent subzero temperatures were recorded from mid-January to mid-March. The month of March was the coldest since 1971 and the cold hung on through the spring, except for a mini heat wave in mid-April that shot temperatures up to a balmy seventy-seven degrees Fahrenheit.

This burst of warmth had a positive effect on the vines, he tells me, causing bud break, the first step in the annual growing cycle of the grapes, which took place between the twenty-fourth and twenty-ninth of April, about two weeks later than usual. But the clement weather was short-lived.

While May began relatively warm, things quickly deteriorated into a burst of exceptional cold, as if winter was trying to make a comeback, with heavy, nearly continuous rain that dumped four and a half inches on Épernay and nearly eight on the Côte des Bar.

Luckily, spring frosts were relatively few, but warmer temperatures in June brought with them a series of violent thunderstorms accompanied by scattered hail that did substantial damage while strong winds broke branches and upset the fragile baby grape clusters.

Happily, the end of June segued into a warm, sunny, and mostly dry July, and, as if seizing their opportunity, the nascent clusters went quickly into flower and pollination. Conditions stayed favorable for the most part, with the exception of sporadic hailstorms, and the pinot noir and meunier began to change color around mid-August, a good two weeks later than what is normal for the region.[2]

"*Et voilà*. That's it, up till now," he concludes. "It's like being on a roller coaster at Disneyland, except there you know how it will end: the ride stops, you get off, you go get an ice cream. Here we have no idea."

Outside Reims we enter a traffic circle, and Eric accelerates quickly to prevent another car from entering in front of him. Eric likes driving and likes cars. He helped locate and supervise the acquisition and restoration of a stunning 1979 Rolls-Royce Silver Shadow II, and he has a vintage automobile of his own that he uses for relaxed cruises around Champagne. But now is no time for relaxation.

It's the beginning of the third week of September and the grapes are only at 65–70 percent veraison, a term of French origin that refers to the color change of grapes from green to red (or golden yellow in the case of white grapes).

"That means we're going to harvest pinot noir and meunier around mid-October," Eric continues. "That hasn't happened here since 1979. A late harvest can be very tricky. The light is different, less intense, so it's harder for the grapes to mature properly. I suspect we'll see many cases of clusters that haven't ripened sufficiently or evenly. There's a much greater risk of problems due to rain, like mildew, oidium fungus,[3] and rot. Then there's the human factor: it's uncomfortable to pick in the rain and the *vendangeurs* [grape pickers] don't work as well."

What's more, because of the wet spring, the grapes have already absorbed an excess of water. At a certain point they can't take anymore and the skin explodes, which causes surrounding parts of the cluster to rot and attracts fruit flies that puncture the grapes. "It's not very pretty," says Eric. "And the meunier, with its soft skin, is especially vulnerable this year.

"It's a very delicate moment," he sums up, quickly accelerating along a straightaway to pass a slow-moving tractor. "Anything can happen."

∾∾

WHEN the ancient Romans first began colonizing the Champagne area around 300 AD, they quickly discovered that the thick vein of chalk beneath the soil made an excellent building material that was fairly easy to excavate, and excavate they did, leaving large conical caverns beneath the ground. (These underground caverns would turn out to be the perfect environment for the aging of Champagne, but that comes later.)

Once they had constructed their fortifications and settled in, the Romans started planting vineyards.[4] Then they discovered something else: despite the difficulties caused by the northerly climate, the poor, chalky soil made exceptional wine.

With the fall of the Roman Empire and the rise of Christianity, winemaking shifted to the monasteries.[5] Besides being necessary for the celebration of the Mass, wine was an important part of the monks' diet as well as a source of income for monastic communities. Monasteries often received land as a gift and, more importantly, had the labor force to cultivate it and the knowledge to transform the grapes into wine. Winemaking thrived in the monasteries of north-eastern France during the Middle Ages, and viticulture made significant advances. Most of the monks who orchestrated these advances remained anonymous; some of them did not.

In the eleventh century, the Cistercian Order was flourishing in Burgundy and the Cistercians were as renowned for the cultivation of grapes and the making of wine as they were for their pristine architectural style. In 1115, a Cistercian monk named Bernard—later *Saint* Bernard—was sent to the Aube in the southern part of Champagne to start a monastery, and he brought his wine savvy along with him, planting vineyards and building wine cellars to support the fledgling community. Thanks in part to the success of its winemaking activities, the monastery, which became known as Abbaye de Clairvaux (Clear Valley Abbey), thrived. The charismatic Bernard rose to great heights in the church and developed a reputation for his holy powers, which attracted so many new monks to the monastery that additional monasteries had to be built to hold them all. Trois-Fontaines Abbey was created near Châlons in 1118 and many other offshoot communities quickly followed, spreading sophisticated winemaking operations throughout the region.

Five hundred years later, another monk had an even greater impact on the development of winemaking in Champagne.

Pierre Pérignon was born to a well-to-do family in early 1639 in the Marne town of Sainte-Menehould and was baptized on January 5 of that year. His father held the respectable position of clerk for the local marshal and was a vineyard owner. At the age of seventeen, Pierre entered the Benedictine Abbey of Saint-Vanne in Verdun and shortly thereafter took his monastic orders.

Dom Pierre evidently distinguished himself during his years at Saint-Vanne because in 1668, at the age of twenty-nine, he was sent to the Abbey of Saint-Pierre in the town of Hautvillers as procurer, an important position that involved overseeing everything that came into and went out of the institution. The monastery, founded in 650, had been devastated during the French Wars of Religion, leaving it with only a handful of monks, crumbling buildings, and sparse resources, and the substantial holding of land it had acquired was in pitiful condition. Pérignon's task was to help get the religious community back on its feet.

The first thing he did was to get the vineyards in order, instructing his fellow monks to prune the vines short and low to the ground in order to obtain high-quality grapes.[6] In addition to the grapes from its own vineyards, the monastery also received grapes as tithes from landowners, and Pérignon insisted that vignerons supply only fruit of optimal quality. He was a stickler for harvesting at just the right moment and demanded that the picked grapes be brought immediately to the winery for pressing.

Dom Pérignon was one of the first on record to recognize the distinct differences of various micro-terroirs in Champagne and was one of the earliest advocates of conscientious blending. It was said he tasted the various lots of grapes as they arrived at the monastery (it was rumored he could tell exactly where they came from just by tasting them) and composed blends of complementary parcels to go into the press. Because at that time the wines of Champagne were prone to spoil quickly,[7] Pérignon favored pinot noir over chardonnay and made major advances in the specialized technique of extracting white juice from red grapes. He also recognized the qualitative differences in the juice produced at various stages during the pressing process—he found the first free-run liquid too weak and the juice extracted by heavy pressure at the end too bitter—and developed sophisticated practices of grape pressing that formed the basis for what became standard procedure and remains so to this day.

Dom Pérignon died in 1715 and was buried in the church at Hautvillers, but the popular myth of him as the father of Champagne was invented much later. Actually, it was invented twice: In 1821, one of his successors at Hautvillers named Dom Groussard attributed the creation of Champagne to Pérignon in order to enhance the reputation of the struggling monastery. A hundred years after that, the image of the monk as the creator of Champagne was put forth yet again by market-savvy entrepreneurs at a company called Moët & Chandon who were getting ready to launch a new Champagne called Dom Pérignon.[8] They were also probably the ones who were responsible for coming up with the now famous image of a blind monk who had just created sparkling wine exclaiming, "Brothers, come quickly! There are stars in my glass!"

In reality, Pérignon, like most other Champenois at that time, viewed bubbles as a flaw and did everything he could to prevent them.[9] Oddly enough, it was his unrelenting efforts to get rid of the bubbles and his strict insistence on quality that led him to make major improvements in winemaking, which spread throughout the area and paved the way for the development of the Champagne we know today.

Another monk who made a significant contribution to the development of viticulture in Champagne was a contemporary of Pérignon named Jean Oudart, of the Saint-Pierre-aux-Monts Abbey in Châlons-sur-Marne, who managed the abbey's vineyards and cellars in Pierry.[10] As Saint-Pierre-aux-Monts and Hautvillers were sister abbeys, Oudart and Pérignon surely collaborated in their winemaking activities and Oudart surely adopted the practices devised by his illustrious colleague. What's more, because Oudart was active nearly thirty years after Pérignon's death (he died in 1742), he was part of the evolution of Champagne from a still wine into an intentionally sparkling one and thus carried Dom Pérignon's legacy into the bubbly era. Oudart made significant contributions to the development of the Champagne method, and the wine of Pierry became quite well known.[11] Unlike Dom Pérignon, however, Oudart was largely forgotten and stayed that way until his tomb was rediscovered in 1972 by Claude Taittinger, who was then director of the house of Taittinger.[12]

During the late seventeenth and early eighteenth centuries, as Champenois continued to strive to refine their winemaking techniques and gradually come to terms with its natural inclination to sparkle, they also began to focus on solidifying the market for their wines, especially at the influential royal court of Paris. But they were not alone. The neighboring regions of Burgundy and Champagne—along with their respective noble rulers, the dukes of Burgundy and the counts of Champagne—had vied against one another for power and influence since at least 987, when Hugh Capet became king of France and instituted the Capetian dynasty, which would rule the country for more than three hundred years. And this competition naturally extended to the regions' wines.

Burgundy and Champagne have always been among France's most important wine-producing areas, and while the chief protagonists of both areas are the same—pinot noir and chardonnay—the wines they produce have always been quite different.

Lying to the south of Champagne, Burgundy has a slightly warmer and slightly less volatile climate, and the soil of its most important grape-growing area, the Côte d'Or, consists primarily of limestone and clay. These factors conspire to produce darker, riper, fuller-bodied wines, while those from Champagne's cooler climate and predominantly loose, chalky soil typically result in lighter-bodied, slightly transparent wines with more pronounced mineral characteristics.

Both Burgundy and Champagne were close to Paris and along the path of the lucrative trade routes to the north, and their wines competed for the favor of the court, just as their respective noble families did. Royal preference in wine, as in most everything else, dictated fashion and had a trickle-down effect that impacted heavily on the image and success of the region that produced it.

On the advice of his doctor, Antoine Daquin, Louis XIV drank nothing but Champagne at every meal, medical advice with which the Sun King was more than happy to comply. But as the king got older, his ailments inevitably increased. In 1693, a doctor named Guy-Crescent Fagon conspired with the king's mistress to undermine Daquin and get appointed as royal physician. Fagon attributed the king's health problems to the unstable nature of the wine from Champagne and insisted that only Burgundy be poured at the royal table. While this certainly came as a big blow to the Champenois, when Louis XIV died in 1715, Dr. Fagon was disgraced and sent into exile, and the competition between the two regions, along with the polemical debate about the relative health benefits of burgundy versus Champagne, raged on.[13]

It should be remembered that the Champagne Louis XIV drank was not the bubbly beverage we know today but rather a still wine (albeit one that frequently had a slight fizz or *pétillance*). And on this playing field, even with Dr. Fagon out of the way, the Champenois were at a distinct disadvantage: their reds were paler and their whites more volatile than those of their southern neighbor. Eventually they came to the realization that the best (if not only) way to gain the upper hand was to play an entirely different game. It would, however, take them a while to figure out what the "other game" was, and the answer would come from a rather surprising place.

ᘒᘒ

VOLATILITY and paleness aside, and long before the game-changing ace in the hole (bubbles) would become apparent, the wine of Champagne did have its loyal admirers. And one of the most fervent of them was Charles de Marguetel de Saint-Denis, seigneur de Saint-Évremond. Saint-Évremond, as he was known in later life, was born in 1613 at the family seat in Saint Denis du Guast in Normandy and studied at colleges in Paris and Caen before joining the military at sixteen. Starting out as a soldier, he was quickly promoted to captain, then field marshal. He later became a statesman and an aide to the influential Cardinal Mazarin, while continuing to study philosophy and pursue literary activities as an essayist, satirist, and political commentator.[14]

But don't be misled by his pious-sounding moniker. More than anything, Saint-Évremond was a gourmand and a hedonist. He loved good food and wine, arguing that sensual pleasures stimulated the intellect, and sought to engage in these experiences as often as possible in the company of like-minded *bons vivants*.

During the coronation festivities of Louis XIV in 1654, Saint-Évremond and some of his colleagues organized a dinner in Paris that was attended by the bishop of Le Mans. And the bishop was appalled: "These gentlemen, in seeking refinement in everything, go to extremes: they can only eat Normandy veal; their partridges must come from the Auvergne, and their rabbits from La Roche-sur-Yon. They are no less particular as regards fruit and as to wine, they can only drink the good *coteaux* [growths] of Aÿ, Hautvillers and Avenay."[15]

The bishop's comments echoed throughout Paris, much to the amusement of Saint-Évremond and his young friends. As their notoriety spread, people started referring to them as *les coteaux*, and before long they decided to form an association to pursue their gastronomic interests known as the Ordre des Coteaux.[16]

In 1661, Saint-Évremond fell out of political favor and fled to London, where he settled into a pleasant life at the center of the freewheeling circle of English high society, which included a beautiful, flamboyant, and apparently irresistible Italian woman named Ortensia Mancini, Duchesse de Mazarin.[17]

Though Saint-Évremond never returned to France, he was never without his preferred beverage. He continued to drink the wine of Champagne, especially "the good *coteaux* of Aÿ, Hautvillers and Avenay," and he rarely drank alone, becoming something of an unofficial but very vocal and very effective ambassador. "Spare no cost to get Champagne Wines, tho' you were 200 Leagues from Paris," he advised.

> There is no Province that affords excellent Wines for all Seasons, but Champagne. It furnishes us with the Vin d'Ay, d'Avenet [Avenay], and d'Auvilé till the Spring; Tessy, Sillery, and Versenat [Verzanay], for the rest of the year.
>
> If you ask me which of all these wines I prefer, without being swayed by the Fashion of Tastes, which false Pretenders to Delicacy have introduced, I will tell you that the Vin d'Ay is the most Natural of all wines and the most wholesome, the most free from all smell of the Soil, and of the most exquisite Agreeableness, in regard to its Peach-Taste which is peculiar to it, and is in [my] Opinion, the chief of all tastes and flavors.[18]

Though Saint-Évremond never intended his writings to be published in his lifetime and remained staunchly antireligious throughout his entire adult life, after his death in 1703 he was buried in Poets' Corner in Westminster Abbey.

Thanks in large part to this witty sensualist with impeccable taste, the wine of Champagne became all the rage in English society, a rage that would take an unforeseen trajectory and later bounce back across the Channel to have a decisive impact on the development of the wine itself.

CHAPTER 3

✦❦ ❦✦

GROWERS, SUPPLIERS, PRESSES

THE Audi slows as we enter the village of Villers-Marmery, population 553, in the Montagne de Reims. Eric turns onto the main drag, rue Pasteur, which is lined with respectable little houses, glides over to the curb, and comes to a stop.

He gathers up his belongings. "We're here and right on time. *C'est bon.*"

As we close the car doors, the sound reverberates through the quiet, still morning: there's not a person or vehicle in sight; the village seems abandoned, as if a big picnic is taking place somewhere and the whole town is there. Moving around the car to retrieve some stuff from the trunk, Eric gives me a short briefing.

"The Moreau family has been supplying grapes to Krug since— well, since forever, three or four generations at least, practically as long as Krug has been in existence. Gérard gives his entire production to us, about three and a half hectares' worth of grapes, mostly Verzy chardonnay, Villers-Marmery chardonnay, and a small amount of Verzy pinot noir.[1] You'll see; he's very timid, a man of few words, but very solid, like the earth."

We walk up to the door, ring the bell, and wait. The three-story house is simple but very proper and well kept. A yellow tractor is parked in the driveway. After a few moments, the door is opened by a short, sturdy, sun-seasoned man with close-cropped grey hair, a healthy paunch, and neatly laundered sky-blue button-down shirt tucked into his belted jeans. He greets Eric warmly and offers me his hand; it has the smooth calluses and deep creases that come from a lifetime of work amidst the vines. His handshake is light, with not even a hint of a squeeze, but sincere.

He ushers us into the dining room–salon at the front of the house, with its shuttered windows facing the street, and we take seats at the shiny lacquered dinner table. Gérard offers coffee, which we both gladly accept, and goes into the kitchen to prepare it.

While Eric takes some papers from his briefcase and starts to examine them, I take a look around the room: little porcelain knick-knacks sit on an ornate end table and framed color photos of children sit atop a bureau; an antique floral-upholstered sofa looks like it has never been sat on, and paintings of nondescript landscapes hang on the walls. What most catches my eye, however, is an entire wall covered with old black-and-white photos: People standing behind wicker baskets full of grapes. A young man sitting proudly astride an old-fashioned tractor. A long formal banquet table lined with men in wide-lapel suits. And, in the center, an ancient hand-tinted portrait of a stoic couple staring staunchly out from the past.

After a few minutes Gérard comes back with a tray holding three demitasses, a dish of sugar cubes, and a *cafetière*, and sees me looking at the pictures. "*C'est ma famille*," he says simply.

Once the coffee has been poured and the sugar added and stirred, the two men, chef de cave and vigneron, get down to business. Eric looks over his sheet and switches his cell phone to calculator function. Names and numbers start flying. They speak in low tones; Eric does most of the talking, punctuated by Gérard replying "*oui*" or "*non*." Sometimes there appears to be a discrepancy that gets quickly ironed out. Quantities are verified. I try to follow their discussion, but there are many terms—*blocage, déblocage, DPLC,* and *reserve personnel*—that are completely mystifying to me, though I don't want to interrupt to find out their meaning.

"Okay, *c'est bon,*" says Eric, putting the papers back in his briefcase and standing up. The two men shake hands sealing the deal. "Shall we go see the vines?" After the coffee cups are brought to the kitchen, we go outside, climb into Gérard's white van, and head out to his vineyards. Each of us takes a row and walks up it, carefully inspecting the leaves and the clusters of not-quite-yet-ripened grapes.

As I know from my time in Italy, tasting grapes shortly before harvest can provide a fascinating glimpse into the growing season and a foretaste of what the wine might eventually be like. But I've never done it in Champagne and I can't wait to try. I take a grape and pop it into my mouth.

"No!" exclaims Eric. "Not like that! You must taste like this."

He plucks a grape and holds it between his thumb and index finger with the small hole where the grape was attached to the stalk pointing up. He puckers his lips, puts the grape between them, and squeezes the bottom with his fingers, extracting the flesh of the grape while leaving behind the skin, which he throws down onto the ground. He sucks in a bit of air and tastes, then a moment later he spits out the pips.

"You must taste only the inside of the grape, without the skin or the seeds."

This is different than how I was taught to taste grapes in the vineyards of Barolo, I point out in my defense.[2] "Yes, but you must remember that for Champagne we do not macerate. We don't get the tannin or the pigment from the skin, so it doesn't figure into our evaluation of the flavor profile, and the seeds only add bitterness. What we want to focus on when we taste Champagne grapes is the ripeness, acidity, intensity of flavor, and individual differences of terroir, how the grapes differ from one vineyard to the next. So no skin and no seeds."

As we quickly continue the march up our rows, Eric points out a cluster covered in what looks like thick grey dust. "Oidium, powdery mildew," he says, "but there's not very much so it's okay."

After a few minutes we stop, turn around, and march back out to the road. It all happens very fast—up and down, a quick glance but an important and telling one. Eric sums up his impressions when we get in the van: "There's not a huge amount of fruit but it's very nice, very nice indeed. Bravo, Gérard!"

We visit two more of Moreau's small plots and finish at one vineyard that consists of only four short rows, a perfect example of one of the most fragmented wine regions in the world. "You see?" says Eric. "*This* is Champagne: 277,000 different parcels in 84,000 acres of vines. That's an average of one-third acre per parcel! It's completely crazy."

Back in the chef-de-cave-mobile on our way to the next visit, Eric pops another piece of gum. "Gérard Moreau is a vigneron: he grows grapes, sometimes he presses them too—he has a beautiful old two-thousand-kilo press and it's in perfect condition—but he does not make Champagne. The people we're going to visit now are *négociant-manipulant,* which means that they grow grapes and make some wine, but they also buy grapes too, and they press grapes for others, such as Krug. There are many different types of winemaking activity in Champagne and different types of *pressoirs,* too, as you will see."[3]

❧

SEPARATING the liquid from the solid parts of grapes is an essential step in the process of making any wine, but it is especially critical in the making of Champagne, where it usually involves the extraction of clear liquid from red grapes. And in Champagne, the technology of extracting the juice, as laid out by Dom Pérignon and his contemporaries, developed right alongside the development of the wine itself.

In the olden days people simply collected grapes in a large vessel and crushed them with their feet. Usually the juice (known as *must*) sat there with the solids throughout the process of fermentation.

When the grapes were red, the liquid in which the crushed grapes were sitting leached pigment out of the skins and took on a reddish color. (The steeping of the grape solids in the juice to extract flavor, color, and tannin is called *maceration*.) At a certain point the wine was strained off and the solids were pressed or squeezed to remove as much liquid as possible.

In Champagne, where the grapes are naturally a bit lighter in ripeness and extract (as well as in natural sugar) and higher in subtlety and finesse, it is especially critical to carefully preserve all their qualities of flavor and aroma during the extraction of the liquid.[4] Because the grapes do not usually macerate before fermentation but rather go directly into the press, stems and all, they are more vulnerable to spoilage.[5] And because most of the grapes used to make Champagne are red, the pressing, as Pérignon realized, must be done very carefully and very gradually and the extracted juice removed immediately so that the skin's pigment doesn't leach into the juice.

Needless to say, this was a major challenge, especially in the early days of Champagne production.

While there have always been many different types of wine presses, the one that was most widely used in Europe during the Middle Ages, particularly by the wine-producing monasteries, is the basket press. It consists of a large wooden receptacle (the "basket") that holds the grapes and a lid that, fitting snugly inside the inner diameter of the basket, is steadily pressed down on them to extract the juice. This was the type of press Dom Pérignon had at Hautvillers, and the system he developed of applying pressure gradually and separating the juice in stages until most of it is removed is known today as *fractional pressing*.

In 1924, a company called Coquard opened in Châlons-sur-Marne and developed the benchmark of basket presses. This press, now often referred to simply as a "traditional press" or "Coquard," with its basket made of thick wooden slats, was the type most widely used in Champagne until the early 1980s and still represents about a quarter of the presses in the area today. The standard press contains four thousand kilos of grapes, which constitutes a basic unit of measurement in Champagne known as a *marc*. A four-thousand-kilo press yields 2,550 liters (about 674 gallons) of grape must. The first 2,050 liters is called the *cuvée* and is generally considered the best part of the pressing.[6] The next 500 liters is called the *taille*. Though it is of lesser quality—a bit harsher, more astringent, and less fruity—all or part of the taille may be blended into the cuvée to make Champagne.[7] Any juice beyond 2,550 liters is called *rebêche* and cannot be used in the production of Champagne.[8] This is all tightly controlled by the authorities and all the data must be fully and accurately recorded in a log called the *carnet de pressoir*, which must be present at the press throughout the harvest period and available for inspection by the authorities at any time. If it is not available or not accurate, the press can be shut down and the proprietor fined. Each year a pressoir is required to send a certain quantity of rebêche to a distillery based on the total weight of the grapes pressed, which, as all rebêche must be entered in the *carnet de pressoir*, provides yet one more level of control.

Today there are many different types of grape presses in Champagne. Most common is a cylindrical press with an elongated pneumatic cushion inside that gradually inflates, gently pressing on the grapes, while the cylinder revolves. There are also much larger machines that are highly automated to efficiently process a huge volume of fruit on a continuous basis with minimal human intervention. However it gets done, the winemakers of Champagne know that minimizing the time between picking and pressing is of the essence, so lining up a pressoir is practically as important as the grapes themselves.

Many of the bigger houses that produce millions of bottles of Champagne per year have their own press facilities. There are many commercial pressoirs-for-hire throughout the region that can handle large quantities of grapes. And there are thousands of smaller Coquard-style presses scattered throughout the 635 villages of Champagne.[9]

AŸ is one of the loveliest and most pristine of Champagne villages, as well as one of the most prestigious, and as we drive into town on this sunny morning, everything seems to hum with a pervasive sensation of peace and well-being. (It has not always been this way, but we'll talk about that later.)

We circle the imposing Gothic cathedral in the center of town and pull into a parking spot behind the church, just in front of the Cave Robert Blanc. After entering a wine shop/reception area to announce our arrival, we are directed by a young woman to an adjacent courtyard where aproned workers are busily engaged in a pre-harvest cleaning of plastic chests and machinery.

"This is a new supplier for Krug," Eric says sotto voce. "And he approached *us*!"

At that moment a robust man in a black beret, black polo shirt, and jeans comes bounding from the door like a rugby player on his way to make a tackle. "*Bonjour et bienvenue chez Blanc!*" he says, opening wide his arms in a grand gesture of welcome. Robert Blanc, current head of the winery, is the complete opposite of Gérard Moreau. Gregarious, extroverted, and self-assured, he poses readily for my photos and speaks with ease and conviction, like a really good salesman who genuinely loves what he's selling. Robert, like Gérard, comes from a long line of Champenois, but the extensive Blanc family has always had a decidedly entrepreneurial bent. They were barrel-makers around the time of the French Revolution and drifted into the vineyards when the wine industry began to take off. During the phylloxera epidemic, an infestation of aphids that destroyed many of Champagne's vineyards and caused practically all of them to be replanted,[10] Robert's great-grandfather and grandfather went to work in the cellars until his father, also named Robert, began to revitalize the family winery in the 1960s. Blanc soon started pressing grapes for many of the local growers and still does.

In addition to growing grapes and producing their own line of Champagnes, the Blanc winery functions as a pressoir, supplying must for many of the larger houses. And now Robert would like to supply Krug as well.

"I get grapes from sixty small growers in and around Aÿ and re-group them myself according to the characteristics of the various lots in order to make a marc," says Robert, standing in front of his tradi-tional four-thousand-kilo press. "I keep the very best grapes from the grand cru and premier cru vineyards for myself—and, of course, for Krug—and I press them separately in here," patting the Coquard. "All the rest I put together in the large pneumatic press and send to the big houses. Everybody's happy!"

"I have a pretty good idea each year what to expect from each vineyard and grower, based on past experience," the effusive Blanc continues, "but sometimes it changes. It gets crazy around here during harvest time with all the growers bringing in their grapes, and me examining them and figuring out what to do. Sometimes it seems like a battle zone! But you must remain calm and you must remain focused. Somehow it all works out."

After a brief tour of the winery we head out to inspect some of Blanc's vineyards.

Here in the Montagne de Reims, the vines are mostly pinot noir and many of them have not completely finished turning red yet, but the drill is the same. We each take a row and start marching down it in sync. Eric points out a bit of rot (once again, nothing to worry about, at least not for the moment), then stops and indicates an odd cluster with a mix of large reddish grapes and tiny green ones. "*Mil-lerandage,*" he says. Hens and chicks (as it is known in English) can occur when there is poor fruit set due to wet, cool conditions during the spring flowering. Sometimes this can cause problems because the tiny grapes never ripen fully. But as long as the other grapes in the cluster reach sufficient ripeness, the tiny, less-ripe ones can contrib-ute a nice touch of acidity.

Blanc takes a small instrument out of his pocket, squeezes a grape on it, and holds it up to the sun. "This is a refractometer," he says, just in case I didn't know. "It measures the sugar in the grapes, which tells us the potential alcohol. Almost nine degrees," he adds, passing the instrument to Eric, who takes a look and passes it to me. "Not bad at all. The grapes are maturing nicely. Shouldn't be much longer now."

"Tout va bien?" Eric asks me. "You okay? Would you like to stop for a sandwich?" We're sailing in the Audi on our way to Ambonnay on the western side of the Montagne de Reims for our third and final visit of the day. It's closing in on four o'clock and we haven't stopped for a minute.

"No, no, I'm fine," I assure him. And indeed I am, though my head is nearly bursting with information and buzzing with French. My ability to understand and speak French was pretty good coming into this adventure (I studied it in high school and university, and later put it to practical use in my restaurant work and travels abroad), and this was, in fact, a prerequisite for this undertaking, as many of the people I would encounter do not speak English. But the strain of trying to follow so many quick and often technical conversations in an array of different cadences was starting to build up, along with the sweet-sour sting on my tongue from tasting so many different grapes.

We glide through a tall cast-iron gate into a cobblestone courtyard and come to a stop next to a prim bourgeois *maison*. As we exit the car I take a deep breath and gear up to dive into another dizzying encounter.

The Bonfils-Brisbois winery was created in 1983 when Jean-Pierre Bonfils, the son of a vigneron, married Francine Brisbois, who brought with her 5 hectares of vineyard as well as 1.3 hectares in *métayage*.[11] The Bonfils family is one of the oldest suppliers of Krug, Eric tells me as we stroll towards the door, and he relates a story about how Jean-Pierre's ninety-year-old grandfather stood up at a dinner at the Krug winery, took out a letter written by *his* grandfather, and read it aloud in a voice practically quivering with emotion: "Dear M. Krug, this year we would be pleased to supply you with five *pièces* of our very good Ambonnay wine."[12]

"The letter was dated 1878," Eric concludes. "M. Bonfils received a standing ovation. I thought he was going to cry. I almost cried myself."

Today the Bonfils-Brisbois holding consists of just over six hectares in the village of Ambonnay. They also acquire grapes from many local growers and, besides making their own line of Champagnes, do a brisk business as a pressoir for hire.

Here we reverse the usual process, heading directly into the vineyards in a three-car caravan with Jean-Pierre, his son-in-law Hervé, who manages the winery, and three of the vignerons that supply them, making a series of quick visits to a handful of different plots of pinot noir. The grapes look lovely. They seem even sweeter and riper than the ones we tasted this morning, as if demonstrating how much the fruit at this stage can mature in a day. Now, as the sun begins to wane, the grapes seem to relax on the vine and breathe a sigh of relief at the first hint of coolness in the air.

Back at the winery, Hervé shows me the old cellars carved out of chalk with stacks of dusty bottles and wooden racks where the riddling takes place. When we walk into the parlor of the house to join the others, it seems as if a boisterous town meeting is going on. As with Gérard Moreau, names and numbers are flying back and forth, except that now the volume is higher, the participants are more animated, and there are many more of them.

Once again, I have no clue what all the commotion is about, but ten minutes later whatever it was appears to have been resolved: the noise immediately subsides, Eric's papers go back in his briefcase, and everyone relaxes. A chilled bottle of Bonfils-Brisbois Champagne is opened and poured around. And, as the light outside begins to fade, we lift our glasses to a good end of the growing season and good harvest to come, and take a sip. The cool, lively bubbles calm my muddled brain after the long day and lift my spirits. This is a good thing, because the next few days are going to be even more intense.

We meet the next morning at eight o'clock sharp on the corner outside my hotel, as workers are hosing down the streets and the city begins to come to life. As waves of commuters emerge from the train station, we begin our journey out of Reims to visit a vigneron in Vitry-le-François. The navigator estimates our arrival at nine forty-five.

Once we settle into the flow of outbound traffic, I ask Eric what the animated discussion at Bonfils-Brisbois was all about.

"For the past ten years I have been taking a strictly parcel-by-parcel approach to sourcing our grapes," he begins.

Krug, like most other houses in Champagne, obtains the bulk of their grapes from outside suppliers, but Krug does it a bit differently than most. Typically, houses contract with a supplier for a certain amount of grapes or must, without specifying exactly where it comes from; the grape variety and town of origin are indicated but the specific parcel is not. This is understandable given that most of the plots are so small and the amount of grapes needed is so large. But Eric and his team have seen that the specific plot the grapes come from actually makes a huge difference, especially given Krug's winemaking approach. In order to guarantee that they get the grapes from the particular plots they want, a separate contract must be drawn up with the owner of each individual parcel specifying the exact surface area and quantity of grapes supplied. And this is not always easy; besides the difficulty of determining the exact size and quantity of each individual parcel, sometimes it is even hard to determine exactly who the legal owner is.

For the two marcs (a little over four thousand liters of must) that Krug will get from Bonfils-Brisbois, eleven individual contracts must be issued. "It's very complicated," says Eric, "but there's really no other way. This parcel-specific approach is absolutely essential in order for us to get the grapes we need to make the Grande Cuvée."

"You know," he continues, as we enter the A4 *autoroute* heading south and accelerate, "it's not just about accumulating a certain amount of grape juice that you manipulate in the winery and magically turn into the kind of Champagne you want. For Krug it all begins here, in the vineyards, each year, by carefully selecting the specific parcels we want, those that produce high quality, yes, of course, but also high personality. The character of the grapes from the individual parcels, and the characters of the individuals that grow them, are preserved by this approach, and all of them will eventually turn up to play their part in the wine."

As we merge onto A26 and cross over the Marne River, I ponder this idea while looking out the window at the landscape passing by, a mostly flat expanse of big square green or beige fields alternating with drab industrial factories surrounded by large parking lots. It seems a world away from where we were yesterday, driving through pristine little villages surrounded by manicured vineyards.

Eric notices me looking. "We're not in grand cru territory anymore, eh?"

"It certainly looks different," I reply. "But what exactly do you mean by 'grand cru territory'?"

Following the turmoil of 1911, during which vignerons in the north rioted over the importation of grapes from outside Champagne and vignerons in the south protested the Aube's exclusion from the official Champagne growing area (discussed in more detail in Chapter 6), a system called the Échelle des Crus was established in Champagne, largely in response to growers' demands for a fair price for their grapes and to prevent cheap imports from coming into the area.[13] A sliding price scale based on a perceived level of quality was established, and, given the huge number of vineyard parcels and subzones in Champagne, it was decided that this scale would be based on *communes* (municipalities).

The towns at the top of the quality pyramid were designated *grands crus* and as such were entitled to receive 100 percent of the set price for grapes in any given year. The second level, *premiers crus*, received 90–99 percent of the price, and all the rest of the towns, referred to simply *crus Champagne*, received 80–89 percent.[14]

All of the grand cru villages are located in the department of the Marne and most of them are in the Côte des Blancs and Montagne de Reims areas.

The Échelle des Crus served an important function when it was first created, but it's not perfect. First of all, the ratings encompass an entire commune, and, while most of the vineyards in a grand cru village might be good, there's a big difference between them: one is good, another *very* good, and yet another superb. A few of them may even be not so good.

But there's something else.

"All the parcels Krug owns happen to be in grand cru villages," says Eric. "It's the classic area of Champagne, and many producers make a point of using only grand cru grapes for their top prestige cuvées.[15] But to me the rating itself is not so important; it's not so much the cru as it is the particular vineyard. I source grapes from all over Champagne. We've even begun working with a cooperative in the Aube who sets aside grapes from one of their member's small plots just for us. I don't really care so much whether the grapes are grand cru or not. The most important thing is the *character*, the expression of the terroir, and what it can contribute to our mix. And I have found that, as long as you source them carefully, grapes from outlying areas can add some really special elements to the list of ingredients we have to create the Grande Cuvée. Stradivarius is great, but it takes more than violins to make a symphony orchestra."

Off the *autoroute*, we are now traveling east on a smaller road lined with scratchy-looking fields and industrial sheds. Near Chagny, scattered vineyards start to appear on gentle slopes interspersed with short crops in the valleys. After about twenty minutes we reach the tiny hamlet of Outrepont, which looks very rural and a bit threadbare, and pull up to a large rectangular metal shed.

Inside, the place is full of big machinery: a huge tractor with immense wheels that can straddle four rows of vines, a tiller with pointed blades to turn the earth, and another vehicle with spray nozzles tinged a chalky pale green.

"Hallo! Anyone here?" Eric calls out. After a few moments a big guy in a heavy beige worker's jumpsuit climbs down from the cabin of the big tractor. His sand-colored hair is ruffled, his big hands are leathery, and his creased eyes seem to be permanently squinting into the sun. When he says "*Bonjour*," I notice his soft voice and amiable smile.

Filip Badowski was born in Outrepont. His father, who emigrated here from Eastern Europe after the Second World War, was a farmer and Filip is too, though, after finishing his agricultural studies, he has devoted himself largely to viticulture. Besides working the three hectares of vines he owns, he provides agricultural services for many growers in the area, which explains all the heavy equipment.

After exchanging pleasantries and checking out Badowski's new tractor, we go back outside and head for the vineyards. Eric cautions the farmer that we're a bit tight on time, and as the roads in the vineyards are rough, we decide to go together in Badowski's work van. The front seat is too small to accommodate the three of us so I start to go around to the back, but Eric stops me and insists on riding in the back himself. After a few minutes, Badowski turns off the asphalt road and into the vines on a steep dirt path deeply rutted by the spring rains. He gives me a wink, and steps on the gas. I grab onto the door handle while the little van rocks back and forth and bounces up and down as it flies up the hill. Looking back through a little window into the back, I see the chef de cave bent over, gritting his teeth with legs spread and hands grasping on to a bar like a cowboy riding a bucking bronco, while the farmer laughs hysterically and charges even faster up the bumpy road.

After reaching the top of the hill, the van turns and comes to a halt. When we open the back doors, I half expect to see Eric badly bruised and shaken, but instead he jumps agilely down to the ground and dusts himself off. "Nice ride," he quips. "I hope your vines are in better condition than your road."

They are. The clusters of chardonnay are full and plump with sugar and crisp acidity, and there are many of them. While bragging about his pruning and the vitality of his vineyard, Filip shows off one plant that has more than twenty big clusters.

"*Regardez comme il est beau!* I could get twenty-five thousand kilos a hectare from these vines," he exclaims.

"Yes, perhaps you could," replies Eric drily, "if the legal maximum this year were not ten kilos."[16]

After inspecting a few more of his vineyards we return to the shed—the downward ride is much gentler than the upward one was—and the comforts of the Audi for our return journey to the north.

"Did you see those grapes?" says Eric. "They're beautiful." These grapes don't have the finesse and chalkiness of the ones we tasted yesterday but they can give a nice full body, robustness, and uncomplicated liveliness to the blend, something slightly wild and crazy but solid, kind of like Badowski.

"Try to remember what they tasted like," concludes Eric, "so you can compare them in your mind. Next stop, Côte des Blancs."

At two o'clock we rendezvous at a clearing by the side of the road in the heart of the Côte des Blancs, where three people are standing around outside two parked cars waiting for us. The entire Krug enology team is here (except for Jérôme, who is holding down the fort at Rue Coquebert), plus a young man introduced to me as an agronomist, who shakes my hand briskly as we set out.

By now I know the drill: we each take a row and march up it quickly, examining the vines, plucking, tasting, and spitting out the seeds, while the agronomist describes in quick truncated French the condition of the plants.

When I taste the grapes, I do as Eric suggested and compare them in my mind to the ones we tasted a few hours earlier. These are less fruity, crisper, with a focused green-apple acidity and stony mineral edge.

We get in the cars and move to another nearby vineyard, along a narrow road paved with asphalt through the vine-covered hills, and repeat the process, then go to another vineyard and do it again, and again and again. We are inspecting the parcels that Krug owns and manages itself in the villages of Aÿ and Le Mesnil-sur-Oger, most of which are chardonnay, though one of them is an old vineyard of pinot noir that Eric tells me is used exclusively for the Krug rosé.[17]

The overall verdict is that quantity is modest but quality is quite high, miraculously high given the late start and rainy spring. The vines are healthy, and the "reasoned struggle," a flexible protocol somewhere in between conventional and organic that the agronomist has been employing in the vineyards, seems to be paying off.[18] The chardonnay grapes will soon be ready for harvest, perhaps in a week or so, depending on how the weather holds. The afternoon sun has completely burned off the morning mist and is now beating down with a vengeance as we march up and down the vines. When we make our way back to the cars to head to our final stop on the tour, Eric mops the sweat off his forehead and glares up at the radiating sun. "C'est pas normale," he mutters to himself. "It's going to be an unusual year, that's for sure, but it's not going to be easy. This year success or failure will depend more than ever on the ability of each grower to choose just the right moment to harvest each of his plots. And we won't really know how well they did until later."

During his visits to the suppliers, besides the contracts, the predetermined dose of sulfites, and written instructions for pressing and handling of the must,[19] Eric has also given a printed message to each of them, as he does each year, a sort of motto to sum up this particular growing season and impending harvest: "Pour cette belle vendange 2013 de fin septembre, la circuit de cueillette restera la clef du succès."

For this beautiful late-September vintage of 2013, choosing the right moment to harvest each vineyard will be the key to success.

Our caravan descends from the densely packed vine-covered hills into the quiet little village of Le Mesnil-sur-Oger, pulls through an open iron gate into a gravel-covered courtyard, and comes to a halt. We are now at the famed Clos du Mesnil, a four-and-a-half acre plot of chardonnay that was originally planted in 1698 and is completely enclosed by a wall. Just inside the entrance is an elegant country house on the left and a grassy, parklike area of trees on the right. Beyond the house and trees, the vines fan out with a subtle rise and sit regally within their enclosure, a boundary that frames and distinguishes them from the houses on the other side without completely separating them. On the contrary, the little two-story abodes seem to buffer their side of the enclosure and peer over the low wall as if keeping a protective eye on the vines while wrapping them in a warm embrace.

The already tiny *clos* is subdivided into five tinier sections; each of them has slightly different characteristics, and they often ripen at slightly different times.

We begin with a small, irregularly shaped parcel next to the house and then proceed to inspect the rest of the vineyard one section at a time. The grapes taste quite good to me; they're ripe and sweet with a nice mouth-puckering tartness and perhaps even a hint of chalky talcum powder at the end. Only an occasional bunch shows any trace of rot. But I notice thoughtful discussion among the four examiners, as well as a hint of concern—maybe even some polite dissension—on Julie's part.

The agronomist has collected a few sample bunches from each of the five sections for chemical analysis. We walk briskly back to our separate cars and exchange a quick *à bientôt* before heading our separate ways. Eric and I have one more visit to make.

We drive in silence for a while. I generally pepper Eric constantly with questions but around this time each day, we have an unspoken understanding to give each other a respite. He breaks the time-out as we enter the town of Ambonnay.

"Our next visit is going to be a bit different. Étienne Bâtonnet is a fifth-generation winegrower but the first of them to be bio. Some of his ideas are a little unusual, but he's very serious and passionate about what he does. And his wine is good."

By "bio" I understand Eric means *biodynamique*, not *biologique*, the French term for "organic." Biodynamic viticulture is an approach to grape growing and winemaking that is based on the agricultural principles of Rudolf Steiner, an Austrian philosopher, artist, and social activist, who also developed a unique system of education that has spawned schools throughout the world. Its principles, which view all agricultural activities as taking place in harmony with the larger planetary cycles and promote the restorative capacity of the earth to heal itself, were first applied to viticulture by Nicolas Joly, an enigmatic winemaker in the Loire Valley. Biodynamic wine growing has found many followers in France (as well as other winemaking countries throughout the world) but not so much in the densely planted, high-yield vineyards of Champagne, an area that is particularly prone to disease due to its high density and harsh climate.

Many conventional winemakers poke fun at practitioners of biodynamics, whose treatments involve esoteric homeopathic preparations that are sometimes placed in an ox horn and buried in the vineyard, and worry that biodynamic vineyards are subject to diseases that may have a negative effect on their adjacent vineyards, much as biodynamic growers fear the harsh chemicals used by neighboring vignerons will negatively affect theirs.

On some of our visits, growers have derisively pointed out haggard yellowing vines with feeble small clusters while smirking, "*Tu vois? Ça c'est le bio.*" But there is no yellowing or feebleness in Étienne's vineyards. The rows don't look as straight and neat as others we have seen and the ground seems coarser and uneven (he says they are plowed by horses instead of tractors), but the pinot noir vines, which are now close to 90 percent red, look beautiful, healthy, and vigorous.

"The biodynamic approach is not easy, especially here in Champagne," says Étienne. "The treatments are more complicated than conventional ones, and all the work must be done at the correct time in sync with the cycles of the moon. But it's the only way to bring life to the soil and allow the vines to grow into strong and healthy individuals that are not dependent on chemicals that drain them of their vigor and character.

"It can be stressful," he continues, "especially around harvest time. The stresses of our work can affect our personal lives and vice versa. But it's stressful for the vineyard too. I prepare both myself and my vines by going into the vineyard and meditating before harvest."

I imagine the young man sitting amidst his vines, legs crossed and eyes closed, while tractors roar around adjacent vineyards spewing clouds and their drivers look down upon him with derision. But Bâtonnet's enthusiasm is compelling; at the very least, it commands respect. And Eric is not laughing.

"Do you believe it has an effect?" asks Eric, genuinely interested.

"Well, I know it makes me feel more relaxed and more centered with my vines," replies Étienne softly. "And I like to think they like it too."

With that, he gets up and pulls a bottle of his Champagne out of a nearby fridge, eases out the cork until it gives a gentle sigh, and pours out three glasses. The color is a pale yellow and the aroma combines faded flower petals with the scent of wild herbs and a hint of decomposed straw. Bubbles float slowly up, as if in no hurry at all. As we sip the cool, crisp, slightly creamy wine in silence, I think of draft horses gallantly pulling plows, a young man meditating in his vineyard, the chalky earth crawling with life, and the nearly red grapes reaching their apex in sync with the cosmos. Is there a direct cause and effect? I like to think that there is. In any case, it is certainly a nice idea.

"*C'est intéressant, non?*" says Eric on the way back to the car. "Each of these vignerons has their own story, their own unique personality, which somehow turns up in their grapes. And this is a big part of where complexity comes from; this mix of personalities contributes as much to the Grande Cuvée as the meteorological events of the season or the terroir where the grapes are grown."

At that moment I realize something else: while the ostensible purpose of these visits is to inspect vineyards and finalize contracts, it appears that Eric also enjoys the personal interactions with the vignerons. Indeed, I have watched him change according to each one—comfortingly reassuring with Gérard Moreau, garrulous with Robert Blanc, feistily sparring with Jean-Pierre Bonfils, reckless with Filip Badowski, and meditative with Étienne Bâtonnet—while somehow still remaining himself. And this subtle metamorphosis creates a more dynamic and synergetic rapport between them. How much, I wonder, does *this* influence the wines they supply him and, ultimately, the Grande Cuvée? While Eric's goal (and the goal of the four generations of Krugs that preceded him) is to maintain the house style and the vision of its founder, surely the gentle touch of the individual behind it does leave its mark.

On the way back to Reims Eric listens to his messages. One of them is from Julie; the two have been calling back and forth all day long. "*Bon*," he says to himself, after he clicks off the audio, "*on commence*." He talks without taking his eyes off the road: "Tomorrow I go to visit a vigneron in the Aube. You can come with me if you like. But perhaps you would prefer to spend the day at Clos du Mesnil? Tomorrow we begin the harvest."

Harvest does not officially start until Saturday, Eric explains, but they're going to start earlier. "We want to catch the grapes at their moment of peak maturity, the point where ripeness reaches its maximum but the acidity has not yet begun to decline. This is absolutely essential. When we visited the clos this afternoon, a few sections appeared to be at that point. We analyzed some samples in order to be sure. And we just got the results."

Each year, the Comité Champagne determines the official start dates of harvest for each of the three principal grape varieties in all 320 communes of Champagne. At the same time, other key harvest criteria, such as the minimum level of potential alcohol at harvest and maximum yield of grapes per hectare, are declared.

This year's start dates were announced two days ago, on Sunday evening, September 22: The official start for picking chardonnay in Le Mesnil-sur-Oger (as in most of the Côte des Blancs villages) is Saturday, September 28. In the Champagne appellation one cannot legally begin to pick before the official start date.[20] However, if you can prove your grapes have reached the minimum level of potential alcohol—this year it's 9 percent—*before* the official start date, you can get permission (known as a *dérogation*) to harvest earlier. In the past, you had to make an official request and wait for a response. But because it sometimes took a few days to complete the process—and a day or two in this case can make a critical difference—now all you have to do is make an official declaration. But you have to be careful: if you harvest early and the grapes fall below the minimum, everything will be declassified.

"Based on the samples we took, the grapes in two sections of the clos are ready and we don't want to wait a minute longer. We're going to harvest those two parts tomorrow and do the rest on Saturday, when the harvest officially begins. So what would you prefer to do?"

I don't want to appear too eager to pass up a day on the road with Eric. And, in fact, I'm not: I enjoy meeting the different vignerons and seeing their homes and wineries and vineyards, and I'd love to visit the southernmost department of Champagne. I even enjoy the downtime cruising around in the Audi. I ask a lot of questions; so much is still mystifying to me. But I also like to keep quiet and look out the window.

When I made my initial proposal, I was afraid the chef de cave, head of the entire winemaking operation chez Krug, would (should he even consent to let me come) resent my presence as a nuisance or an intrusion. But, far from grudging tolerance, I am happy and relieved to discover that not only is he being incredibly open, generous with his time, and patient with his explanations, but he's also humorous and personable.

After only several days on the road (though long and busy days they have been), we are beginning to develop a more relaxed and friendly rapport, in spite of my less-than-perfect French. When he introduces me to people, Eric now refers to me as his "copilot," "navigator," or "*petit ombre*."

I'd gladly shadow him to the Aube. But the possibility of being present at the very beginning of the 2013 harvest, and in the famed Clos du Mesnil to boot, is too good an opportunity to pass up.

Eric, waiting for an answer, looks over at me inquisitively. After a moment I reply.

"I think I'll go to the clos."

As we drive, I gaze out the window and think about bubbles. So if neither Dom Pérignon nor Jean Oudart put the sparkle into Champagne, who did? The answer is surprising and might even be a bit disconcerting to some Francophiles.

In the second half of the seventeenth century, England was laying the foundation to become a world power and London was becoming one of the financial capitals of the world. The Bank of England set up shop in 1694, colonists were creating new markets in America, and English maritime traders were gaining the upper hand from East Asia to the New World.

The Brits were working hard, and they were thirsty. They could produce all the beer, mead (an alcoholic beverage made from fermented honey and water), and cider they needed at home, not to mention whiskey in Scotland and Ireland. But what they really craved was wine (even more so, perhaps, because it was nearly impossible at that time to grow grapes in England) and they got a lot of it from France, at least during periods when the two countries were not entangled in some bitter conflict.

The wine from Champagne was shipped in barrels, like wine from most everywhere else at that time. But, unlike the wine from most everywhere else, a lot of the wine from Champagne had not completely finished fermentation, due to the onset of cold autumn temperatures. The following spring, after the wine had reached its destination and the temperature rose, the remaining sugar "woke up" and went back to work on the remaining yeast, resulting in a distinctive fizziness.

This was nothing new; the same thing often happened in France, and many people were working very hard to try to find a way to prevent it. But what *was* new is that for many English patrons this wasn't a problem: they *liked* the fizziness (not surprising, perhaps, given their fondness for effervescent beer and cider). They referred to it as "brisk," and many people actually started specifically seeking out the wines that had it.

It didn't take long for English merchants to catch on and start asking their suppliers in Champagne to give them the fizzy wine, the brisker the better. More ambitious merchants even started to make it brisk themselves.

In 1662 an English physician and scientist named Christopher Merrett (the name is sometimes spelled with only one *t* at the end) presented a paper to the Royal Society called "Some Observations Concerning the Ordering of Wines" describing how adding sugar or molasses to wine or cider makes it sparkle and exploring the reasons why. Little was known about the science of fermentation at the time, but Merrett noted that, besides making it fizz, the added sugar also increased the level of alcohol.

It soon became common practice for English wine merchants to add a bit of sugar, and the bubbly wine of Champagne became all the rage in England; everyone was talking about it, most everyone was drinking it, and poets and playwrights were writing about it.[21]

Back across the Channel, when Champagne merchants noticed the spike in sales and learned the reasons behind it, they started making sparkling versions of their own.[22] In France, with its long history of wine production and consumption and the ingrained attitude that bubbles were a flaw, it took a while for the idea of sparkling wine to catch on. But there were some early influential fans.

When Louis XIV died in 1715, Louis XV was crowned king of France. But, as he was only five years old, Philippe II, Duc d'Orléans, was appointed regent, which made him a very influential man in-deed. Unlike the royal predecessor, whose vinous partialities vacil-lated back and forth according to his physician-of-the-moment's advice, the duke's preferences were clear: he liked Champagne and he liked it bubbly. From then on, the sparkling wine of Champagne flowed like a fountain in the palace of Versailles and all the royal houses of France. And when visiting dignitaries went back to their countries of residence, it flowed there too.

The craze for *mousse* (foam) spread quickly. The new wine was off to a brisk start and its future looked very promising. But there were some problems.

One of them had to do with the bubbles themselves: now that everyone loved them, the problem became trying to find a way to preserve them. English merchants had discovered that the process of adding a bit of sugar and yeast to the wine to induce a second fer-mentation worked better in individual bottles than in large barrels, and that the closed container captured the fizziness inside until the wine was consumed (which usually didn't take very long). But this led to a second, even more serious problem: exploding bottles. The carbon dioxide gas given off by the second fermentation sometimes turned these little bottles of bliss into tiny time bombs with a ten-dency to spontaneously explode, and many of them did.

Here, too, the English had a technical advantage.

In 1623, Sir Robert Mansell, along with his Welsh partner, James Howell, received a royal patent for a technique they developed for the production of glass in ovens fired by coal instead of wood. The heat of the coal-fired ovens was much higher and the glass that came out of them was much stronger. Glassblowers took to adding iron and manganese to the raw materials, which made the glass even stronger, and it could be blown thicker to make the bottles even more resistant. This technology eventually made its way to France but it took about a hundred years to get there.

Another critical issue was keeping the bottle closed. The ancient Romans were familiar with the use of porous tree bark to close small flasks (though most of their wine was shipped and stored in earthen amphora), but the practice had been lost during the Middle Ages. In France, bottles were a rarity: most wine was sold in barrels, and when it was necessary to ladle it into a smaller container, a small piece of wood was wrapped with oil-soaked cloth and stuck into the opening. This worked okay to keep the liquid from spilling out but certainly didn't do much to help keep the bubbles in.

The English, however, who had had a much longer experience with effervescent beverages and had a long-standing economic relationship with Portugal (long one of the world's most important producers of cork), had been using cork as a bottle closure since the end of the sixteenth century.[23]

Cork is a good material for a bottle stopper, particularly for a bottle of wine. Its spongy consistency allows it to contract and expand, so it fits tightly into a narrow-mouthed bottle of solid English glass without cracking the mouth. It is dense enough to keep the liquid from spilling out yet porous enough to allow a slight transference of air in and out of the bottle, should anyone desire to mature the wine for an extended period of time (which, as it later turned out, many would).

In 1728, after strong lobbying from aldermen in Reims, Louis XV issued a royal edict permitting the transportation of Champagne in bottles (though the quality of French glass was still not as high as British); up until that time, Champagne, like all other wines in France, could only be sold and shipped in barrels for tax reasons. This was a real boon to the "brisk" wine of Champagne; not only did it help retain the bubbles in the wine, it also facilitated shipping and took bottling of the wine back from the British middlemen. And with this development, the commercial potential of sparkling wine exploded.

CHAPTER 4

VENDANGE

I WAKE before dawn and walk through the desolate damp streets to Rue Coquebert, where the maroon-colored, spear-topped iron gates are firmly shut, standing sentinel over the deserted winery. After a few minutes, a red Peugeot pulls to the curb and stops. I get in. In the back is a child's car seat holding a collection of stuffed animals and in the front is a groggy Julie.

"*Bonjour, ça va,*" she says in a raspy early-morning voice without any hint of the interrogative. She seems drowsy and edgy at the same time. Inside the car I pick up faint residual scents of coffee and cigarette smoke.

"I'm good," I say a little too spritely. "How are you?"

"*Eh bien, on démarre,*" she replies, shrugging with her voice as if to say, "How do you expect I should be? It's time to start picking."

While Eric is the chef de cave, Julie is responsible for the Clos du Mesnil. And Julie is concerned. The grapes, she says, are ready—maybe more than ready. They have been carefully monitoring and analyzing the situation in the clos for weeks, but with the recent bursts of heat, the ripening has accelerated and Julie is afraid it might have gone too far.

"This isn't Burgundy, you know," she says.

In Burgundy, as in most other wine-producing areas, maximum ripeness is sought in order to achieve sufficient sugar to reach the desired degree of alcohol during fermentation, as well as to obtain good body and a rich flavor profile. In many areas, growers allow grapes to hang on the vine long after adequate sugar levels have been reached in order to let them mature completely. This is not the case in Champagne.

Of course, the Champenois want ripeness and must have a minimum level of natural sugar in the grapes before they can legally pick them. But what they *really* want is acidity. Acidity gives life to the wine; it brings out the minerality of the soil and balances the sweetness of the grapes. It helps keep the wine fresh and lively through the second fermentation and over many years of aging.

"Without good acidity the wine is flat and boring," says Julie. "Without good acidity you cannot make good Champagne."

After a moment of silence she concludes: "It's definitely time to pick these grapes. In a few parts of the clos it might even be past time. *On verra.*" She remains silent for the rest of the ride.

Each year the Comité Interprofessionnel du Vin de Champagne (CIVC), now known simply as the Comité Champagne, sets the legal harvest dates for each of the three principal grape varieties in each of the 320 communes of Champagne. But how exactly is this determined? I go speak with Thibaut Le Mailloux at the Comité Champagne headquarters in Épernay to find out.

"We have over five hundred growers throughout the Champagne region who report to us regularly on the condition of the grapes in their vineyards," Le Mailloux says. "We collect all of this information and monitor the development of ripening throughout the growing season, taking into account all of the various meteorological events that occur."

As the end of the season begins to draw near, they make a preliminary determination of the maximum yield of grapes per hectare based on the level of existing stock. These estimates are relayed to

each of the 320 communes in the appellation, after which the growers hold a meeting to discuss them and get back to the Comité with
any comments. About a week before harvest is going to begin, the
organization finalizes all the parameters, defines the minimum level
of potential alcohol based on the amount of sugar in the grapes, and
makes the official announcements.

I am amazed at the complexity and specificity of this process. In
most other places growers decide for themselves when their grapes
are ready to be picked.

"That's true," replies Thibaut, "but the dynamics in Champagne
are different."

He reminds me that in Champagne there are three different
grape varieties, each of which ripens at a different time in different
parts of the zone.[1] Given the large expanse of the growing region,
there are significant differences between north and south, and even
within a given village (cru) or grape variety, there are often huge
variables relating to differences in microclimate, exposition, and
soil. Because the Champagne appellation uses only a single geo-
graphical indication—Champagne—and is regulated under a single
set of production rules, there has to be some guarantee that the juice
meets minimum requirements. What's more, in Champagne chaptalization (adding sugar to the must to boost alcoholic fermentation)
is not only permitted but the norm. Without minimum natural sugar
requirements, producers could theoretically make up for extreme underripeness by adding more sugar during fermentation, which would
undoubtedly lower quality. Finally, without strict dates for the commencement of harvest, many growers would be tempted to harvest
early in order to jump-start the production process and avoid the risk
of bad weather.

"So you see," Le Mailloux concludes, "in Champagne these seemingly complicated regulations are absolutely necessary to ensure the
level of quality and consistency outlined by the production guide-
lines and protect the appellation. Anyway, we only determine the
start date; growers can always wait a bit longer to harvest if they wish."

The Clos du Mesnil, a historic walled estate in the town of Le Mesnil-sur-Oger in the heart of the Côte des Blancs, is one of the dozen or so precious jewels of Champagne known as *clos*.[2] Besides the vineyard, the garden, and the house, the property has a winery that contains a traditional four-thousand-kilo Coquard press (the only pressoir Krug owns and operates itself), a battery of small stainless-steel tanks, and space for the wooden barrels.

As we pull into the gravel courtyard, Jérôme drives in right behind us, and I can almost feel Julie breathe a sigh of relief to have the support and camaraderie of her young colleague. Jérôme, high-spirited and enthusiastic, gets along well with everyone, but he and Julie seem to have an especially amicable rapport.

Inside the house, Jérôme pulls out a thermos of sweetened coffee and a bag of croissants, which are quickly wolfed down. Then he and Julie get to work setting up a command post in a little room just inside the foyer, unpacking computers, plugging in cell phones, and arranging a makeshift laboratory of glass vials and instruments to measure the grape must. As they go about their business, they chatter playfully, creating a buoyant counterpoint to the underlying sense of restrained anticipation.

Not wanting to further clog the already cramped quarters, I set up my own little command post on an oak table in the parlor. I have been in this house several times before but always with a group of people during some glamorously orchestrated event. Now that I am here alone, waiting for harvest to begin instead of the next course of a fancy dinner to be served, I can almost imagine what this place must have been like when it was the home of a well-to-do Champenois family.[3]

Just before eight o'clock, a small caravan pulls into the courtyard and a ragtag group piles out of the vehicles: men and women, young and old, French and non-French (mostly non). Some of the women are wearing colorful turbans wrapped around their heads while others are draped in long scarves.

After a quick exchange of greetings, a young, blue-jeaned Champenois gathers his group in front of a table in the courtyard. On the table are three large paper place mats with sample grape clusters on them. The first one, labeled "*Acceptable*," has two healthy grape clusters on it; the second, "*Unacceptable*," holds moldy, rotten clusters; and the third, "*Attention!*" has bunches with a little mold or some unripe berries that can be harvested but need to be cleaned. The blue-jeaned Champenois quickly but thoroughly explains the three categories to the group.

While some vineyard owners pay by the hour or the shift, most pay by the weight of the grapes harvested, which can sometimes create a conflict of interest: pickers want to pick as many grapes as possible in the least amount of time while winemakers want to ensure good quality in order to make good wine, which makes the presence of a good group foreman (like M. Blue Jeans) especially critical. I learn that this year the going rate for pickers is twenty-two cents per kilo. As a good picker can pick one thousand kilos of grapes in a day and work six to seven days a week during harvest, this adds up to quite a good income for a few weeks' work, even after a small percentage is paid to the person or agency who hired them and a portion is withheld for taxes.

"Any questions?" he asks. "Okay, *allons-y!*"

The group, peeling off down jackets, putting on gloves, or securing headdresses, marches around to the back of the house and into parcel number one. Though they might have seemed like a motley contingent when they first straggled in, once they hit the vineyard they morph into a well-ordered brigade.

The bulk of the group breaks into pairs; each person grabs a small plastic basket with handles, places themselves on either side of a row, and begins cutting the grapes, working their way quickly down the row. As the baskets begin to fill, a runner appears and seamlessly exchanges the full baskets for empty ones so the pickers don't miss a beat, carries the full baskets to the head of the row, and gently empties them into a large rectangular plastic chest with perforated bottom, several of which are placed at intervals along the central aisle, then rushes the empty baskets to other pickers who need them.

When, after about thirty minutes, the first chests are full, a porter arrives with an odd sort of yellow metal wheelbarrow—really no more than a hollow rectangular frame that holds two or three of the plastic chests—and one of the basket runners helps load the full chests onto the cart, which the porter shuttles down to the base of the vineyard and stacks two or three high.

While the grape pickers, the basket runners, and the chest porters continue their choreographed activities, Julie keeps a watchful eye from the sidelines, picking a stray leaf or two out of a chest as she inspects the grapes. "Tell them not to overfill the chests," she says to the blue-jeaned foreman; overfilling would cause the grapes to be crushed when the chests are stacked. Every now and then one of the pickers in need of an empty basket yells out, "*Panier!*"

At nine o'clock another group arrives on the scene, shuffles up the rise through the central aisle to the head of the vineyard, and gets to work, exponentially increasing the level of activity in the little clos. At about the same time, a tractor pulling a flatbed trailer lined with wooden pallets arrives at parcel number one. The driver, a ruddy local character sporting an impressive handlebar mustache and long leather apron, nimbly swings out from the tractor to the trailer, and as two beefy comrades lift the crates up onto the bed, he stacks them three high atop the wood pallets. A marker with the name of the picking group is placed in each pallet of chests, and the tractor ferries the grapes around the corner to the front of the house, where Julie and Jérôme inspect them: "*C'est beau!*" "*Oui, c'est très beau,*" they whisper back and forth.

At that moment, an orange forklift operated by a stocky middle-aged woman wearing a regulation yellow safety vest comes zipping out of the winery. She gracefully scoops up the first pallet with the big iron fork and zips it into the winery, where the contents are weighed on a big scale and the net weight is entered on the receipt.

The grapes are then transported around corner and into the pressoir, where an équipe of four guys wearing bib aprons, rubber gloves, and steel-toed safety shoes is waiting for them.

The men swing into action: Two of the taller, stockier guys grab a chest on either side, lift it, and spill the contents into the press. This, they tell me, is called *charger la presse*. A third guy takes the empty chests and begins stacking them near the door. Just as the first pallet of grapes is emptied, the forklift arrives with another. When one side of the press begins to fill with grapes, the guys move around to the other side and begin dumping them in there.

Though the inside of the old press didn't look that large when it was empty, it is surprising how much it holds. As the interior begins to fill, another man—shorter, balding, quiet, but very agile—shovels the newly added grapes up towards the center into a pile that resembles a soft green volcano.

"It's very important to have the peak in the center to get the right pressure, an even pressure, when the grapes are pressed," he tells me.

I remember Eric's words: "There's nothing like a traditional Coquard press, operated by someone who knows how to do it."

And François, the agile man, knows: he began working at the Clos du Mesnil in 1982, when he was twenty-two years old, and has been *chef de pressoir* here since 1990. During the rest of the year he works at one of the well-known houses, but he takes time off from his regular job to come here each year to supervise the pressoir during harvest. "Working the press at Clos du Mesnil is my personal tradition," he says, in a simple, matter-of-fact way. "It's my life."

As François puts the final touches on the contents of the now full basket, I begin to hear the faint trickle of juice falling into the first of three white-tiled wells called *belons* behind the press, the first free-run juice coming from the grapes on the bottom of the basket under the weight of those on top.

"Okay, *on y va*," says François, giving the grapes an affectionate pat with the bottom of his shovel. With that, the two semicircular wooden wings of the lid are lowered over the grapes and locked horizontally into place with two iron arms on each side. When the green button on the wall is pressed, the wooden lid slowly lowers and a gentle but decisive pressure is exerted on the grapes by a hydraulic arm. A moment later, the slight trickle increases to a steady flow that resembles the sound of a lightly babbling mountain brook.

I go over and peer into the well, where a stream of golden-yellow liquid pours out of a stainless-steel tube from a hole in the tiled wall of the well, through a small mesh filter hanging over the end of the tube, and down to the bottom. The undulating surface of the juice is covered by creamy white foam.

"Can I taste it?" I ask François.

"*Mais oui, pourquoi pas?*"

He grabs a small glass off a shelf, leans nimbly over the protective rail to put the glass under the spigot, and, straightening back up, passes it to me.

"*Voilà*," says François, smiling, "the very first glass of Clos du Mesnil 2013!"

The stem of the glass is a little sticky. The color resembles a light, slightly turbid golden-yellow honey, and as I tilt it to my mouth, the smell suggests fresh wildflowers and cut grass. The first palate impression is of sweet-sour, syrupy grape juice with a hint of golden raisins. Then comes a nice burst of tart green apple, followed by a slightly resinous finish.

After about forty-five minutes, the press stops and the lid is lifted. Using plastic shovels, the guys do the first of several *retrousses*, breaking up the compressed solids of grapes around the inside edge of the basket and shoveling them in towards the center to re-form a peak. The lid is lowered again and the gentle but persistent pressure resumes. This process will be repeated four times, and each pressing is called a *serre*.

While the juice continues its steady flow into the first well (now almost half full), I go outside to see how things are progressing. The sun is shining. The courtyard has several towers of full chests on pallets and the forklift continues to zip back and forth, weighing and shuttling them into the winery.

In the vineyard, the choreographed activities continue at a steady pace, with pickers picking (I notice a new third group has just got to work at the top of the vineyard), basket runners running, and porters hauling full chests to the pickup area, where the stocky aproned guys lean up against the tractor, smoking and chatting about soccer.

Suddenly Julie, who had just stepped out to survey the activity, runs up the center aisle of the vineyard waving her arms and screaming, "Arrêtez, arrêtez!" When she gets to the top she engages in an animated discussion with the foreman while the frozen pickers, who have no idea what all the fuss is about, look blankly on. The group, it turns out, was about to start picking the wrong section of the vineyard. But the pickers silently move to the other side of the aisle and everything returns to organized efficiency.

Back in the winery, the juice continues to flow out of the old Coquard and François uses a long plastic stick to measure the amount of must in the first well, which is now nearly full. When the quantity reaches 2,050 liters, the spigot is closed and transferred to the adjacent well. The press is stopped, the lid comes up, and the upper half of the wooden basket is removed, making it easier to get to the compressed grapes for the last retrousse and serre.

Remember, the standard marc of four thousand kilos of grapes yields 2,550 liters of juice: the first 2,050 liters is the cuvée and the next 500 is the taille.[4] Any juice beyond 2,550 liters is called rebêche, which cannot be used for Champagne and is usually sent to the distillery. The cuvée, now sitting in the first large well, is considered the best part of the pressing, and this is the only part that Krug uses for its wines. (The taille is used to season new barrels or is given away.)

While the pressing continues, François dips a beaker attached to a long stick into the first well, then pulls it up and pours the contents into a cylinder that is sent to the makeshift lab, where Jérôme performs some rudimentary tests to determine the levels of sugar, acidity, pH, and density, which he enters into his laptop and onto a small printed form.

At twelve thirty everything stops: the pickers wipe off their clippers, the runners drop their baskets, the porters park their wheelbarrows, and everybody goes off to find a shady place with their compatriots of choice to consume bag lunches, while Julie, Jérôme, and I, along with the pressoir team and the tractor guys, sit down at a long Formica table set with paper napkins and wicker baskets of bread in a utility room off the interior courtyard.

The woman who was zipping around in the forklift all morning has traded her orange vest for a checkered apron and is now carrying large platters of *choucroute garnie* into the room and plopping them on the table. Her name, I learn, is Anne-Marie. She has worked at Clos du Mesnil for forty-two harvests, first as a teenage picker, then as cook and forklift driver. And this is her last vintage before retirement.

"So this is the first of the last suppers," says the tractor guy when Anne-Marie takes her seat at the table. "Yeah, the party's almost over," jokes another.

"For you, perhaps," retorts Anne-Marie. "For me it's just beginning!"

Everyone laughs and digs into the food, shoveling mounds of sauerkraut and various cuts of braised pork onto paper plates. Mustard makes the rounds. Someone pops open a label-less bottle of red wine that was left over from last year, while others opt for lukewarm beer or water. All raise their clunky glasses to Anne-Marie with a collective *"Bonne chance!"* and begin to eat.

After lunch, everyone gets back to work: the pickers resume picking, the runners shuttling baskets, and the porters wheeling chests. The pressoir guys dismantle the bottom portion of the wooden basket so they can remove the compressed disk of grape pomace and hose down the press. After everything is thoroughly cleaned, the basket will be reassembled and the press will be ready for the next bunch of grapes, which Anne-Marie, zipping around again in her forklift, is already depositing in the pressoir.

While all this is going on, the first marc of grape must embarks on its journey to becoming wine. François attaches a tube to a spigot at the bottom of the well; the contents are pumped into a stainless-steel vat in the *cuverie* next door that comfortably holds 2,050 liters, and the vat is labeled with a code linked to a new file containing the data of Jérôme's initial chemical analysis of the must. Additional data will be added to the file over time and the code will follow the liquid throughout its entire life.

The must is allowed to sit for about forty-eight hours, during which time the heavier particles known as *bourbes* (seeds, skins, little bits of stem) sink to the bottom and the lighter particles float to the top, leaving the still-turbid liquid in the middle. This process is known as *débourbage*.

Next, the juice will be transferred to a *cuve de mixtion* (mixing vat) where the required amount of sugar (to boost alcohol) and yeast (to induce fermentation) will be added. But I'm getting ahead of myself. . . .

At four o'clock, the pickers finish the first two sections of the clos and leave. About half the vineyard has been picked and the second of two marcs is underway in the press. The mistake made by the group of pickers in the morning appears to have been a prophetic one: as it turns out, those grapes are ready, too, and everyone will come back tomorrow, still two days before the official start of harvest, to pick the rest of the clos, the total of which will yield a little less than five marcs.

After the clos is finished, grapes from Krug's other vineyards in the Côte des Blancs will start to arrive and they will be treated in the same way; each parcel—or group of small parcels assembled to make a four-thousand-kilo marc—will be kept separate throughout the entire process.

From this point on, beginning with the chardonnay (and the small quantities of other white grapes), followed by the black varieties, the harvest activity will quickly accelerate until all the grapes in all of Champagne's 33,500 hectares of vineyards have been picked and pressed and have begun their multifarious journeys to becoming wine.

∿

LOCATED along the trade routes between Flanders, Germany, Paris, Marseilles, and Italy, Champagne was an important production and trading center in the Middle Ages, especially for textiles. Major trade fairs took place throughout the year in different parts of the region; producers from the north brought cloth to sell to Mediterranean merchants, who in turn brought spices and dyes from the Orient, and transactions were carried out through an elaborate system of promissory notes that was sanctioned by the counts of Champagne and monitored by a special police force. This vigorous commercial activity made Champagne one of the wealthiest and most important banking centers in all of Europe. By the seventeenth century the textile fairs died down and the trading activity became diffused, but a well-established well-to-do merchant class remained a fixture in the region's principal economic centers of Troyes in the south and Reims in the north.

Though not part of the nobility, these merchants owned land and had capital. Many of them made a small amount of wine on their estates for their own personal consumption and to give as gifts to their textile customers. But when the craze for the bubbly version took off and it became legal to sell and transport the wine in bottles, many of these savvy entrepreneurs saw a good business opportunity and went for it.

Nicolas Ruinart, scion of a wealthy textile family in Reims, was the first to start commercializing their sparkling wine in 1729.[5] Six years later, business was so good that he abandoned textiles altogether in order to focus exclusively on the production of Champagne. Ruinart was soon joined by others.

In 1730, brothers Jacques-Louis and Jean-Baptiste Chanoine created a wine trading company in Épernay, excavating an underground cellar for the production of sparkling wine. And in 1734, another wealthy textile merchant, Jacques Fourneaux, constructed a grand château in Pierry to house his new wine business while carefully observing and learning from the practices of his neighbor, Jean Oudart, whose adjacent vineyards Fourneaux later acquired.[6] An Épernay-based wine merchant named Claude Moët was the best networker of the early entrepreneurs, and his winemaking operation, which commenced in 1743, was among the very first to focus exclusively on the production of sparkling wine. Besides being an energetic businessman, Moët was a consummate salesman. The key to his success was personal contact, and it seems he got as much personal satisfaction out of hobnobbing with the rich and famous as he did out of making a sale. Even before starting his own winery, he networked extensively with noble attendees at Versailles and was one of the few merchants authorized to supply the royal court. One of the people whose favor he particularly courted was Jeanne Antoinette Poisson, otherwise known as the Marquise de Pompadour, and this was a very good move indeed: Madame de Pompadour, Louis XV's chief mistress from 1745 until her death in 1764, helped ensure that Moët's wine was a fixture at the royal table and thus at many other aristocratic tables throughout the kingdom.

Claude Moët's son, Claude Louis Nicolas, had joined the firm in the mid-1750s, and when he died in 1792, his son Jean-Rémy took over direction of the company, greatly expanding the distribution of their wines and acquiring the Abbey of Saint-Pierre and its vineyards, where a century earlier Dom Pérignon had laid the foundation for the Champagne industry. Along with his sharp business acumen, Jean-Rémy also apparently inherited his grandfather's modus operandi, for he became a personal friend of Napoleon Bonaparte, who regularly stayed at Moët's palatial château in Épernay on the way to or from his campaigns and loudly proclaimed his fondness for his host's wine.

In 1798 Claude Jacquesson, also a wine trader, set up shop with his son Maurice ("Memmie") in the town of Châlons-sur-Marne and quickly became archrivals with Moët for market share and for the favor of Napoleon Bonaparte. While the emperor's stated preference was Moët, Bonaparte was also a big fan of Jacquesson, awarding the house a Médaille d'Or in 1810 "for the beauty and richness of its cellars," which sealed the reputation of Jacquesson & Fils as one of the top producers of Champagne.

And then there's the famous widow of Champagne. In 1798, Barbe-Nicole Ponsardin, daughter of one of Reims's most prominent cloth merchant families, married François Clicquot-Muiron, son of the other. While this arrangement effectively merged the interests of the two powerful families and ensured their dominant position in the cloth industry, what François really wanted to do was make wine. And with the support of his new wife (whose maternal grandmother was, coincidently, the daughter of Nicolas Ruinart), François finally convinced his father to let him try his hand at turning the wine his family was already making into a bona fide business.

Though the popularity of wine—particularly sparkling wine—from Champagne continued to increase, the Napoleonic Wars of the early 1800s created major difficulties for commerce, and as production levels increased to meet rising demand, technical problems created increasingly serious economic obstacles. François struggled passionately to try to make the business work until he took ill and died seven years later, leaving his dream unrealized.[7]

At that point, one might have thought that Barbe-Clicquot would retreat into mourning with her infant daughter, perhaps even eventually remarry, and live out her life in the comfortable trappings of her well-to-do family. But instead the young widow (*veuve*, in French) chose to continue the wine business and convinced her father-in-law to bankroll her—twice. With the support of Jérôme Alexandre Fourneaux (grandson of the founder of the Fourneaux winery) in the cellar and an intrepid traveling salesman named Louis Bohne promoting the wines far and wide, production began to stabilize and the reputation of the house slowly began to grow.

Despite the fact that competition was stiff and a number of other, more prominent companies had been at it longer, the widow orchestrated two coups that bumped her fledgling enterprise to the forefront.

In 1813, her company was on the verge of total bankruptcy and her cellars were full of wine that could not be sold due to naval blockades during the Napoleonic Wars. Feeling certain that Napoleon's siege of Russia, a very promising market for Champagne, would not last long, the widow Clicquot made an all-or-nothing gamble: she arranged for a secret shipment of her wine to be smuggled to Amsterdam and held there until the blockade was lifted, and she sent her trusty representative Bohne to St. Petersburg with samples. With Napoleon's surrender and pitiful retreat in 1815, her gamble paid off: Veuve Clicquot was the first Champagne to reach Russia, and it remained the only one there for months, thus cornering the huge emerging market and securing pride of place as the only wine Tsar Nicolas I would drink.[n]

The Russians, it was well known, liked their Champagne especially sweet, and Mme. Clicquot was happy to oblige. Which brings us to her other coup.

By the first decade of the nineteenth century, adding sugar to induce the second fermentation and make the wine bubbly had become common practice. But it also created a few problems. One of them was that after the yeast finished its work on the sugar, creating bubbles of carbon dioxide gas that became trapped in the wine, the dead yeast particles remained in the bottle. This sediment, besides being unsightly, would often become suspended in the wine, creating a slimy effect known as *ropiness*.

In order to avoid this, conscientious producers had taken to pouring wine from one bottle into another (a process called *transvasage*), leaving the sediment (most of it, anyway) in the original bottle. This helped minimize the problem but it also lost a lot of fizziness, as well as wine, in the process, making it an immensely time-consuming and costly operation.

Most of the Champagne bottlers were struggling to come up with a solution to the sediment problem, but Veuve Clicquot & Co. was the first to finally do it, developing a technique called *remuage* ("riddling," in English), which involved inserting the capped bottles neck-first into oblique holes in an upside-down wooden V called a *pupitre*. Starting out from an almost horizontal position, the bottles are turned a fraction each day over a period of weeks while gradually edging them up to an almost vertical position in the rack, until all the sediment forms a solid mass at the mouth of the bottle. At that point, the bottle is righted, the cap is popped off, and the pressure shoots the sediment out of the bottle—disgorging it, as it were—which is then quickly resealed, thus eliminating the gunk with a minimal loss of fizz, wine, or time.

While Barbe Clicquot Ponsardin is generally credited with the creation of this technique (it is said she designed it one sleepless night out of a kitchen table), it was likely invented sometime around 1816 by her cellar master, Antoine de Müller, a German emigrant who assumed the post in 1810, in response to his boss's incessant entreaties for a solution to the problem.[9] In any event, the procedure, which greatly streamlined production and increased quality and consistency, gave Veuve Clicquot a strong advantage over its competitors, until knowledge of it eventually leaked out. The technique, or some variation on it, remains an essential part of the Champagne process to this day.

❧

IN the aftermath of the French Revolution of 1789, the country was in political turmoil. Numerous attempts were made by other European kingdoms to restore a monarchy and the country was quite vulnerable, especially during the War of the Second Coalition, while General Napoleon Bonaparte was away campaigning in Egypt. Upon his return, Napoleon seized control in the so-called Coup of 18 Brumaire in 1799,[10] overthrowing the Directory of the Republic and replacing it with a consulate of which he was the chief.[11]

After taking control in 1800, one of the first things Bonaparte did was install Jean-Antoine Chaptal as minister of the interior.

Chaptal was a distinguished chemist, statesman, and social activist who believed above all else in the application of science—specifically chemical substances—to industry for the betterment of society and its citizens. Accordingly, he revamped the hospital system and created numerous trade schools and factories for the production of chemicals, such as one for the production of hydrochloric acid to create chlorine, which, he said, could be used to turn paper refuse and rags into writing paper and an effective cleaning substance for prisons. He was also a teacher and the prolific author of numerous books, including *Traité Théorique et Pratique sur la Culture de la Vigne* (Theoretical and Practical Treatise on the Cultivation of the Vine) and *Art de Faire, de Gouverner et de Perfectionner les Vins* (The Art of Making, Managing, and Improving Wine), both published in 1801.

Chaptal's treatise on winemaking advocated the addition of sugar to grape must deficient in natural sugar in order to boost the alcohol, a technique today known as *chaptalization*. While the treatise was distributed to grape growers throughout France, it had particular value for a wine-producing area like Champagne that chronically suffered from cold growing seasons and underripe grapes. Not only did the addition of sugar to sugar-deficient grape must increase the alcohol to an acceptable level of 10–11 percent, it also helped avoid the problem of blocked fermentations and created a generally more stable wine that had less of a tendency to go ropey after the second fermentation took place.

Besides maximizing the economic efficiency of the country's wine industry, one of the minister's chief objectives was to make France as independent as possible, especially during the frequent naval blockades that occurred during the Napoleonic Wars. Having demonstrated that it didn't make much difference what *kind* of sugar was used and that it was possible and economically feasible to make sugar out of beets, Chaptal aggressively lobbied for the planting of sugar beets throughout France (and especially in the Champagne area) to reduce (if not eliminate) the amount of sugarcane imported from South America.

Napoleon later gave Chaptal the title of Comte de Chanteloup and made him a member of the Legion of Honor (a legion which the emperor himself had created). Jean-Antoine Chaptal was admitted to the Chamber of Peers (the upper house of the French parliament from 1814 to 1848) in 1818, and his name is one of seventy-two inscribed on the base of the Eiffel Tower.

It must be remembered that the addition of sugar Chaptal was promoting—that is, adding sugar to the must of underripe grape juice to boost fermentation and make a more stable wine with a higher level of alcohol—was different than the practice developed by British merchants, and later adopted by the producers of Champagne, of adding sugar to a finished wine to induce a second fermentation and make it bubble.

The benefits of chaptalization in an area like Champagne were clear. But having wines with higher alcohol and more residual sugar also exacerbated another serious and longstanding problem: exploding bottles.[12]

As demand increased and new markets for the sparkling wine were cultivated in places far and wide, production rose to never-before-seen levels, and so did the incidence of spontaneously bursting bottles. During the first quarter of the nineteenth century, while bottles of wine were stacked up in the cellar awaiting disgorgement and distribution, it was not uncommon for some—actually, many—of them to explode. Thirty to forty percent was not unusual; sometimes the reverberation of one bottle bursting would set off a chain reaction, causing thousands and thousands to explode like a series of land mines, leaving few survivors and a mess of sticky liquid and shattered glass behind. This obviously meant a huge loss of income for producers, not to mention the possibility of physical damage to workers caught in the crossfire.

The fizzy wine of Champagne had caught on: people wanted bubbles and so sugar must be added. But how much?

In the 1830s, a modest pharmacist named Jean-Baptiste François in the commune of Châlons-sur-Marne began exploring the question. After closing up shop in the evenings, he undertook a series of experiments in which he evaporated the alcohol in samples of wine, measured the weight of the residual sugar, and developed through trial and error a table of how much sugar should be added in order to make the wine sparkle without making the bottles burst. He published the results of his findings in 1837 in a small pamphlet called *Traité sur la Travail des Vins Blancs Mousseux* (Treatise on the Work of White Sparkling Wines), and his technique for calculating how much sugar to add for the second fermentation became known as the *Réduction François*.

Though not perfect, Réduction François drastically reduced the incidence of exploding bottles to a very manageable 3–8 percent, and this in turn helped propel the industry into the next big phase of expansion.

After François' untimely death in 1838 at the age of forty-six, the work of the quiet, low-profile pharmacist was carried on and refined by others, but his method formed the basis of the fine-tuned procedure that is employed today to give Champagne its sparkle without the bottles exploding, for which, I think you'll agree, we can all be thankful.[13]

∽☙∽

I RETURN to Champagne at the beginning of the second week of October. Though barely a week has passed since I was last here, everything has changed. Harvest is now in full swing and the place is crawling with people, as if the sedate vineyards and villages of Champagne had somehow been turned into a giant human anthill. The roads are clogged with vehicles—buses large and small, vans, caravans of cars—transporting pickers from one place to another, and diesel-belching tractor-trailers piled high with crates full of grapes chug back and forth, rushing their loads to the press. Parked vehicles line the already narrow roads festooned with cautionary signs proclaiming "*Attention! Vendange en cours*," and the vineyards are speckled with red, grey, and orange crates and peppered with people moving up and down the rows.

It's an incredibly diverse group. In addition to the North Africans, Algerians, and Champenois who were already here, there are now hoards of others: students from throughout France and beyond, "People from the North" (Belgium, Holland, the Picardy region of France, and the northernmost Nord-Pas-de-Calais region, which was once part of the Netherlands), and Romani, who are referred to here in Champagne as Manouche. The large *maisons* have opened up their long whitewashed barracks that are used once a year to accommodate their armies of pickers, students crash in farmers' homes, and the Manouche have staked out vacant lots by rivers to set up camp, with campfires smoking, children playing, and work clothes hanging up to dry.[14]

The advance party that was here at the beginning of harvest seems to have swelled into a battalion, and judging by all the focused, well-ordered maneuvers, it seems as if a battle is about to take place. In fact, a battle is already underway, and the principal adversary is time.

While the white grapes have pretty much all been picked, most of the red grapes, which make up nearly three-quarters of *la Champagne viticole*, have not. And though many of the clusters had not even finished changing color last time I was here, now they're completely red and plump and juicy, begging to be snipped. The clock is ticking down, and the race to get the grapes picked and pressed before they become overripe or rotten or damaged by some storm is at its peak. And if the good condition of the chardonnay was essential, with the red grapes, the vast majority of which will be used to produce white juice, it's even more critical that they be perfectly healthy and pressed as quickly as possible so the pigment from the skins doesn't leech into the liquid.

The normally tranquil Clos d'Ambonnay, Krug's other prized parcel, in the grand cru village of Ambonnay in the Montagne de Reims, is buzzing like a beehive. Located behind a gated wall in front of a small square across from the village cooperative on one side and Étienne Bâtonnet's winery on the other, the Clos d'Ambonnay vineyard—a miniscule 1.7 acre—is even smaller than the one in Mesnil and is planted entirely with pinot noir.

Here I actually get to help pick the grapes, moving down the rows with the basket, snipping off the tight little black clusters and laying them carefully (but quickly) in the basket, and yelling out *"Panier!"* when it's full. Sometimes I help load the full crates onto the funny little wheelbarrow, and occasionally I pause to taste the mature berries just as Eric taught me: intense grapiness with a touch of ripe strawberry and black currant, and a mouth-puckering tartness.

Despite the strange season and the extended, unusually late harvest with high risk of rot and hail damage, the grapes are lovely and perfectly healthy, with only occasional incidence of mold. In other areas, I did notice some *millerandage* but, as Eric suggested, not enough to create any problem whatsoever. The anomalous vintage of 2013 is turning out to be quite a promising one indeed.

It takes only a few hours to harvest the entire vineyard, after which Eric pops open a bottle of Champagne—Clos d'Ambonnay, naturally—to toast with the pickers, many of whom are Krug staffers from the communications, sales, and hospitality divisions, getting a token taste of harvest to help them better understand the product they represent. For me, tasting this Champagne made from the grapes of this same vineyard in the vineyard itself, after having just picked the grapes that will one day become a wine much like this one though with its own unique personality, is a pure and heady experience indeed.

Unlike at Clos du Mesnil, there is no pressoir here—the long rectangular brick building that runs perpendicular to the vineyard houses a large *cuverie* and fermentation facility to accommodate the wooden barrels—so the grapes are brought over to Bonfils-Brisbois a few minutes away to be pressed.

In stark contrast to the buoyant joviality of the clos, the ambience of the Bonfils-Brisbois press house is frenetic. Outside the hangarlike entrance of the pressoir, tractors and pickup trucks carrying grapes are lined up and down the driveway and farmers stand outside their vehicles chatting, smoking, and looking at their watches, while inside the two pneumatic presses (plus the old Coquard in another wing) are going full-speed. Two forklifts zip back and forth, unloading grapes from trucks, which are weighed—the weight is shouted out to a young woman in a glass booth who records it in a ledger and provides a numbered paddle to place in each lot—then deposited off to the side to await their turn in the press.

Back at the clos, cisterns containing grape juice arrive in a steady stream (in order to avoid backups, their arrival time is tightly scheduled). Lucien oversees a team of eight blue-jumpsuited workers, and Jérôme has set up his makeshift laboratory in an office in the *cuverie*. After each truck arrives, Jérôme has the driver lower a beaker in to get a sample, which he analyzes in the office while a hose is attached to the cistern and the juice pumped into a *cuve de mixtion*.

While there's no press here, Ambonnay is a much larger operation than Mesnil, though not nearly as large as the main facility at Rue Coquebert, where the number of cisterns arriving is nearly double.

Though the weather has held and the grapes are, by and large, lovely, the harvest road is not without its potholes.

In the car one morning when *vendange* is nearing its peak, Eric gets a call from Marie in the office: it seems that there have been some last-minute changes with some of the contracts and she is upset.

"*Ecoutez-moi*, Marie," says Eric calmly and reassuringly. "Relax, have a cup of tea. Everything will work out; I'll go talk to everyone and we'll sort it all out. À *tout* à *l'heure*."

Pressing the disconnect button on the dashboard, Eric says "Marie is great. She's worked at Krug for thirty-five years, going back to the time of Paul II; she knows the intricate regulations and procedures of Champagne like the back of her hand, and she manages my schedule, which is not always easy. Neither is harvest."

After a momentary pause to enter a new address in the GPS, he concludes: "Harvest is a perpetual game of variables. And our parcel-by-parcel approach doesn't make it any easier. But there's no way around it. Good thing it happens only once a year!"

Less than a week later, harvest activity peaks. Then it is over. At the conclusion of picking and the last run of the press, many growers hold a traditional festive harvest meal called a *cochelet* for their *vendangeurs*. The name is said to come from the word for rooster (*coq*) and there are a number of explanations of why. One is that once the press was shut down and cleaned, it was decorated with a bouquet of flowers tied onto the end of a pole, which some thought resembled a rooster weather vane or a chicken on the end of a spit. Another apparently stems from an ancient custom of bringing a live rooster to the post-harvest dinner and making it drink the new wine until it became tipsy and flew around in a drunken state, to the great amusement of the (probably also tipsy) onlookers. And yet another is that coq au vin (made perhaps from the drunken chicken?) was a dish traditionally served at these dinners.

While coq au vin—not to mention drunken chickens—are no longer de rigueur at these gatherings, food and wine and celebration are, and many still prepare a traditional *tarte aux maroilles* with the stinky cheese that was typically brought to Champagne by the pickers from the north.

Once the festivities are over, everyone gets ready to return to their normal routines, backs a bit sore, perhaps, and hands still stained with grapes, but bellies—and pockets—full. And as the northerners head north and the caravans of Manouche head back to their established encampments, they sound their horns jubilantly on the way out of town to announce the end of harvest and say goodbye to Champagne until next year.

After that, silence returns. The days grow steadily shorter and colder, and, while the once crawling, now grapeless vineyards drift into dormancy and the raucous *cochelet* celebrations quickly fade to a distant memory, the activity moves indoors.

∽◉◡

FOR the early producers and consumers of Champagne, wine was primarily a foodstuff, and thus its nutritional value, rather than the subtlety of its flavor, was at the top of their list of priorities. And while the monks did much to further the knowledge and practice of winemaking, the aesthetic qualities of the product, not to mention its intoxicating properties, were not high on their list of priorities, either. The bubbles initially happened on their own, spontaneously, as if by some act of God or fluke of nature. When, however, a large number of consumers (the king of France among them) began to express a fondness for fizz, producers did a quick about-face and put all their energy into perfecting the process of getting (and keeping) the bubbles in the wine.

This concerted effort to first eradicate and then wholeheartedly embrace the bubbly proclivities of the wine from Champagne can be seen as a kind of innocence or naiveté on the part of its frustrated yet well-meaning producers. But it would not last for long.

The transition from innocence to intention is exemplified by the overlapping careers of Dom Pérignon and Frère Oudart, and confirmed by the first big wave (there would be others) of sparkling wine producers in Champagne, about whom there was nothing "innocent" at all. With them, bubbles didn't just happen; they were *made*, intentionally and specifically in response to market demand. And this in turn helped their industry weather the upheavals of the French Revolution and other conflicts that followed. Louis XVI— and, consequently, the entire aristocracy—was a great patron of the sparkling wine of Champagne, as was Napoleon, who came after him. In fact, while European nobility continued to drink it, the triumph of "*liberté, égalité, et fraternité*" over *noblesse oblige* opened up whole new populations of consumers in places near and far.

It is no accident that the post-revolutionary period was dominated by the amazing conquests of an ambitious upstart soldier from Corsica who became emperor during a period that also corresponded with an intellectual revolution known as the Enlightenment.

Before that time, wine was consumed to quench hunger and thirst. It was used to celebrate the Mass, though this wine did not sparkle (the very idea of using white wine made from red grapes for this purpose would have been anathema) and the celebration of communion was a sober one indeed. The wine of Champagne, first the still wine and later the sparkling one, flowed at the heavily laden tables in the palaces of the aristocracy, but for them overabundance and wildly festive banquets were an everyday affair.

But then something else began to happen.

Between 1805 and 1814, Napoleon made numerous trips through the Champagne region on his way to battles, and on the way back, developed a ritual of celebrating his incredible victories of military wit over the might of much larger forces with bottles of the effervescent wine. There was something about the now reliable "pop!" of the heavy glass bottles that resembled the sound of cannon fire, while the foamy liquid that burst forth mimicked the soldiers' euphoria, and the sweetness (to say nothing of the alcohol) echoed their happiness to still be alive. Some of the Hussars were in such a hurry to get the bottle open that they sliced the top off with their sabers, a trick that was to be (and sometimes still is) repeated at other particularly feisty moments of celebration.[15]

And it wasn't only about cannon fire and military victory. When Napoleon chose Champagne to serve at his wedding to Marie-Louise of Austria in 1810, the foamy geysers that spewed forth suggested an altogether different kind of explosion.[16]

In 1812, Napoleon's long string of victories finally came to an end with the failed assault on Moscow. And as the fallen emperor's once Grande Armée hobbled home, the victorious Russians toasted his defeat with the French sparkler. One can even imagine the pragmatic entrepreneurs of Champagne, relieved that the decade-long series of Napoleonic wars was finally at an end, making a celebratory toast with their ebullient wine before rolling up their sleeves and getting back to business. It is likely the vanquished general got some too, for he is quoted as saying, "In victory, one deserves Champagne; in defeat, one needs it!"

In these and countless other occasions around the same period, the bubbly wine from Champagne became not just another incidental alcoholic beverage (much less a source of nourishment) but a central part of the festivities; the go-to, practically de rigueur libation that both reflected and enhanced the exuberance of whatever it was people were celebrating.

And this celebratory significance would only increase as time went by.

PART II

COMING OF AGE
LA BELLE ÉPOQUE

CHAPTER 5

✦✦✦

FERMENTATION

EVER since I started coming to Rue Coquebert in the spring of 2013, the wooden barrels have been standing there in the rear of the courtyard, clustered together like huddled masses waiting patiently to be inspected and processed before embarking on a journey or, perhaps more appropriately, like an army of rigid soldiers waiting to be sent into action.

For nearly three months (beginning in mid- to late June, depending on exactly when the previous year's harvest began and ended), a crew of workers in blue jumpsuits devotes the majority of their time to them. The foreman of the crew is Jean Nguyễn. He was born in Vietnam but immigrated to France when he was a child. His father worked in the Krug cellars for twenty-five years, becoming a proficient *caviste*, and Jean joined him as soon as he was old enough to work. "My father taught me everything," he says in his heavily accented French, punctuated with little nods and rapid blinks of his dark eyes.

By August, the preparation of the barrels is at its peak. "Last winter, after the barrels were emptied of wine from the 2012 harvest, we washed them out with hot water and treated each one with a dose of sulfur to kill any bacteria," Jean explains. "Then we let them alone until the summer. Harvest is still months away but we must start early. It takes time and everything must be ready when the grapes are."

"The first thing we do is look," indicating a guy who is thoroughly engrossed in inspecting each barrel for any visible flaws such as cracks or warps. "Then we listen." He raps his knuckles on the top and sides. "The sound it makes is important," says Jean, "but you have to be trained to hear it. If it echoes with a ping, it is good," he says, knocking on the barrel. "If it has a dull thud, it might not be so good."

Any potential problem areas are marked with chalk and the barrels set aside for closer inspection and possible repair. The rest are rolled to another area where they are hosed down with water, which collects in the top (known as the *head*) like a shallow pool. The water is left to sit there for a day. And sit there it should; if the water leaks through the head, there's a good chance something is wrong. The barrels are then turned over and the process repeated on the other side.

Due to the large number of barrels at Krug, this operation must be done in overlapping phases. The men can handle about a hundred barrels a day, and the whole thing takes about three months.

Once the barrels have passed the water test, they must be kept damp until they are used; a dry empty barrel is prone to shrinking and cracking and would soak up the wine put in it like a thirsty sponge. To prevent then from drying out, lawn sprinklers are set up to spray gently over the barrels on a daily basis.

The barrels Krug uses—the typical Champenois *pièce* with a capacity of 205 liters—are produced by two *tonnellerie*, Taransaud and Seguin Moreau. And they are used for as long as possible: during the 2013/2014 season the oldest barrel in use was put into service in 1966, making it nearly fifty years old.

Keeping track of all theses barrels is not easy, but it is much easier now than it was prior to 2006, when a system was devised in which a metal plaque with a barcode is affixed to each barrel.

"*C'est super!*" said Laurent, one of whose principal responsibilities is monitoring the barrels. "When I got here in 2004, I had no experience with barrels. It was crazy! Each one had a handwritten number on it and we had to keep track of them manually. Now we can simply scan the barcode and get the entire life story of a barrel: when it was bought, who made it, when it was put into operation, what parcel it was used for each year, and whether it had undergone any repairs. It's a little complicated; there's no precise temperature control in the barrel and each one is a bit different. But the use of barrels is central to the way wine is made here at Krug."

Krug uses the barrels only for fermentation, which is followed by a period of natural clarification by gravity, during which the coarse particles settle to the bottom.[1] They are not used as aging vessels and the wood is not intended to contribute any flavor whatsoever.

Because barrels will eventually outlive their usefulness and must be retired, new ones must periodically be acquired. But they are not put into use immediately.

New barrels are first soaked for months with warm water and then filled with *vin de taille*, which Krug does not use for its Champagnes. This is done for three years. After the third year, the *vin de taille* is tasted: if there is any hint of woodiness, the barrel will get the treatment for another year; if not, it is ready to be put into use. But even then the "new" barrels (which are now already three or four years old) are used with discretion, as I would later find out.

In earlier times just about everyone in Champagne used wooden barrels, for the simple reason that that was all there was. When stainless steel appeared on the scene in the late 1940s/early 1950s, most producers happily switched: the new steel tanks held more, were much easier to clean, and lasted forever. Moreover, the temperature inside the tanks could be easily controlled, which gave producers much more control over the delicate fermentation process.

Only a few houses stubbornly hung on to the traditional use of wood barrels, and even fewer as standard practice for all their wines. Why?

"Stainless-steel tanks are much less expensive in the long run; they are much less labor-intensive and much less finicky than wooden barrels," says Eric. "For the majority of producers it's the logical choice. But for Krug, fermentation in small wooden barrels is absolutely essential for the style of the wines we want to produce, and especially for the Grande Cuvée."

"The principal importance of using barrels is that it allows us to keep each and every parcel separate," Margareth Henríquez told me later, "which in turn enables us to evaluate each lot of wine individually and eliminate any which may fall short of our standards. The first consideration is isolation and flexibility, because the number of barrels can be adjusted as necessary to the actual amount from any given parcel. Then comes the nature of the individual wines and the complexity they may add to our Champagne."

The barrel provides a perfect cocoonlike vessel for the fermentation, allowing the liquid to gently breathe while it's becoming wine. And each barrel is different: each one has its own unique history, its own particular personality and nuance of character, its own slightly different grain and toast. Even the individual who crafted it makes a subtle difference.

"These factors add a whole other dimension," Eric concludes. "I could try to explain it to you but in a short time you'll see for yourself."

∂₀₂₀

ON the twenty-seventh day of October in the year 1800, in a large timbered house in the bustling city of Mainz, a boy, the third, was born into the flourishing Krug household and christened Johann-Joseph.[2] His father was a butcher, as his father's father had been before him, and business was good. Though not ostentatiously wealthy, the family was quite prosperous and there was, needless to say, always meat on the table.

Not long before this inconspicuous event took place, Napoleon Bonaparte had beaten the Austrians and annexed the territory, making Mainz—or rather, Mayence, as it was then known—the capital of the new Département du Mont-Tonnerre on February 17, 1800. Thus Johann-Joseph was, technically speaking, born in France.

Located on the west bank of the Rhine River at its confluence with the Main, Mainz has always been a city of cultural and strategic significance. It was founded by the Romans in the late first century BC as a fortress outpost of their empire, and it was later the seat of an electorate to the Vatican. Gutenberg, inventor of the movable printing press, was born here, and the city has long been home to an important university.

Mainz has also always been a bit of a black sheep. Despite the fact that the Protestant Reformation launched by Martin Luther in 1517 quickly spread throughout much of Germany, Mainz remained staunchly Catholic, and Catholic is how young Johann-Joseph was brought up.

For the first fourteen years of his life, French was the official language of Mainz, the one he learned and spoke at school, though German was still spoken at home. The occupiers also attempted to inject a bit of French culture into the area, including French wine, but it is unlikely it ever made its way onto the table in Johann's home. Wine from the nearby Rhine Valley probably didn't make it to the table much either, for it is probable that Herr Krug, like most of his fellow Mainzians, preferred beer.

Johann's mother died when he was seven years old, after which his father quickly remarried and had six more children, though three of his siblings died when he was young.

After Napoleon's fall in 1814, the French were ousted and Mainz became the capital of the province of Rheinhessen; people went back to speaking German in public, and the foamy beer steins filled to overflowing. But for Johann-Joseph it probably didn't much matter, for by now the different languages and cultures had already been well amalgamated into his persona.

Life went on. The little boy turned into a young man and went complacently through the motions of his unremarkable life. Until one day in 1824 he made a drastic decision: Johann-Joseph decided to leave home.

Documentation from this early period—indeed, from much of his life—is practically nonexistent. But one of the few documents that remains is a passport issued by the Grand Duchy of Hesse for Joseph Krug (the "Johann" was dropped), merchant and traveling salesman, twenty-four years old, five feet two inches tall, brown eyes, brown hair, and black beard. With this piece of paper in his pocket and a little bit of cash, Joseph set out to seek his fortune forty-five miles away in Hanau, a city that had long been an important center for gold craftsmanship.

It is not clear why Joseph decided to go there in the first place or what he did while he was there. After ten years he was self-sufficient and reasonably successful; he had food to eat and clothes on his back. But something else glittered off in the distance and, once again, he followed it. In 1834, Joseph Krug went to Paris.

Krug arrived in Paris at an auspicious moment in time.

Following the abdication of Napoleon in 1814, the four principal victors—Great Britain, Austria, Russia, and Prussia—got together at the Congress of Vienna from September 1814 to June 1815 and decided that a return to (more or less) pre-Napoleonic borders and the restoration of the Bourbons to the throne of France under a constitutional monarchy, would offer the best prospects of lasting peace and stability.[3]

Louis XVIII (formerly the Comte de Provence) took the throne in 1814 and sat on it until he died heirless in 1824, at which point his younger brother, Charles X, took his place. Unlike his predecessor, Charles was a strict authoritarian, offering restitution to nobles for losses suffered during the revolution, reasserting the power of the Church, and drastically curtailing freedom of the press. People were not happy.

In the stifling Parisian summer of 1830, discontentment boiled over into a popular insurrection led primarily by the bourgeoisie (*petite* and *haute*, but mostly *petite*) who wanted more political and economic freedom. Following "Three Glorious Days"—July 27, 28, and 29—of rioting in the streets, the Bourbon government was toppled and Charles X, who was off hunting in the countryside, hastily fled the country.

Afterwards, the more liberal Orléans branch took over. Louis-Philippe adopted a more middle-of-the-road position and proclaimed himself "king of the French" rather than the more proprietary "king of France." This was a subtle but significant distinction, for it greatly diminished the image of the king as supreme and immutable ruler, and seemed to somehow incorporate and empower the common man. Louis-Philippe kept a low profile, dressing less flamboyantly and generally comporting himself in a less regal manner, which led to his popular soubriquet, the "Citizen King."

While much of this was merely appearance—the poor (which remained a large segment of the population) continued to live in dire poverty on the fringe of society, the wealthy noble class still dominated politics, and political unrest continued up until the revolution of 1848, when the last king was ousted and the monarchy in France came to an end—it did signal a fundamental shift towards national sovereignty and greater economic opportunity. And this, needless to say, had a positive impact on the further expansion of Champagne.

In Paris and beyond, "normal" people of the petty bourgeoisie could now toast their newfound freedom and expanded opportunities with a bottle of the bubbly wine that was once available only to those of extreme wealth and privilege. And one of these normal people was Joseph Krug.

Upon arriving in Paris, Joseph took lodgings and quickly landed a job. But he soon received an even better offer that would significantly change his life.

Based on a recommendation by a certain Herr Daumer, the German agent for Jacquesson & Fils, Joseph was offered a position at the firm's headquarters in Châlons-sur-Marne. There is nothing to indicate that Joseph had ever tasted Champagne before he got to Paris, much less sought a career in the wine industry.[4] Four years into the July Monarchy, however, commerce was flourishing; Germans (who were generally considered to be well-organized and good with figures) were in great demand, and Champagne was flowing as swiftly as the Seine. Notwithstanding Joseph's naturally thrifty tendencies and Germanic air of sobriety, it is probable that he at least tried it. And he surely realized that the opportunity to get into the bubbly business with one of Champagne's most prestigious producers was too good to pass up.

Joseph gave notice to his current employer and, at the end of November 1834, met Adolphe Jacquesson at the Hôtel d'Espagne and traveled with him to Châlons to begin his new job.

Though very different—Adolphe Jacquesson was gregarious and had been born into a wealthy family enterprise whereas Joseph was the introspective son of a butcher and had been working odd jobs for the past ten years—the two were the same age and hit it off immediately.

Joseph quickly settled into his new job processing orders, keeping track of accounts, overseeing production logistics, and coordinating shipping. He worked well and quickly became a valuable and trusted employee, while his relationship with his boss continued to develop.

Three months later, on February 16, 1835, Adolphe's father died. With the responsibility of managing the large company entirely on his shoulders, Adolphe relied on Joseph more than ever, and it didn't take long for him to decide to make Krug a partner in the business: "The two of us will, I hope, succeed in reaching the objectives we desire: For me, consolidating the firm my father created by so much effort on a more solid base; and for you, dear M. Krug, ensuring for the rest of your days an easy living, associated with the quiet satisfaction of having, through your good advice and efforts, contributed so valuably to the prosperity of the house."

Joseph humbly accepted the offer: "It is too flattering for me, both by virtue of the friendship you are so good to show me and the evidence of your satisfaction with my poor services. I am over-whelmed and I do not know how to express my gratitude. I shall therefore limit myself, dear M. Jacquesson, to saying—count on me all your life long and I shall count on you."[5]

Things went well. Jacquesson & Fils continued to grow, despite strong competition and occasional cash-flow pinches, while Joseph became ever more intimately involved with the business, and in more ways than one.

Some years before, while living in London to promote the inter-ests of Jacquesson in the important English market, Adolphe had become enamored with the daughter of a Frenchman named François Jaunay and his English wife, who were the proprietors of the hotel where he lived. Following a short engagement, Adolphe Jacquesson and Louisa Jaunay were married in the Anglican church of St. Martin-in-the-Fields, and shortly thereafter the couple moved back to Châlons, where Adolphe was made assistant director of the firm. Louisa's sister, Emma, came for a number of extended visits, during which she met Joseph and a romance was kindled.

After François died, the hotel fell on hard times, Mme. Jaunay and daughter came to live in France, and on February 17, 1841, Emma and Joseph were married at a chapel in the British embassy in Paris. Because Emma was Anglican, Joseph obligingly converted. Emma brought with her a dowry of twenty-five thousand francs that had been generously provided by her brother-in-law, Adolphe, and on January 3, 1842, their first and only child was born, whom they named Paul.

With that, the transition was complete: in a mere handful of years the butcher's son had become a father, the traveling salesman had become a Champenois (and a partner in a very prestigious firm), and Herr Krug had become Monsieur.

The Krug family—a blend of French, English, and German ancestry—settled into middle-class bliss in the bourgeoning (if pro-vincial) society of Châlons. As the business developed so did Joseph, whose knowledge and appreciation of Champagne deepened as his position continued to expand. Before long, the objectives of the partners had been met, the business was thriving, and the Jaunay women were happy. It was an ideal situation for everyone. Everyone, that is, but Joseph Krug.

∼❧∼

ABOUT forty-eight hours after pressing, the still-turbid grape must is siphoned out of the *débourbage* tank and pumped to another stainless-steel container called the *cuve de mixtion*, after which the leftover *bourbes* in the bottom are cleaned out and sent to the distillery along with the rebêche.

Yeast is added to the tank,[6] along with just enough sugar to bring the potential alcohol after fermentation up to 11 percent, and mechanical paddles gently mix everything together.

"We use selected Champagne yeasts that were developed by the Comité Champagne," says Laurent. "They're neutral—they don't contribute any particular flavors or aromas—but they are strong enough to keep any other wild yeasts from interfering with the fermentation and prevent it from getting stuck."

Mature grapes are coated with a dusty layer of yeast particles and there are numerous airborne yeasts circulating throughout wine areas during harvest time. These are referred to as *wild yeasts*. So what's wrong with just allowing the must to ferment spontaneously with the natural yeasts that are already on the grapes and in the air?

"We already have many variables," Eric replies. "Each barrel already has its own particular characteristics, and the fermentation begins and ends at slightly different times in each one of them. To run the risk of different yeasts controlling the fermentation in the different barrels of different parcels of wines would create problems. You must remember that we are dealing with three different grape varieties and many, many different parcels, most of which will be used at some point in the Grande Cuvée. In order to allow each wine to express its own unique character as purely as possible, we want to remove the variable of different yeasts governing the fermentation. Using the same neutral yeast in all the different wines gives us the clearest possible expression of all the different terroirs."

From the *cuve de mixtion*, the liquid—now somewhere between grape juice and wine—is pumped into the barrels where fermentation will take place. Because it must enter through the small bunghole of each barrel, this operation is a bit delicate, and an attachment with a long pointed nozzle and a handle to stop and start the flow is used.

"We call this *charger le fût*," says Jean Nguyễn, as he inserts the nozzle in the opening and eases open the valve. As he finishes a barrel, a rubber stopper is placed in the hole and two guys roll it away and line it up on a wooden frame with the other barrels of the same marc, stoppers facing up. Once there's a row of five barrels, four are stacked on top and three more on top of that, forming a three-level flat-topped pyramid, with wooden wedges stuck underneath the barrels to stabilize them.

"We choose the barrels randomly. The only thing we do is put the new barrels on top. In a few weeks you'll see why."

While Jean and his crew are finishing charging the barrels at Clos du Mesnil, the same thing is starting up at Clos d'Ambonnay and Rue Coquebert but on a much larger scale. The Clos du Mesnil facility is used to accommodate mostly chardonnay from the Côte des Blancs that are pressed on-site, d'Ambonnay holds mostly pinot noir from the Montagne de Reims, and Rue Coquebert handles all the other musts the house acquires from throughout the Champagne region.

One afternoon about a week after the end of harvest, I walk through the ground floor of the Rue Coquebert cellar, now filled with row upon row of elongated truncated pyramids of barrels, with Eric and his team as they inspect the different parcels like a team of doctors making their rounds.[7] Laurent is holding a clipboard with a printout containing all the vitals of the various lots, and the distinctive smell of fermenting grapes, in which the grapey sweetness develops an edge of malty rising-bread-dough aroma and a touch of gaseous fumes, fills the air.

As Eric suggested, each of the different lots—and, indeed, each of the different barrels within the same lot—are at a slightly different point in the process of becoming wine (a process which the barrels at Clos du Mesnil have now already completed) and must be closely monitored to make sure it proceeds correctly. As we arrive at a pile, Laurent recites the data from his sheets—source of the must, date of pressing, and date of *mixtion*, along with other vital statistics—while Eric removes the stopper from one of the barrels and inhales deeply; the rest of us follow suit.

"This one is in full fermentation," he says, while barrels in another pile are winding down. Some of the aromas suggest the smokiness of a fireplace in which the fire has died down, or citrusy orange peel, or fresh-cut grass and hay. After smelling a barrel in one pile, someone has a flashback: "That smells exactly like my grandfather's garage!" When we arrive at a barrel in another pile in which the wine is foaming and bubbling up through the bunghole, Eric shows me a trick: "If you do this," he says, rubbing his index finger on the side of his nose just above the nostril and then putting it into the bubbly foam, "it stops." And indeed it does, though no one has any idea exactly why.

Even at this very early stage, each barrel-in-the-act-of-becoming-wine seems to have its own character and personality.

"Once, everyone used barrels," Eric tells me, "then almost no one did. Now it's become kind of fashionable."

Many of the people who use barrels nowadays use them for aging, which contributes a hint of oaky richness to the wine. But Krug uses barrels *only* for fermentation, and only because of the flexibility to accommodate different-sized parcels and the unique ambience these small wooden vessels offer for this critical process. "By allowing the wine to breathe a little during fermentation, the barrels help give life, longevity, and personality to the wine and allow the individual terroir to come through. The last thing in the world I would want is the flavor of wood to interfere with that," Eric scoffs.

The barrels I watched being tapped and sulfured and rolled around and showered for months in the courtyard of Rue Coquebert are now finally being put to use. And now I can see that the analogy of a co-coon was not merely a poetic one: a sort of gestation process is in-deed taking place inside the small cylindrical casks, but it's taking place a bit differently in each one of them.

The grapes are the outcome of a particular plot of soil, the sun, the rain, and everything else that happened during its growing cycle, as well as the care and attention of the vignerons. The grape juice I watched coming out of the old Coquard press at Clos du Mesnil is the product of this collaboration between human beings and nature, but it is very fragile. Grape juice, like any fresh product, is perishable; fermentation helps preserve it, locking certain characteristics into the liquid while allowing it time to evolve and better express all its unique particularities.

Fermentation is a dynamic process in which the yeasts "eat" the sugar and turn it into alcohol. During this transformation, the liquid bubbles, the temperature rises, and carbon dioxide gas is given off. When the barrels are charged, the 2050 liters of must are spread out over twelve barrels, leaving a bit of room at the top of each for all the turbulence to take place. The carbonic gas escapes out through the pores of the wood or through the bunghole of the barrel (sometimes, when it's particularly active, the gas can back up and shoot the rub-ber stopper out of the hole).

While a small amount of air can be beneficial for fermentation, af-terwards, an excess of oxygen becomes the enemy. Once fermentation is complete—it usually takes about a week—the wine in the two top barrels is redistributed throughout the remaining ten, to fill them up. As Nguyễn said, the barrels being put to use for the first time are always placed on top, so that any slight, lingering aggressiveness from the wood is ultimately spread out over the other ten barrels.

Each of the individual parcels is kept strictly separate throughout the fermentation process and beyond, right up until they are used. "You'll have ample opportunity to see how that works later on," Eric tells me. "But for now you must be patient; fermentation has only just begun!"

It has, and I will.

⁓❦⁓

ADOLPHE Jacquesson was a trustworthy and generous man, as he demonstrated time and time again. He had given Joseph Krug, a recent arrival to France with no previous experience in Champagne, a job. He then made him a partner in his prestigious family business (not to mention providing his wife-to-be's dowry), thereby ensuring Joseph and his family certain prosperity and, as he had said, an easy life for the rest of his days. Which makes what happened in the autumn of 1842 even more shocking.

Joseph Krug, reneging on the promise he made to his friend and benefactor to remain his partner "all his long life," abruptly announced in a letter to Adolphe his intention to leave Jacquesson and start his own Champagne house.

The news couldn't have come at a worse time. Adolphe was seriously ill and away with his family in Paris receiving treatment from a doctor, and Emma and young Paul were there with them. Krug sent Emma a sealed letter to give Adolphe, and when Emma found out what it said, she was as surprised and dismayed as her brother-in-law was.

Unfortunately, none of Krug's letters survive, but several of Emma's do, and they offer precious insight into the critical events that followed.

One letter, dated August 29, 1842, reads in part:

I cannot tell you what sorrow your decision has caused. You had been talking of leaving for some time but I always hoped the

matter would resolve itself. Now that it has become serious, I am
most sad. When I think of leaving mother, Louisa and the
children—to whom, as you know, I am very attached—I cannot
believe it possible. Such a separation seems to me like a death:
and that it should be deliberate, and on our part, saddens me.
Poor Adolphe will do anything to make us happy. If office work
does not agree with you, go away more often; he does not ask you
to work. Only supervise. Be fully the master. [. . .] Why worry
about creating an establishment? You are not ambitious and, for
myself, I have never complained about my position. [. . .] Make
me happy by changing your resolution that has been for you, I am
sure, a painful one. We shall stay, shall we not?[8]

The idea of leaving Jacquesson and starting a house of his own
had evidently been on Krug's mind for some time. Emma dissuaded
him and hoped it would eventually just go away. But it didn't.
Throughout this difficult correspondence Emma demonstrated a real
affection for her husband. And Joseph obviously cared for her, too,
because he gave in to her entreaties and agreed to stay.

In a subsequent letter Emma was ecstatic and grateful, as well as
relieved. She also urged him to

Yield a little and, instead of regretting that you have not the cellars, think that this will make you freer. And we must confess that
Clauzet knows this business much better than you.[9]

Krug gave it his best shot. But it was no use: a few weeks later he
again resolved to leave, and this time there was no going back.
Emma, still away in Paris, tried to be upbeat, but the tone of her next
letter, written almost exactly a month after the first one, was glum
and defeated, even a bit annoyed. She said, in part:

I am extremely embarrassed by this sorry business both for myself
and for my people. I am anxious that we should all stay together.

Apart from the challenge of establishing yourself, I still fear the worry and the weight of the responsibilities you would have to bear might be harmful to your health. . . . [Adolphe] is quite willing to forget all that has taken place and live happily together but never speak of this business anymore. He would like to shake hands with you when he comes back and forget the whole thing. Do think carefully, my dear Krug, before taking a final decision. Is it not preferable to overlook an unpleasantness and live in peace rather than look for troubles and sorrows of the heart? We shall have a nice talk and see whether, while you are right, you could not yield a little for the happiness of being together. . . . I hope you have said nothing to Clauzet. It is best that our family matters should remain unknown to strangers, especially to those who live in Châlons. Clauzet would mention it to his wife and the whole town would speak of nothing else.[10]

What was it Joseph wanted so badly that he was willing to walk away from an extremely comfortable situation and risk everything? What was Emma referring to by "this sorry business," and what was it that she suggested he should yield on? Who was Clauzet? And, most importantly, what did Joseph Krug, who, as far as we can tell, didn't even know what Champagne was until eight years before, possibly want to do with the cellars?

On a chilly grey afternoon in early January, I sit in a little salon just off the reception area at Rue Coquebert speaking in hushed tones with a historian named Isabelle Pierre, who works in the Heritage Department, which oversees the Krug archives, and who has closely studied every historical shred related to the house and its founder.

"Unfortunately, most of the personal documents of Joseph Krug that were preserved by his son Paul were destroyed when their house was bombed during World War I," she says. "It's very frustrating; so little remains. But when you piece together all the fragments, a clear portrait of this enigmatic man begins to come into focus. At first he seems very serious, very sober, very Germanic. I think much of this had to do with his education and perhaps also with his large family and the early death of his mother; Joseph Krug was clearly taught not to show his feelings or emotions. But, despite outward appearances, I think he was really a very passionate person; beneath his cool exterior there was a fire burning."

When Isabelle utters these last sentences in a soft whisper (which seems to betray some hidden fire of her own), something ignites in my head.

Joseph Krug is forty-three years old. Throughout his life he has always demonstrated a decidedly rational nature, a quiet reason, a Teutonic temperance, and, at least on the surface, a stiff absence of emotion. But now he is different; now he is completely *un*-rational. His actions perilously fly in the face of reason and put everything he has achieved, along with his wife's happiness, his son's future, and his own good name, in jeopardy. The perennially steady and stoic Joseph Krug seems thrown off balance, out of kilter, even perhaps a little bit desperate, not unlike someone enmeshed in a fatal attraction.

Then it hits me: strange as it might seem, it would appear that the self-controlled, rational, mild-mannered M. Krug is madly, hopelessly in love.

And, indeed, he *is* in love, but with a wine—Champagne, to be precise—or rather, with his vision of a kind of Champagne that did not yet exist. And, as with any infatuation, he is irresistibly compelled to pursue this dreamy obsession at all costs and, by doing so, consummate this strange emotion that has mysteriously taken over and radically upset his life.

Once this thesis presents itself, facts begin to emerge to reinforce it, like circumstantial evidence about one caught out in an illicit affair. The longer Joseph stayed in Champagne, the more Champagne he drank, both Jacquesson's and that of their competitors. And the more experience he acquired, the more he began to develop his own ideas, both about the business and about the wine itself, and the less satisfied he became with the wine Jacquesson was producing.

There is also evidence that, beyond merely developing opinions about what the wine should be like, Krug had actually began blending Champagne himself and, even more surprising, that he appeared to be a quite good at it. Which brings us back to the mysterious Clauzet.

Hyacinthe Maurice Clauzet was born on November 3, 1801, in Sainte-Menehould, though he spent nearly his entire life in nearby Châlons. He began apprenticing in the Jacquesson cellars as a child and, over the nearly three decades that followed, painstakingly worked his way up to a position of importance in the company.

By the time Joseph arrived, Clauzet (who was just about the same age as Krug and Adolphe) was a key figure in the company's operations, and, like Joseph, he became even more so after Adolphe's father passed away. While Krug became a partner in the company, Clauzet kept a firm grip on the cellars, overseeing the production of the wines as well as making occasional sales trips to promote them. Having spent practically his whole life in the winery, he naturally felt a proprietary sense of entitlement, and while the company might have fallen short of the mark in Krug's opinion, for Hyacinthe, things were just fine as they were.

For Adolphe, Clauzet was a sort of safety net, a comfortable link of continuity, and a valuable asset, especially after his father died. For the enamored Krug, however, Clauzet was a nemesis, an annoying obstacle standing between him and the realization of his desire to consummate his love and create the perfect Champagne.

This was the "serious" situation Emma alluded to in her letters, and it presented something of a stalemate: Hyancinthe was not about to loosen his grip on the Jacquesson cellars. Adolphe, much as he liked Joseph, was not about to replace the tried-and-true Champenois with a foreign newcomer, especially in the cellars. And Krug, try as he might, could not dispel the obsession that had seized control of him and content himself with simply managing the office and having a very comfortable life.

Thus, there was nothing for him to do but to leave. And that's what he did.

It took Krug nearly a year after leaving Jacquesson to finalize the deal, but it was worth waiting for. His new partner, Hyppolite de Vivès, one of Reims's biggest wine merchants, wanted to step back from the daily operation of his establishment and wanted Krug to take it over—badly. Krug, it appears, was a talented and highly sought-after blender. There is evidence to suggest he had collabo-rated with de Vivès as far back as 1840, secretly blending wines for his company, and had been doing so for a number of other houses as well.[11] In any event, Krug managed to get de Vivès to give him a very generous package: 50 percent of the business for putting up one-third of the capital, a solid existing customer base, the contents of de Vivès's winery at 8 rue Saint-Hilaire in Reims (which included a substantial stock of wines), and, most importantly, complete control of the operation.

Thus, in 1843, Krug et Cie., as the new company was called, was born.

⌁

THOUGH Joseph Krug was driven more by passion and desire than entrepreneurial zeal, he could not have picked a better time to start a new Champagne venture if he'd tried. In fact, it is not unreasonable to suggest that a company like Krug could *only* have been conceived precisely when it was. Before that time, producers spent most of their energy trying to figure out whether the wine was supposed to sparkle or not and, after they did, trying to keep all their bottles from explod-ing, whereas after that time, a nearly continuous series of social up-heavals kept producers busy trying to keep their businesses afloat.

By 1843, the reputation of the bubbly wine was firmly established and spreading like wildfire; the production process had been refined, all of the major kinks had been worked out, and demand was rising exponentially. For the amorous Krug, this meant that not only could he entertain the luxury of imagining a truly beautiful Champagne, but he could also devote the bulk of his attention to bringing his

vision to life rather than cleaning up the mess left by exploding bottles. And the seemingly limitless international appetite for Champagne offered the prospect not only of realizing his dream but also of
substantial wealth and success.

The Marne Valley in the mid-nineteenth century was in many ways
like Silicon Valley in the late twentieth—lots of excitement, lots of
money flowing in, lots of speculation, and many people hustling to
get in on the action.

This was fertile ground for a whole slew of new companies to
sprout up, including Perrier-Jouët, Laurent-Perrier, Billecart-Salmon,
Roederer, De Venoge, Pol Roger, and Mercier, while many existing
ones morphed and merged to better position themselves in a rapidly
developing marketplace.

In 1832, Jean-Rémy Moët (grandson of founder Claude) retired
and left the company in the hands of his son Victor and son-in-law
Pierre-Gabriel Chandon de Briailles, and the following year the
company's name officially became Moët & Chandon.

Nicolas-Louis Delamotte took over the activities of the house
founded by his father, François, in 1760 and formed a partnership
with Jean-Baptiste Lanson in 1798. When Nicolas-Louis died in
1837, the company became known as Lanson, though the Delamotte
name would later make a comeback.

In 1856, Alexander Pommery created a company devoted primarily to textile trading (along with some wine trading) with partner
Narcisse Greno. When Pommery died two years later, his widow,
Louise, shifted the company's focus to sparkling wine production,
establishing huge underground cellars in the ancient chalk pits of
Reims to produce and store vast quantities of Champagne, starting a
trend that many others followed.

And after Florens-Louis Heidsieck died in 1828, the textile and
wine business he established in 1785 splintered into three wineries
bearing the Heidsieck name: the original company became known
as Heidsieck & Co. Monopole in 1834; Piper-Heidsieck was created

in 1838 by Christian Heidsieck with a former employee of his father's named Henri-Guillaume Piper; and finally Charles-Camille Heidsieck—son of Charles-Henri, who distinguished himself when he purportedly showed up in Moscow in 1811 astride a white horse with samples of wine and a notebook to take orders—created his own house named Charles Heidiseck in 1851 (we'll hear more about Charles-Camille later).

Along with Joseph Krug and the Heidsiecks, many of the second-wave start-ups were created by other transplanted Germans in the 1820s and '30s, such as Mumm, Bollinger, and Deutz, who, having settled in Champagne and gained experience working in wineries, decided to start their own enterprises. Some came from other places, like Edmond de Ayala, Paris-born son of a Colombian diplomat of Spanish descent, who in 1855 made a visit to the Vicomte de Mareuil and fell in love with the his niece Gabrielle Albrecht. The two married in 1858, and upon her uncle's death, Gabrielle inherited the Château d'Aÿ and surrounding vineyards, and the Ayala Champagne house was founded in 1860.

All of these houses—and a multitude of others—were born during this period not only to take advantage of a good business opportunity but also to help meet a steadily growing demand for the sparkling wine of Champagne. Besides markets in France, Europe, and the United Kingdom, export channels were now firmly established in the Baltic, South America, and the United States. And it seemed that people couldn't get enough of it.

Around the time of the French Revolution, a total of approximately three hundred thousand bottles of sparkling wine were shipped from the Marne. By the time Joseph Krug started his house in 1843, the total was over six million, and when he died in 1866, the number had nearly doubled, with three-quarters of the nearly twelve million bottles being shipped to destinations outside France. What's even more amazing is that this incredible growth took place during a period of social and political turmoil, including the revolution of 1848, which forced the "Citizen King" into exile, ending the French monarchy once and for all; the subsequent rise of Louis-Napoleon Bonaparte, nephew of *the* Napoleon, who became first president of the new republic and, three years later, orchestrated a coup d'état and created the Second Empire with himself as emperor; the Crimean War; the Second Opium War; and the second French intervention in Mexico (known as the "Mexican Adventure").

Not only did Champagne survive this constant tumult, it thrived. People throughout the world were clamoring for it. And the honest, hardworking merchant-producers of Champagne hustled to sell it to them. So did many of the less honest ones.

With the greatly expanded market, a number of significant things happened: the wine, which up until this time had usually been labeled under the generic term *vin mousseux* ("foamy wine"), began to be widely referred to as *Champagne*; people throughout the world began to think of the bubbly wine with the exotic name as the go-to libation of festivity; and a new breed of unscrupulous hucksters, both in the Champagne area and outside of it, began to make facsimiles of it.

While all this activity was going on, Joseph Krug had consummated his desire to have his own house and, once the tumult of leaving Jacquesson died down, quickly settled back into his typically reserved persona and set about building the business and creating his wine. He'd made a huge gamble, and it paid off; the venture, while not large in volume, was financially solid, the brand developed an excellent reputation and a loyal clientele, and he was able to provide well for his family while remaining true to his vision.

Now an established business owner and respected Rémois, Joseph became a bona fide French citizen in 1846. He maintained a polite veneer of amicability with his in-laws: Emma got to see her mother and sister quite often, and young Paul had a cordial relationship with his uncle Adolphe, who, in turn, was a constant pillar of support for his nephew. The house of Jacquesson continued to thrive after the departure of Krug,[12] and Adolphe himself was responsible for yet one more refinement of the Champagne process, inventing a wire cage called a *muselet* that fits snugly over the cork and twists around the lip of the bottle to keep it from popping out. This was a great improvement over the piece of string that was used previously and it went on to become the norm for Champagne and, indeed, most other kinds of sparkling wines throughout the world.

Having started his house at what was then the rather advanced age of forty-three, Joseph knew his son would have to take it over before too long, and he began grooming him for the task at an early age. Paul was quite receptive, showing a natural affinity for the Champagne business. And Joseph kept a detailed notebook to pass on to him, mapping out his theories and practices. His last entry was an account of his net worth of 1,407,921 francs, a considerable sum at the time, especially for the immigrant son of a butcher.

Paul Krug himself made the last entry in the notebook, noting the death of his father on August 5, 1866; the division of the estate between his mother and himself; and the creation of the new business entity, of which he was the head. Then he carefully wrapped up the notebook and tucked it away for safekeeping, where it remained, untouched and largely forgotten, for nearly a hundred years.

CHAPTER 6

✦❦ ❦✦

TASTING, TASTING, TASTING

ONE by one, the barrels in the flattened pyramids stop bubbling, fermentation gradually tapers off to a finish, and the liquid in the upper barrels (a liquid that can now accurately be called wine, albeit very new wine, but certainly not Champagne) is transferred to the ones beneath to fill them up. And there it remains.

On my next trip to Champagne in late November, I notice the countryside has once again been transformed: the hoards of people from far-off places have disappeared, the frenetic activity has shifted down to a very low gear just barely above a standstill, and the endless rows of what were once vibrant green vines have dropped their leaves and closed up shop for the winter, leaving dark, gnarly outlines against the dull gray sky. The only sign of life now is the occasional vigneron squatting on a low wooden stool amidst the endless vines, like a lone fisherman on the wide-open sea, getting a jump-start on pruning.[1]

Behind the gates at Rue Coquebert, as in countless other wineries throughout Champagne, the moment has finally come. We congregate just before eleven o'clock in the tasting room of the enology department, beneath the outward-facing clock under the eave. Julie and Jérôme are already there, chatting quietly, when Laurent comes in with a plastic crate cradling glass bottles filled with liquid in various shades of pale yellow and bearing handwritten labels on the front. Laurent and Jérôme arrange the bottles on the table and take a seat in one of the tall black swivel chairs. I too am sitting at a chair at the table, off to the side, trying to be inconspicuous. A moment later Eric saunters in, says hello to everyone, takes his place, and opens his big black notebook. "So, shall we begin?"

One of the bottles is passed around: "*La mise en bouche*," Jérôme whispers to me, "just to cleanse your palate." I watch as each person pours a small amount into the glass in front of them, twirls it around to coat the inside of the glass, tips the contents into their mouth and swishes it around, then spits it out into the sink set into the table in front of them. I do the same.

"*Alors*," says Eric, as he begins writing in the notebook, "let's see what we've got."

Jérôme, sitting at Eric's left, reads out the label of the first bottle and, while Eric enters the information in his notebook, pours a bit into his glass, then Eric's, and then passes the bottle around for others to do the same. When it gets to me, I pour two fingers' worth of wine and, being the last, place the bottle at the end of the table.

Everyone silently examines the wine in their glass, looking at it, swirling it, sniffing it, inhaling deeply, jotting down a few notes, taking a taste, slurping decisively to take in air, swishing it around, spitting it out into the sink, and making some more notes. After a minute, two at most, Eric begins.

"White flowers, grapefruit, mandarin peel, a touch of grilled bread; lively in the mouth, quite *net*, precise, almost crunchy. Sixteen."

Laurent: "Excellent structure, clean and well-balanced. Closed now, certainly, but for me there is much more to come. Sixteen, almost seventeen."

Julie: "The acidity is there but just barely. I find a bit of over-ripeness, even a hint of rot. Good but not extraordinary. Fifteen."

Jérôme: "Very good. The aroma reminds me of a caramelized apple tart with apricot glaze just coming out of the oven. Sixteen."

Silence. A moment later Eric looks up from his notes, his eyes peering at me across the table over his black frame glasses.

"Alan?"

Caught off guard, I practically choke. I had intended to be a mere observer, a passive fly on the wall. But that, apparently, is not going to happen.

"Would you care to offer some comments on the wine?" Eric prods.

"Well, um, yes, okay," I say, looking over my scratchy, barely legible notes. I feel everyone staring at me, waiting to see what I will say. Then I just dive in: "I liked the aroma a lot; white flowers, lilies, with a bit of tart green apple and fresh peach. The acid was very pronounced at first, almost harsh, but then it began to soften and open on the palate, as Laurent suggested. I like the chalky mineral finish, and, um—well yes, it seems good to me."

After a moment of silence, Eric says, "Thank you. Okay, next." Everyone dumps the remaining wine into the sink, Jérôme reads off the label on the next bottle, and the whole thing starts over again. And again and again.

I have been to many wine tastings: I often participate in panel tastings for a magazine where we blind-taste and critique thirty or forty wines at a sitting to determine whether they merit being included in the magazine or not; I have regularly attended a weeklong annual sit-down tasting for journalists in the Barolo area of Italy at which nearly a hundred just-released full-bodied, tannic red wines are tasted each morning; and I have been to countless trade tastings and wine fairs where a multitude of wines from many different places are sampled and assessed.

I have tasted very old wines, very new wines, and wines out of cask that have not yet completed their vinification process.

But I had never experienced a tasting quite like this.

First of all, it was fast—*very* fast. I'm a pretty quick taster but the speed of this one took my breath away: look, twirl, smell, taste, spit, comments, next. There's no pondering or equivocating, and the process of evaluation takes place like a snap of the fingers. Eric, I noticed, takes the entire contents of the glass into his mouth in one gulp, holds it there a second, then spits it out. Done.

At first I was startled by the sheer rapidity. But after the first four or five wines I began to get into a groove. The quickness, the lack of time to overthink and reflect about what I was tasting, actually became kind of liberating, and the act of tasting itself became, by necessity, more of a visceral automatic response than an in-depth intellectual examination.

Another issue for me was the wines themselves. Initially, they seemed thin, metallic, and razor-sharp; I was knocked off-kilter by the palate-numbing acidity, which felt like it was cutting holes in the back of my mouth. But after the first few wines, my taste buds adjusted, and other particularities began to emerge through the heavy metal mesh of mouth-puckering tartness. White lilies, spring blossoms, wildflowers, green apple, tart berries, ripe peach, leaves (green, dried, tomato), citrus, tree bark, smoke, buttered toast, bread dough, talcum, cement, wet gravel . . . A whole hidden world of scents and flavors began to unfold, accompanied by a multitude of different physical sensations—sharp and prickly, soft, warm, milky, reserved, a quick burst and fade, a slow crescendo. These distinctions were often not immediately obvious—after all, these wines were all the same grape variety (chardonnay) from the same 2013 vintage and the same general area—but rather subtle nuances that had to be carefully listened to, discerned, registered, and evaluated—and all in the blink of an eye.

Language was an issue too. It's hard enough as it is to describe your sensory impressions of a wine (especially wines like these), but it's even more difficult when you're trying to do it in a language that is not yours.

After this first tasting, Eric asks me what my impressions are. I tell him that it was a bit difficult for me at first to keep up with the pace and evaluate the wines, but that I found it totally fascinating.

"You're doing fine," he says. "And don't worry about trying to evaluate the wines. Just taste them; register your impressions, but keep an open mind. This is just the very beginning. These wines are brand new and a bit rough, like newborn babies being held up to the light: some of them are still wrinkly or blue, with messy hair or spittle on their chin. It's normal. This is just a first pass for us too, a quick snapshot to get an idea of what we've got."

The wines in these sessions, he reminds me, are samples siphoned off from one barrel per lot of wine before the wines have been racked (*soutirer* in French) and all the barrels of a particular parcel combined together. On several occasions during this series of tastings, a wine was immediately disqualified for some defect, barely perceptible to me but crystal clear to most everyone else, that might stem from a problem with an individual barrel. In such cases a note is made, another barrel of the same lot sampled later, and the questionable one carefully monitored to see whether it was a temporary isolated issue or not. In the event the problem does not go away, the contents of the barrel will be discarded and the barrel itself closely examined. Each barrel is, after all, different, and it is fascinating to see the effects this has on wines from the same parcel.

There are three tastings of the new wines that week, and by the end of the week it is starting to feel much more natural. I even begin giving numerical scores with my comments like everyone else. With over two hundred different wines from the 2013 vintage, these sessions continue for three to four weeks, until all the new wines have been tasted at least once. After that, the enology crew, like everyone else at Krug and elsewhere in Champagne, takes a break for the holidays.

"*Joyeux Noël et Bonne Année*," Eric says as I get ready to leave for the airport. "And remember what you tasted, because the same wines after *soutirage* will be completely different."

⁓◦◦⁓

AFTER decades—centuries even—of almost continuous domestic and international hostilities, a period of peace and prosperity finally arrived in France. By 1871 the Franco-Prussian War was over, the third (and last) Napoleon had fallen along with the Second Empire, and the monarchy had been abolished once and for all. A new political structure called the Third Republic was established, which finally institutionalized the revolutionary promises of liberty, equality, and brotherhood, while the Industrial Revolution, which was now in full swing, offered never-before-seen opportunities for the attainment of wealth and the enjoyment of prosperity, a prosperity made even more enjoyable by advances in science and technology. The invention of the camera, created by Louis Daguerre and presented to the French Academy of Sciences in 1839, changed the way people viewed the world. By the 1870s, this new vision helped give birth to a new artistic movement known as impressionism, which sought to represent impressions of subjects and moods of light rather than capture strict reality.

By 1870, Baron Georges-Eugène Haussmann's massive makeover of the center of Paris, begun in 1853 under Napoleon III, was largely completed, leaving a coherent layout of elegant parks, grand boulevards, and monumental squares that were well illuminated at night by gaslights. The new home of the Paris Opera, the Palais Garnier, with its extravagant Beaux-Arts façade and even more extravagantly ornate interior, was completed in 1875. And the Hôtel Ritz, opened in 1898 by Swiss hotelier César Ritz and his partner, chef Auguste Escoffier (emblematic champion of classic French haute cuisine and forerunner of today's celebrity chef), set a new standard for opulence, luxury, and comfort, with bathrooms, telephones, and electricity in each room.

The Universal Exposition that took place in Paris from May 6 to October 31, 1889, was a celebration of optimism and affluence, and the strikingly modern yet graceful tower designed by Gustave Eiffel for the occasion immediately became (and remains) an iconic symbol of unlimited possibility and the glory of France.

During this period, a whole new class of people known as *nouveaux riches* blossomed. They had money and wanted to celebrate their good fortune, and celebrate it they did—with Champagne—but unlike the royal extravaganzas of time past, this was not a private party: now everyone (just about) was invited. The expression "Tout-Paris," which once referred to the upper crust of entrenched high society, came to mean anyone who was someone of interest in some way: wealthy entrepreneurs, old nobility, foreigners, actors, musicians, artists, courtesans.

Dance halls, cafés, and cabarets sprang up all over Paris, including the fashionable bistro Maxim's, opened by a former waiter named Maxime Gaillard in 1893; the Palace Theatre (now the Casino de Paris); the Moulin de la Galette in Montmartre, where festive balls immortalized in paintings by Renoir and Toulouse-Lautrec regularly took place; and the lavishly decorated, fabulously risqué club called the Folies Bergère. In Édouard Manet's famous painting *A Bar at the Folies-Bergère*, the predominance of gold foil–topped bottles on the bar gives a clear indication of the preferred beverage of the period, the very same period in which Champagne became inextricably linked with the aura of celebration.

The Belle Époque (or "Beautiful Time"), as it would later become known, was a time of high spirits, big dreams, and seemingly unlimited possibilities. And at most every table in every café, and at raucous cabarets and unbridled festivities, a glass of Champagne was lifted high in celebration of this ebullient time by a cast of larger-than-life personalities who were both a product and a reflection of this unique moment. While this cast of characters was a large one indeed, there are three in particular that exemplify not only the era but also Champagne's important role in it.

Just as his father was one of the first to realize the commercial opportunities that Eastern Europe and tsarist Russia offered Champagne, Charles-Camille Heidsieck was among the very first to set his sights on America. Having just started up his own eponymous house with his brother-in-law and partner Ernest Henriot, Charles made his first exploratory journey to the East Coast of America in 1852 and quickly found someone to represent his wines there. Americans liked him: the thirty-year-old Frenchman was witty, charming, adventurous, and personable. Even more importantly, they liked his wine.

When Charles returned to America five years later, the brand was extremely popular: annual sales were at an incredibly strong three hundred thousand bottles, notwithstanding the financial panic of 1857, and he was treated like a celebrity, with fancy dinner parties and festive receptions up and down the East Coast, where he immersed himself in American high society. Due to his affable nature, he fit in quite well; he seemed to genuinely like the brasher, more down-to-earth Americans, who, in turn, took to affectionately calling him "Champagne Charlie."

With the bourgeoning American market already forming a significant part of his company's business, Champagne Charlie made another visit in 1860 to bolster sales in the South, especially in the former French territory of New Orleans, and this is when things started to get complicated.

A year later, his US agent informed Heidsieck he was having difficulty collecting money owed in southern states due to growing domestic hostilities. As these outstanding payments represented a substantial portion of his company's revenue, Heidsieck had no alternative but to go back to America and try to resolve the problem. When he got there, the country was on the brink of civil war, and with all financial transactions between the North and South suspended, he went south to try to get the money himself.

In Kansas, with his customers practically bankrupt, he agreed to accept cotton in place of cash and attempted to smuggle it to Europe on two separate ships, but they were both sunk by Union forces. With access to Louisiana tightly controlled, a now not-so-ebullient Champagne Charlie sought assistance from the French consul in Mobile, Alabama, who gave him a diplomatic pouch for the consul in New Orleans to get him through the military blockades. When

Heidsieck arrived in New Orleans in 1862, the city was under siege by Union forces, and when the pouch he was carrying was found to contain documents from French textile manufacturers for the production of Confederate uniforms, Charlie was promptly arrested as a foreign spy, despite his pleas that he had no idea whatsoever what was inside the bag.

This set off an escalating diplomatic situation between France and the (not so united) United States that became known as the Heidsieck Incident. After Napoleon III appealed directly to Abraham Lincoln, Champagne Charlie was finally released on November 16, 1862, but he was not able to recover the money he was owed and hobbled back to France in very poor health, with his spirit broken and his business bankrupt.

It appeared that the impetuous entrepreneur's luck had finally run out.

Then, out of the blue, Champagne Charlie received a letter from the brother of the New York agent who had defaulted on the payments and inadvertently thrown Heidsieck into great difficulty. To help right the wrong, the deceased agent had left Heidsieck a number of deeds for what amounted to a rather large holding of land in the state of Colorado, in an area that had been undergoing tremendous expansion and would soon become known as the city of Denver. The deeds were promptly sold for a significant amount of money that not only repaid all the outstanding debts but also left a substantial amount of operating capital to put Champagne Charlie's house back in business.

The American market for Charles Heidsieck Champagne quickly got back on track after the Civil War ended, and because of the strong brand recognition created by its intrepid founder, the house was perfectly positioned to take advantage of the huge increase in demand during America's post–Civil War corollary to the Belle Époque, which became known as the Gilded Age and had its own colorful cast of extremely wealthy, colorful, and very thirsty individuals. Champagne Charlie, however, never returned to America and enjoyed his prosperity from the comfort of his home in France, where he died in 1893.

During his heyday, news of Champagne Charlie's American adventures bounced back across the ocean, and he also became something of a legend in Europe. In 1866 a music hall performer called George Leybourne (his real name was Joe Saunders) wrote a song called "Champagne Charlie," which he premiered at Leeds Town Hall. The song was a huge hit; it became popular in music halls throughout England and beyond, and Leybourne's weekly income quadrupled. Further adding to his income, Moët & Chandon paid Leybourne a fee to have their company name worked into the lyrics. The success of this number induced another music hall performer named Alfred Vance (aka "The Great Vance," real name Alfred Peak Stevens) to write a competing song called "Clicquot, Clicquot," which was sponsored by the competing house. Occasionally the two would even appear together in a kind of sing-off, with each performing at opposite sides of the stage swilling their respective Champagnes of choice.

Though Leybourne's song poked fun at the foppish, dandy-like upper-class character of Champagne Charlie—the music hall audience was, after all, largely middle-class—his manager urged him to capitalize on the success as much as possible by fully playing the part even offstage. And he did. In fact, he practically became his character: Leybourne wore long weeping whiskers; dressed in striped pants, a smart cutaway jacket, and top hat; and drove around in a four-horse carriage drinking nothing but Champagne (and lots of it) while chasing women and extolling the high life, helping create a whole new type of music hall persona known as the *lion comique*.[2]

Louise-Joséphine Weber was born in 1866 in the town of Clichy-la-Garenne, just outside Paris, into a Jewish family from Alsace. While her father was away fighting in the Franco-Prussian War, her mother ran away with a lover, leaving Louise, brother Henri, sister Marie-Anne, and illegitimate baby sister Victorine-Madeline in a convent.

And when her father returned from the war in 1871 with his legs severely mutilated, the children had to remain there.

While this was surely not an easy situation, Louise and her siblings were resilient, one might even say happy, and full of *esprit de vie*. Most of all, Louise liked to dance. She had her public debut at the age of six at a Christmas party for distressed children of Alsace-Lorraine at the famed Elysée Montmartre ballroom hosted by Victor Hugo and the Comtesse de Chabrillan. Seeing the darling hand-holding sisters, with their pink cheeks, blonde hair, and white pinafores, the comtesse asked Louise and Marie-Anne to do a dance and they happily complied, to the great pleasure and applause of all present. Louise didn't realize that Victor Hugo was a huge celebrity (sitting on his lap, she asked the kind man with the full white beard if he was Père Noël) or that the Comtesse de Chabrillan was a big celebrity too. And she could never have imagined that she and the elegant woman had a lot in common.[3]

In 1873 Louise's father died, and the following year the children were removed from the convent and raised by their maternal uncle, Pierre Courtade, in the nearby town of Saint-Ouen. As a teenager, Louise helped out at the laundry where her older sister worked and began exploring the seedy edges of Paris, in particular the village-like quarters of Montmartre and Montparnasse. Louise left home at sixteen to live with her boyfriend, who was also of Alsatian descent, and discovered places like the Moulin de la Galette, La Closerie des Lilas, and the Bal Bullier. Working at the laundry during the day, she also began posing for painters and photographers and frequenting the cabarets at night, where she happily joined in the dancing, attracting the attention and admiration of all.

Three years and two lovers later, with the coaching and encouragement of Céleste Mogador (Comtesse de Chabrillan) and another well-known dancer-choreographer by the stage name of Grille d'Égout ("sewer cover"), she got her first paying job as an entertainer in a new revue at the Cirque Fernando in Montmartre along with

Boum-Boum the clown.[4] After that she became a fixture in the city's hottest dance halls, joining the ranks of performers like "Camélia dite Trompe-la-Mort," "Nini Pattes-en-l'Air," "la Môme Fromage," and Jane Avril (better known as "Jane la Folle") and, like most of them, regularly engaged in prostitution to make extra money. But Louise stood out.

Noticed by impresarios Charles Zidler and Joseph Oller, she was immediately hired for their new venue, the Moulin Rouge, which opened in 1889. The cancan, a saucy variation of other dances like the galop, the quadrille, and the chahut, was all the rage, and Louise brought it to new raunchy heights: she lifted her leg so high that a heart embroidered on her culottes could be clearly seen; she raised up her perfumed skirts and ruffled them right in the faces her dumbfounded spectators; and, slipping off her shoes, she sneaked up on unsuspecting customers and knocked off their top hats with a brisk kick of her foot.

Dancing boisterously through the hall, she would grab a glass of Champagne off a table and down it in one gulp without missing a beat, then another and another. Champagne was her favorite, and chilled bottles and perspiring glasses were everywhere. One night the Prince of Wales was in the audience, incognito and trying to keep a low profile, when her voice boomed out across the room, "Hey Wales, tonight the Champagne's on you!" And it probably was. She seemed to have an inextinguishable penchant for the stuff, but no one seemed to mind: the sweet bubbly wine renewed her energy and made her lift her legs even higher. For this reason she was given the sobriquet La Goulue, "the gluttonous one."

The Moulin Rouge quickly became the undisputed palace of the Belle Époque, and the ravenous La Goulue its reigning queen. In 1895, La Goulue, now rich and famous, decided to set out on her own, forming an act that toured all over France. And that's when things began to unravel.

Fabulously famous/infamous though she was, outside the gritty streets and dance halls of Montmartre, the spectacle of La Goulue and company fell flat, like a Champagne that had lost its bubbles. At the end of that year she returned to Paris disillusioned and financially depleted. Several years later, after giving birth to a son she named Simon-Victor (father unknown), she began working in circuses as a lion tamer. In 1910 she married a circus magician named Joseph-Nicolas Droxler and they created a lion-taming act together, but after only a few years the two drifted apart.

La Goulue, former queen of the cancan, eventually made her way back to Paris where, now destitute, alcoholic, and severely overweight, she sold peanuts, matches, and cigarettes to revelers in front of her old haunts in Montmartre and slept in a wagon parked by the side of the road. Though most people had no idea who she was, when someone did occasionally show up to pay their respects to the once famous *danseuse*, La Goulue was always happy to appease them by discreetly lifting her skirt and doing a little turn, eyes closed, singing to herself, feeling once again the warm sticky air of the Moulin Rouge and the admiring eyes of all fixed upon her, while her dance, and the cool bubbly Champagne she so enjoyed, became an enduring image of the Belle Époque.[5]

Another thing that characterized the Belle Époque was *la grande geste*, the tendency (facilitated by new technologies) to do things *and* let people know about it on a large scale, and few succeeded at both better than a man named Eugène Mercier.

Eugène Edouard Mercier was born in Épernay on April 20, 1838, to Jeanne Marguerite, a twenty-two-year-old daughter of a grape grower who had become pregnant out of wedlock and left her family home in disgrace.

As soon as he was old enough, Eugène was sent to a school run by the Frères of Épernay, and he began working in the vineyards when he was thirteen. Even at this young age, the child always seemed to be in a hurry to get somewhere. (As an adult, Mercier, who purportedly slept only three hours a night, would be quoted as saying, "I rest very quickly.")

From the vineyards, Eugène followed the grapes into the winery, where there was work all year round, and here the young man began to nurture a dream: one day he would have his own house that would make excellent Champagne that everyone could afford. While this might have seemed a preposterous idea for a fatherless child with a young mother struggling to keep her small family out of the poorhouse, Eugène didn't think anything was impossible and set about making his dream a reality.

After working several years at the winery of Philippe Bourlon in Cramant, Mercier proposed to his boss that he create a *union des propriétaires* with a handful of other small producers and open an office in Paris to market their wines. This was in 1858; Mercier was twenty years old, and the business did quite well. But it was just the beginning.

In 1867, Mercier married Bourlon's daughter, and four years later he undertook the realization of his childhood dream of building a winery of his own. And this is where his true nature as a visionary entrepreneur who thought on a grand scale became evident. "Don't think in meters, think in kilometers!" he told his architect when planning the new winery. And indeed, this cellar was quite unlike anything ever seen before. It took six years to complete; over a million square feet of chalky earth were excavated, creating forty-seven galleries extending for nearly five miles sixty feet below the surface, with a direct connection to the Paris-Strasbourg railway. This was indeed a grandiose project, but there was a practical side to it as well: if Mercier's objective was to make Champagne for the masses, it had to be relatively inexpensive. In order to keep the price down, he realized, he had to produce a large quantity, and in order to sell a large volume, people needed to know about it. This trail of reasoning led to one of the earliest examples of brand marketing in the modern sense of the term.

For Mercier, the new wine cellar was not merely a production facility but a tourist attraction. He was one of the very first to open his wine cellar to the public, offering tours of the extensive subterranean labyrinth in a horse-drawn carriage, where huge bas-reliefs carved out of the chalk walls by a Champenois artist named Gustave-André Navlet could be admired and the entire process of making Champagne could be observed. He was also among the first to install the new technology of electricity in his cellar, both to provide light and to power some of the machinery.

Just after construction of the new winery began, Mercier started working on another large-scale project: building the largest wine cask in the world. After he sent his cooper (who happened to have the propitious name of Jolibois, or "pretty wood") to Hungary to personally select the ancient trees that would be used to construct the mega barrel, the undertaking, which would take over a decade to complete, began in earnest. This project too had both a practical objective—creating a container that could be used to blend a huge quantity of wine—and a promotional one. With a capacity of 160,000 liters (about 42,000 gallons or over 200,000 bottles of wine), the "Cathedral of Champagne" was hauled to Paris by twenty-four oxen and eighteen horses and unveiled at the 1889 Universal Exposition, where it attracted almost as much attention as the Eiffel Tower and, needless to say, spread the Mercier name far and wide.[6] But the restless entrepreneur didn't stop there.

The first manned flight of an aircraft, a hot-air balloon created by brothers Joseph-Michel and Jacques-Étienne Montgolfier, took place in Paris in 1783, and hot-air balloons were subsequently refined and adapted for military use and as an amusement. But it was still something of a novelty when Eugène Mercier used it as a publicity vehicle at the Universal Exposition of 1900 in Paris from April 15 to November 12, tethering a balloon with MERCIER in huge letters and taking people for a ride a thousand feet into the air, rising like a big bubble of Champagne, while they sampled his wine. Thousands of people got to partake of the unique experience, and millions more watched it from the ground and had the name of the Champagne producer imprinted on their consciousness. On the last day of the fair—which happened to be a rather windy one—the balloon accidently broke loose of its tether and sailed northwards until it dropped gracefully into a wheat field in Belgium. When the authorities arrived, they found the wayward balloonists toasting their good fortune at having survived their impromptu journey. Mercier was fined for having illegally imported Champagne into the country, but he didn't mind: the event was reported in newspapers throughout Europe, and Mercier said merrily that it was the cheapest publicity he ever paid for.[7]

As if the balloon escapade wasn't enough, Mercier also took advantage of yet another monumental technology developed by another set of French brothers to promote his brand, contracting Louis and Auguste Lumière (who had debuted the first moving picture in 1895) to create a film about Champagne shot in and around Mercier's winery. The film, entitled *Champagne from Vine to Glass*, was shown to throngs of people during the Universal Exposition of 1900 and is widely considered to be the first publicity film ever made.

In all of these high-profile exploits, not only did Eugène Mercier make good Champagne accessible to more people than ever before, he also recognized the importance of publicity and took the promotion of brand—intrinsic to Champagne from the very beginning—to new heights, laying the foundation for a modern concept of marketing that continues to this day.

∽⦿⤳

WHILE less adventurous than Champagne Charlie, less risqué than La Goulue, and less ostentatious than Mercier, Joseph and Emma Krug's son Paul was also a reflection of the buoyant period in which he lived. As a child he spent a lot of time with his mother and his aunt's family while his father was engaged with his business activities. But Joseph loved and nurtured the boy; he encouraged him to study hard in school and, when he was traveling abroad with his mother in England, urged him to perfect his language skills and be observant of the things around him, requesting detailed descriptions of what the young boy saw. At home, as Paul grew into a young man, Joseph involved him more and more in the world of Champagne, bringing him into the vineyards to inspect the vines (he even sometimes stayed over with a vigneron), and into the winery and tasting room to familiarize him with the complicated techniques of making Champagne.

By the time Joseph died, twenty-three-year-old Paul was well equipped to take over management of the firm, with the support of his father's partner, de Vivès, and his uncle, Adolphe Jacquesson. Paul inherited a financially solid business with an established clientele, but he deserves credit for taking it and riding the big Champagne wave of the Belle Époque for all it was worth, turning the house his father built into a bona fide grande marque. While Joseph overcame huge risks to create a viable business, during Paul's tenure the company realized wealth and prosperity beyond what his father could even have imagined. The volume of production increased considerably and, thanks in part to steadily rising prices, revenue more than quadrupled.

Besides his business, Paul also inherited his father's exceptional knack for blending Champagne: in addition to personally blending all of Krug's wines, Paul continued his father's practice of blending Champagne for other houses, which continued to be an important activity for the house and accounted for a sizable amount of the revenue for years to come.

Unlike his father, Paul was large and robust; he had a predilection for loud laughing and having a good time and was an avid sportsman who loved to hunt. He got married in 1868 and, like his German grandfather, had ten children. In 1872, to accommodate his growing family and the growing business, Paul acquired property at the corner of boulevard Lundy and rue Coquebert where he built a new winery (the same one that exists to this day) and a palatial mansion called Le Quarante in the classical style, with turreted mansard roofs and chimneys.[8] He also purchased a summer estate on the coast of Normandy in a small town called Bénouville.

Paul was one of the first to foresee potential threats to Champagne, particularly concerning the often tenuous rapport between growers and shippers, and the growing number of counterfeit products that were appearing on the market. And he was among the first to push for an organization of producers that could work with vignerons to protect the reputation of Champagne.[9]

The Belle Époque was the time when Champagne—with its distinctive "pop" of the cork and bubbly effervescence—became *the* symbol of celebration, the harbinger of good times, and the epitome of the good life, and not just for the lucky few. During this time Champagne became an obtainable luxury, almost a necessity, for a substantial segment of the population rather than just a handful of rich nobles behind closed doors, and not just in Paris or France but throughout a significant portion of the world, including Europe, Russia, Scandinavia, the United States, and South America.

Champagne took on this celebratory aura during what was for many a time of peace, prosperity, and opportunity. And, as often occurs during such periods of what someone would later refer to as "irrational exuberance," there was a natural tendency to think it would last forever.[10] Alas, it would not.

☙❧

IT'S January in Champagne: the holidays are over, winter vacations in snowy mountains or some faraway sandy beach fade to a pleasant dream, and the new year stretches far ahead into the future. People, back from wherever they were, get back to work. And for the enology team that means tasting. The pre-holiday tasting of the brand new wines from barrel was just a warm-up. Now tasting begins in earnest.

The first order of business is a thorough examination (or rather, reexamination, since each reserve wine is retasted each year until it is gone) of the stock of reserve wines.

Krug, like many other houses in Champagne, keeps a significant amount of wine in reserve. But Krug keeps more of them than most other houses, and for longer (as much as fifteen years, in some cases). And, following its practice of vinification by individual parcel, Krug keeps them all separate.

There are between 100 and 150 different reserve wines in the Krug cellars at any given time, spanning up to fifteen different vintages. Naturally, the largest quantities tend to be wines from the most recent vintage—2012 in this case—and the smallest quantities are from the oldest. (In 2013/2014, the oldest wine in reserve was a 1998 from Avize.) As the reserve wines get used each year, they are transferred to progressively smaller containers in the cellar. When the remaining amount of a wine gets too small to fill even a small container, it is combined with other compatible remaining wines to make up enough volume to fill a small vat.

Needless to say, this carries a huge expense, but because an ample library of reserve wines is essential to the production of the Grande Cuvée, it is an absolutely crucial one.[11]

While sourcing wines of different grape varieties and from different areas began with the Champagne wine trade itself, intentionally laying aside wines from good vintages to make up for the shortcomings of less favorable subsequent ones came later. Because the wine of Champagne was particularly volatile—one of the problems that Dom Pérignon had worked so hard to rectify—and storage in barrels made it even more so, producers sought to sell off everything they possibly could as soon as possible. It is likely that good wine from a bountiful vintage may have exceeded market demand and the leftover wine could (and surely would) have been kept and mixed in with the following vintage or two. But initially this happened more by chance than by intention.

With improvements in winemaking and the diffusion of the glass bottle and cork stopper, the longevity of wine increased, and by the 1830s and 1840s, it was not unusual for Champagne houses to maintain an inventory of wines from past vintages that could be used to boost their production if necessary or as a blending tool to improve their product and satisfy customer demand.

When Joseph Krug took over the cellar of de Vivès in 1843, he inherited a stock of wines (including wines of Aÿ and Verzenay), as well as candles, string, and empty bottles.

While the use of reserve wines may have historically begun as a way of making something passable in a poor vintage, for Joseph Krug it offered yet another tool for creating the kind of superlative Champagne he envisioned every year, regardless of the climatic vicissitudes, while still maintaining a consistent character and style. For this reason, this Champagne (which would later become known as Krug Grande Cuvée) became the standard bearer of the house, the essence of what Krug is about, and it remains so today. It is also, according to Eric, the most demanding of their wines to make.

In order to guarantee the continuity of the Grande Cuvée, it is absolutely essential to maintain an ample collection of reserve wines. And this sometimes necessitates some difficult choices.

I ask Eric for an example of the house's priorities. "As you may remember," he says, "2012 was a strange year. The weather was terrible all spring and summer with nearly continuous rain and devastating hailstorms just before harvest. Production was down by thirty to forty percent. But, much to our surprise, the grapes that were picked were excellent and many of the wines were extraordinary. And it was definitely a year with an interesting story to tell. We could have made an excellent vintage Champagne. But the quantities were limited and, what's more, our reserve holdings were seriously depleted. If we had made a vintage that year, our production of Grande Cuvée could have been compromised for decades to come. So we didn't. The wine went into reserve."

With that, he stands up and grabs his black notebook. "Speaking of reserve, let's go taste."

Being back in the tasting room has the familiar feel of a homecoming; I slip easily into my usual place at the far side of the table near the windows looking onto the courtyard and, when the first bottle arrives, automatically pour a bit of wine into my glass, swish it around my mouth, and spit it into the sink to wake up my palate. I heeded Eric's advice before the break and tried to lock in the memory of the 2013 wines we tasted when I was last here. And as we dive into the reserves, I can immediately detect a world of difference.

We begin with six 2012s from Villers-Marmery (Gérard Moreau's town) which score mostly in the thirteen-to-fifteen-point range. These are good solid wines, with full body and ripe caramel–lemon curd flavors. While they might seem a tad short on personality and verve on their own, wines like these, I imagine, could function as building blocks to help form a solid foundation for a blend. The character level goes up a notch in the three 2011s that follow—one of them is fresh and lively with a touch of smokiness and a surprising level of maturity (I give it fifteen points); another has a buttery caramel-toffee nose and slightly muddy palate (an acceptable twelve points); the third, a pronounced aroma of shoe polish and soy with a brambly rustic edge (I gave it fourteen).

And the level goes up yet again with three 2010s: the first is elegant and meaty, like beef bouillon (fifteen points), another is subtle and delicate (fourteen), and the last suggests bitter orange rind, resin, and tobacco (fifteen points). A 2006 (again from Villers-Marmery) is the standout with a lovely aroma of jasmine flowers and tropical fruits, and dried plum on the palate (seventeen points), while the last wine, a 2010 from Trepail with fluffy lemon meringue and firm acidity (fifteen to sixteen points), is not far behind.

As usual, Eric assiduously records comments and scores in his black notebook. The whole thing takes less than half an hour, but the pace seems less frantic and frenetic than it did before. After the last wine, Eric snaps shut his notebook: "Good, thank you. So what is there to drink?" Jérôme goes over to the fridge in the corner and comes back with a label-less magnum;[12] after he gently eases out the cork, the bottle gets passed around the table and we fill our glasses. The wine—pale golden, straw-colored, with a subtle aroma of leather and faded flowers; sour grapefruit peel acidity, baked pineapple, and burnt sugar on the palate; and a long slow finish, during which a myriad of flavor sensations float by—turns out to be Krug Vintage 1998, and it's excellent. Needless to say, no one spits.

The final reserve tasting is devoted mostly to pinot noir. Standouts for me are a 2009 from the Aube commune of Les Riceys that has a lovely floral aroma, a soft yet tart berry palate, and a dry white pepper finish (sixteen); a 2001 from Aÿ with a distinctive yellow color, grilled bread aroma, and almond paste palate (seventeen); and a 2012 red, also from Aÿ, that sang out fresh strawberry, rosehips, and phosphate (seventeen).[13] The session is capped off by a 1997-based Grande Cuvée from the fridge (layers of rich and buttery puff pastry with taut lemon confit acidity, fine persistent bubbles, and a long luscious finish), and it puts the entire series of reserve wine tastings into perfect perspective.

Midway through the tastings, I have to remind myself that while many of these reserve wines are excellent and some of them have significant bottle age, they are still not to be evaluated as finished wines, the way one would, say, five- to ten-year-old burgundies, though it is still hard for me to articulate exactly how they *should* be evaluated.

Eric meticulously records our brief comments and numerical scores on each wine, as if compiling clues to a complex theorem he is determined to eventually work out. I could understand jotting down comments to get an overall idea of flavor profile, but what, I ask myself, is the point of giving a numerical score to a wine that's not even finished? I will have to wait until a bit later to find out.

∾ఴఛ

WHILE the tasting panel charges through the reserve wines, Jean Nguyễn and the rest of the blue-jumpsuited workers are completing the *soutirage* of the new wines of 2013.

The rubber stopper is removed from the hole in the lower front of the barrel and a spigot with a long tapered nozzle is quickly inserted.

As the spigots are opened, the wine falls into a trough beneath the pile of barrels and is pumped into a stainless-steel vat. When the barrel is close to empty, Jean tips it slightly forward to get the last of the liquid but is careful to leave the sedimentary sludge at the bottom of the barrel. This procedure will be repeated until all the barrels of a pyramid have been emptied and mixed together in one stainless-steel vat, combining together all the individual micro-vinifications, with the subtle differences and unique characteristics of each wooden barrel, into one cohesive expression of the particular parcel.

These *après soutirage* wines are now known as *vins clairs* ("clear wines") and, after a week or so, they will be ready to begin tasting too.

This is the second of two weeks devoted to tasting the reserve wines, and an intense, hectic, and fascinating week it is. During this winter period I'm coming to Paris from New York instead of Italy, so the trip is considerably longer and there is a six-hour time difference. I usually leave on Sunday or Monday evening and arrive at Charles de Gaulle early the next morning, get the 6:22 TGV (high-speed train) to Champagne-Ardenne, and take the local Transport Express Régional train to Reims, where I drop my suitcase at my hotel and head straight to Rue Coquebert in time for the daily coffee chat with the crew.

Reims is by now quite familiar. During the early visits I stayed in different hotels—my main priorities were proximity to both the train station and Krug, working wifi, and reasonable cost—but I quickly gravitated to two preferred places: the Best Western Plus Hôtel de la Paix and the Grand Hôtel des Templiers. The Hôtel de la Paix is located on a side street off the Place Drouet-d'Erlon a few minutes from the station and has a sleek modern decor in a renovated shell of several old buildings that were probably destroyed during the First World War. The rooms in the back look down onto a courtyard and out over rooftops to the striking towers of the cathedral, impressive during the day but even more beautiful at night, when it is illuminated and you can even hear the soft comforting thud of the bells tolling the hours. The Hôtel des Templiers is a bit further from the station but closer to Krug (right around the corner, in fact), just off of boulevard Lundy.

Located in what was once a nineteenth-century residence, Templiers is smaller and more intimate, with the feel of a prim bourgeois Belle Époque *maison*. Madame Mauget, the proprietress, warmly welcomes me by name each time I return and usually gives me the same room each visit, a large salon-like *chambre* with elegant old-fashioned furnishings and a huge marble bathtub. While I generally pass on breakfast, I occasionally splurge and have it—a pot of French coffee, a basket of miniature croissants, some fruit, and a yogurt—in my room while still sporting my plush Templiers-monogramed robe and slippers, just to prolong the sensation of feeling like a Rémois burgher.

Besides meeting all my stated prerequisites, both these places have one additional amenity: a swimming pool. After a long day of tasting, spitting, critiquing, listening, note-taking, and trying to follow nonstop rapid-fire French, often while still fighting off serious jet lag, I go back to my hotel, put on my bathing suit, and jump into the hotel pool, blowing bubbles out of my nose underwater while attempting to perform a proper stroke. I love these moments of quiet solitude—it's off-season and I'm usually the only one there—during which I can turn off my brain and methodically plow through the heavy water, which muffles the sounds without and within. Sometimes, however, and quite unconsciously, my aquatic efforts blend with my vinous ones and I imagine I am floating in a big tub of Champagne, sending my not-so-elegant bubbles up to the surface.

After my swim, I have a good sweat in the sauna, then go back to my room, take a cool shower, get dressed, and head out for dinner. I usually skip lunch, but dinner is another story.[14] Besides providing my main nourishment of the day, dinner is also the time I get to relax, reflect back over the day's events, and actually savor wine with food and see how it evolves during my meal. While the consumption of calories is a necessity for every human being and a break from intensely focused activity is always welcome, for the wine professional, sitting down and savoring wine is just as important. For in the end, all of the tasting and critiquing and analyzing and research and fine-tuning of the faculties of sensory perception come back to this: the pure pleasure of enjoying excellent wine with food and watching it develop over the course of a meal. (You could also add "sharing the experience with other people" to the list, but, though there are other diners in the restaurants, not to mention the waiters and hosts, my dinners during these trips are always taken alone.) These occasions also offer me the valuable opportunity to try some wines of Champagne that I am not familiar with.

As with the hotels, I initially tried a number of different restaurants but quickly gravitated to two that became my favorites. Both are on the same street—practically next door to one another, in fact—on rue de Mars just around the corner from the Porte de Mars, one of the few remnants of the ancient Roman origins of the city, and right in front of the art deco Boulingrin market.[15]

Brasserie Boulingrin has been in the area since 1925, and I went there the very first time I visited Reims, when it was in its original location across the street beside the market.[16] The interior was a bit tired and so was the food, but with its slightly threadbare yet cozy ambiance and nonplussed, long-aproned waiters, it had an appealing old-world feel that made me want to go back.

At the end of October 2013, after having been closed for nearly seven months, Brasserie Boulingrin reopened. The new incarnation, on the conical corner of rue de Mars and rue Henry IV, was more elegant that the original one, with lots of shiny mirrors, polished brass, and cushy red banquettes on two floors connected by a wide marble staircase. But it still retains its comfortable old-world feel. Better yet, the service, provided by friendly young men and women dashing briskly to and fro, is markedly improved, and so is the food.

I quickly became acquainted with the maître d', Cyril, who always greets me by name and gets a big kick out of showing off his English ever since he found out I was American. I sat upstairs a few times, but he soon took to seating me at a corner banquette on the ground floor in the room with the big bar, where I can observe all the activity and chat with the wait staff.

Here I focus on traditional bistro fare—that is, for the most part, meat. I love the *jambon de Reims* (a local take on the Burgundian classic jambon persillé) and the *fromage de tête, à volonté*, a head cheese terrine of moist shredded morsels held together by a densely flavored (but not too stiff) gelatin abundantly flecked with parsley and black pepper. À *volonté* means "as much as you want," so they plop the whole terrine down on the table with a sharp knife and leave it there until you wish to surrender it. And when I have it, I think they are often surprised by how much is missing when I finally let it go.

My favorite main course is the classic Alsatian brasserie dish *choucroute garnie*: warm, thinly sliced sauerkraut flavored with vinegar and juniper and cooked in beer, with a variety of different pork cuts—smoked pork chop, pork belly, garlic sausage, frankfurter—steamed potatoes, and spicy mustard. But sometimes I opt for a simple *filet de boeuf au poivre* or *onglet* (hanger steak) with *frites*.

At Boulingrin, after the obligatory *coupe de Champagne*, I usually want something red (although with the *choucroute* I often get a tall cool glass of hoppy Kronenbourg 1640 Alsatian draft beer). Here I discover, and fall in love with, two anomalies of Champagne, both representatives of the *other* two appellations of the region: a nonvintage Coteaux Champenois Bouzy Rouge by Lanson and a Rosé des Riceys 2008 by Alexandre Bonnet.

Because wines of these *other* appellations are largely relegated to obscurity and not readily found on restaurant menus, not even right here in the heart of Champagne, these are my first real encounters with them, and I immediately become a fan.[17]

Bocal, just a few doors down from Boulingrin, is a small cozy place that specializes in fish. In warm weather, which is when I first started going there, they put a few tables out on the sidewalk under the awning; just inside the door is a large glass case filled with crushed ice, on top of which are displayed the day's offerings, and in back is a cozy little dining room with windows looking out onto rue Henry IV. Bocal works closely with the Boulingrin market and sources shellfish, oysters, and smoked fish from small artisan producers throughout France.

Here too, after the first few visits, I am warmly welcomed by the energetic maître d', Nathalie, and shown to my "regular" table next to a shelf holding a large round bowl with a big bug-eyed goldfish that I dub Jacques. It might be my imagination, but it seems that Jacques becomes a bit more animated each time I sit down, swimming around hysterically with his big eyes bulging even wider and staring at me and what I'm eating, which is, inevitably, fish—impeccably fresh and simply prepared—paired with an interesting bottle of Champagne from their small but excellent list, like a 100 percent meunier blanc de noirs Champagne from a small Aube producer named Trudun or a fantastic Coteaux Champenois blanc from Bérêche & Fils that, with its pronounced mineral quality and subtle yet persistent *pétillance* (fizz), makes me imagine what Champagne must have been like before it was intentionally made *mousseux* (sparkling).

Sometimes, as my meal progresses (and my bottle empties), I inconspicuously sprinkle a few breadcrumbs into Jacques's bowl—which he gobbles up—just to show I mean no harm.

∽❧∽

AT its peak at the dawn of the new (twentieth) century, it must have seemed that that the Belle Époque would never end. Or perhaps on some level people knew it wouldn't last, which is precisely why they went about enjoying the good times with so much gusto for as long as they could. While it was in full swing, the Belle Époque didn't even have a name: the name came only later (the first use of the term is thought to have been in 1904), when things weren't quite so beautiful any more, in a kind of nostalgic longing for the good old days.

There were three main things that signaled its demise, particularly in relation to what had become the era's ubiquitous icon:
Champagne. And the first of them was a tiny insect.

Throughout the 1800s, as the Industrial Revolution unfolded and
the wine industry continued to grow, trade between America and
Europe steadily increased. Thomas Jefferson, wine lover and American ambassador to France from 1785 to 1789, traveled extensively
throughout the country, observing winemaking practices, visiting
vineyards, and collecting cuttings of *Vitis vinifera* vines to bring back
and plant on his Virginia plantation in an attempt to expand and
improve winemaking in America.[18]

This worked in reverse as well: having heard stories about the
tremendous vigor of native North American grape varieties—not
European *Vitis vinifera* but rather indigenous wild species such as *Vitis
rupestris* and *Vitis labrusca*—some French winemakers began importing vines from America and planting them in their vineyards in the
hopes of getting more virile, higher-producing plants. These experiments were unsuccessful; people just didn't like the taste of the
grapes, which they described as "foxy." Then something even worse
happened: vines in adjacent vineyards started dying. At first it was a
mystery. But when people began pulling up the dead vines, it didn't
take long to determine the cause, for the shriveled roots were covered with tiny insects.[19]

Phylloxera (*Daktulosphaira vitifoliae*), a type of aphid, is an insatia-
ble stalker of grapevines. It likes to lay its eggs on the undersides of
leaves; after the insects hatch, they devour the greenery, then bur-
row down into the earth, attack the roots, and suck the sap out of the
vine. When the vine is dead, they move on to the next, and the
next. As if that weren't bad enough, the second generation grows
wings so that when one area is destroyed they can quickly fly on to
another.

Over time, indigenous American species had developed a resistance to phylloxera, but European *Vitis vinifera* had no such resis-

tance. The problem first appeared in the Languedoc area of southern France in 1863 and quickly spread throughout south-central France from east to west, then on to Spain, Portugal, and Italy. The blight was devastating. In France alone, during the last quarter of the nineteenth century, more than 40 percent of the vineyards were lost and total wine production fell by more than 75 percent. Despite a plethora of drastic attempts at finding a solution—including burning, flooding, and ripping out vineyards, dousing vines with carbon bisulfide, burying live frogs in the ground, and performing rites of religious exorcism—the insect seemed unstoppable and the cultivation of the grapevine in Europe seemed to be in serious peril.

By the late 1860s and early '70s, a number of people were beginning to claim that grafting was the best—if not only—option for eradicating the problem.[20]

Grafting is an ancient viticultural technique that involves fusing a branch (known as the *scion*) of one vine onto the rootstock of another. To do it, you cut a notch in the top of the rootstock, insert the end of the branch (which has been sharpened like the tip of a screwdriver) into the notch, and secure the intersection with cloth or tape until the two grow together into a new compartmentalized plant that retains the characteristics of the grape variety on top and the vigor of the roots below. Often this is done *in situ* to change an existing vine from one variety to another utilizing the existing roots. Now, however, advocates of grafting as a solution to phylloxera were proposing to graft European *Vitis vinifera* vines onto imported American roots.

"*Quelle horreur!*" cried the grape farmers, envisioning the bastardization and ruination of their cherished (and clearly superior) vines, despite assurances by the proponents that the essential qualities of the vine would be preserved. Many growers resisted; some even outright refused, preferring to lose their vineyards (as many of them did) rather than compromise their vines.[21]

Thanks to Champagne's position in the north, phylloxera didn't arrive there until much later, but arrive it did. The first appearance of the insect occurred in 1888 in the Aube, but this was largely disregarded by most vignerons in the north, who considered it a southern problem. Two years later it turned up in the department of the Aisne, the western outpost of *la Champagne viticole*, adjacent to the Marne, in a vineyard that Moët & Chandon promptly took it upon themselves to purchase and burn to the ground. But it was only when it turned up in Le Mesnil-sur-Oger in the heart of the Côte des Blancs two years later that people in the Marne really began to take it seriously.

The Champagne bottlers, who were used to sourcing grapes from throughout the region and keeping a constant eye on supply, had been the first to recognize the true gravity of the situation, and grafting Champagne vines onto American rootstock had been proposed back in the 1880s. But many of the vignerons who owned the bulk of the vineyard area resisted.[22] Though most other viticultural areas of France had already been through this painful predicament and the replanting of grafted vines was already well underway, the majority of vine growers in Champagne refused to take any decisive action against phylloxera until they could see it kill their vines with their own eyes, which, alas they did. At that point most of them realized that, while grafting might not be a perfect solution, it was the only viable option. The beautiful days were over.

By the beginning of the twentieth century more than half of the vineyards of Champagne were decimated, and the rest were destined to follow. While this affected just about everyone in the region, vine growers, many of whom barely eked out a subsistence living from their tiny plots of land, were hit hardest. Some, thinking the benefits not worth the expense, threw in their cards and left the area or switched occupations. But most, hardened by experience (or without other options), bit the bullet and got to work replanting their vineyards with grafted vines.

There were some upsides to this. The necessity of replanting gave growers the opportunity to reduce the extremely high density of plants, thus improving quality; grow varieties that were most suitable to their area (and/or most in demand by merchants); and plant their vineyards in a more systematized way. But, as a newly planted vine requires five to eight years to reach full production and not all newly planted vines survive, these benefits would take a long time to realize.

The Champenois were stretched to the breaking point by phylloxera. But there was another crisis looming on the horizon.

In ancient times it was the indigenous peoples against the Roman invaders. Later it was landless serfs against landed nobility. After the French Revolution, peasants, who'd finally gotten a small piece of land of their own, were resentful of the wealthy merchants who had huge estates. At a certain point the hot commodity shifted from textiles to sparkling wine, and the farmers' principal activity shifted to grape growing. As demand for Champagne rose, so did the price of grapes, and the vine growers did a bit better, especially the ones who were able to acquire enough capital to start up a press. But there was still a sharp divide between the farmers who grew grapes and the merchants who produced, bottled, labeled, and sold Champagne.

This division has characterized the Champagne region since the moment the sparkling wine began to take off, and it remains so to this day: the vignerons who grow grapes in Champagne own about 90 percent of the land but produce only around 30 percent of the Champagne on the market, while the maisons who make and commercialize nearly 70 percent of the Champagne on the market own only about 10 percent of the vineyards.[23]

While the growing of grapes and making (and marketing) of Champagne are two very different activities, both of them are critical to the industry, and thus the two groups, vigneron and maison, are inexorably locked in a close interdependence. But this has not always been easy.

At the dawn of the twentieth century, as the fame and demand for the sparkling wine of Champagne continued to skyrocket throughout the world, so did imposters. A multitude of sparkling wines began to turn up in places well outside the region and even outside of France, such as Germany, Eastern Europe, and even the United States. They were bubbly and said "Champagne" on the bottle—so how was anyone to know the difference?

Many Champenois were quick to understand the potential danger of this and rally to combat the problem.[24] But how could one realistically attempt to protect Champagne and prevent abuse of its name if no legal restriction existed and if the vine-growing and wine-producing area was not even officially delineated?

While some were trying to figure out how to deal with outside threats, other Champagne bottlers, faced with scarce supplies, rising costs, growing competition for market share, or simply a desire for higher profits, began sourcing less-expensive grapes from outside the immediate vine-growing area, and many were also adulterating their products with ingredients that had nothing whatsoever to do with grapes.

Vignerons, already stretched to the limit by phylloxera and a series of dismal vintages and struggling for their very survival, were nearing the breaking point. Champenois against "counterfeiters"; farmers against merchants; vignerons of the northern department of the Marne against those in the southern department of the Aube—tension was building in many different directions and hostilities were percolating.

The French government, having been petitioned by both growers and merchants, stepped in to resolve the situation. And on December 17, 1908, an official decree was made that clearly delineated the territory from which grapes could be used to make the wine called Champagne. In a clear nod to the influential houses and vocal growers in the Marne, which had become the commercial center of production, all of the towns in the *arrondissements* of Reims, Épernay, and Châlons were included, along with selected towns in the Marne *arrondissement* of Vitry-le-François and in the neighboring department of the Aisne. The southern department of the Aube—ancient home of the comtes de Champagne and Saint Bernard's Clairvaux

Abbey, and present home of many small growers who worked the vine-covered hills of the Côte des Bar—was entirely excluded. Though clearly unfounded, the reasons behind such a decision are not difficult to understand.

Located in the southwestern section of the region, the Aube has always been a bit disconnected from the north, geographically, geologically, and psychologically. Bordering the region of Burgundy (Champagne's historic rival), the Côte des Bar, the department's main wine-producing area, is actually a geologic extension of Burgundy's Côte d'Or and is geographically closer to Beaune than to Reims.

In the Aube, vignerons worked their small plots of land and made wine that, due to the more southern climate and less chalky soil composed of limestone and clay, was more full-bodied and vinous—a bit more Burgundian, in fact—than the wine of the north.

While the Aubois largely missed out on the Champagne boom, which was centered squarely in the commercial centers of the north, most of the Aube growers had come to depend on selling their grapes to the big northern bottlers, many of whom had, in turn, come to count on the steady supply of bigger-bodied wine from the Aube to fill out their Champagnes. Northern farmers, on the other hand, resented the "intrusion" of the less-expensive grapes from the south on their turf.

When the news came out that the region had been excluded, the vignerons of the Aube were devastated. They too had been hard hit by phylloxera and a series of disastrous vintages: while they might hate the *négociants* of the Marne, being cut out of the Champagne appellation was even worse; in fact, it was essentially a death sentence for their livelihood. People grumbled and complained; two more painful years followed, then the volatile situation ignited.

In 1911 public protests and strikes broke out in towns throughout the department. On March 19, a big demonstration took place in Bar-sur-Aube at which an effigy of the president of the regional council was burned, followed by an even larger one in Troyes on April 9 that brought the city to a complete standstill. While the demonstrations were not violent, they were angry and loud enough that Paris heard them.

Meanwhile, up in the Marne, large amounts of grapes from far outside the Champagne region were still being brought into the area with impunity, and the northern vignerons were angry too.

In the early morning of April 11, 1911, a small group of vignerons broke into cellars in the Vallée de la Marne towns of Cumières and Damery whose proprietors were suspected of importing grapes from the Midi, and ransacked everything. These gangs, and many others like them throughout the area, then descended on the small village of Aÿ and proceeded to unleash their vengeance on other wineries thought to be importers of outside grapes, smashing bottles, hacking apart barrels, and destroying equipment until the gutters were coursing with rivers of wine. A number of buildings were completely destroyed by fire, as were vineyards belonging to the suspected houses, and by dusk the little village was shrouded under a thick blanket of grey smoke.

The next day the group of rioters, which had now grown to over five thousand, started towards the nearby city of Épernay while shocked municipal governors made frantic appeals to Paris, which hastily sent in the dragoons. Close to forty-five thousand soldiers from throughout the surrounding area descended on the Marne to restore order and prevent additional violence.

People throughout Champagne, and indeed all of France, were shocked at the virulent outbreak. And the government in Paris, already dealing with serious external issues that threatened national stability and afraid of a civil war within its own country, set about resolving the critical issue of Champagne.

Shortly thereafter, the 1908 decree was annulled; a new map was created and even stricter regulations regarding use of the name *Champagne* were put into place (including the provenance and type of grapes that were used to make it). At about the same time, a set system of pricing called the Échelle des Crus was enacted by Champagne houses and growers. Most significantly, the Aube was reintegrated into the *Champagne viticole*, but only as a *deuxième zone*, a secondary area, like a sort of second-class citizen.

The Marne vignerons were pacified, at least momentarily. The Aubois felt the sting of insult even while they celebrated. But it was better than nothing: at least they were part of Champagne and could continue to sell their grapes (albeit at a lower price than their Marne counterparts) to the northern merchants, who, in turn, were pleased to legally retain their channels of supply. The most incendiary sentiments were assuaged for the time being.

While it was not perfect, it was a beginning: the vignerons had been heard, officials had recognized the problems, the first real steps had been taken towards addressing them, and there was hope that the regulations could be further refined and improved. They could, and they would. But, unfortunately, it would take much longer than expected because another, and much graver, conflict was about to emerge.

On June 28, 1914, a nineteen-year-old Bosnian Serb named Gavrilo Princip shot and killed Archduke Ferdinand of Austria, heir to the throne of the Austro-Hungarian Empire, triggering a series of events that would quickly escalate into an international conflict the likes of which the world had not seen before.

One month after the assassination, Austria-Hungary declared war on Serbia and invaded the country. While Russia rallied to support Serbia, Germany invaded neutral Belgium and Luxembourg, in violation of the 1839 Treaty of London, prompting Britain to declare war on Germany. Shortly thereafter, Germany declared war on France and France reciprocated by declaring war on Germany and mobilizing troops to retake the regions of Alsace and Lorraine that had been forfeited after the Franco-Prussian War of 1871.

When German armies moved into France on their way towards Paris, they encountered French and British forces that repulsed them back towards the border to where the Germans had created reinforced trenches sturdy enough to withstand the Allies' assaults. And there they remained, entrenched German soldiers on one side and entrenched Allied troops on the other, in a jagged line that reached across northern France and Belgium to the English Channel.[25]

Though at the outset both sides were convinced that their victory would be swift and the conflict short-lived, that is not how it turned out. The jagged line in the sand formed by the two opposing forces that became known as the Western Front was established in 1915, shortly after the onset of hostilities, and would last right up to the end of the war. And it tore right through Reims and the surrounding vineyards of Champagne.

Due to its geographically strategic position, Champagne was no stranger to war. But this one was different. This time Champagne found itself right in the middle of a conflict on an international scale. And, coming as it did at the tail end of the Industrial Age and at the beginning of the technological revolution, the nature of the conflict was different too. Whereas past battles were fought on horseback and foot, with sabers and muskets, this conflict introduced machine guns, tanks, and powerful artillery, as well as the military use of aviation and (though officially prohibited by international treaty) poison gas.

While weary but determined soldiers on both sides huddled in their mazes of deep trenches and pounded one another, weary Rémois retreated into the protected galleries of their underground cellars. People lived in them; schools, hospitals, and chapels were established in them. And people continued to work in them too. Miraculously, though the vineyards were badly battered (especially the ones located right on the front line of battle) and most of the male workers had been conscripted, work went on despite great risks.

The threat of bombs falling on the vineyards took the place of the threat of hail. Women tended the vines, harvested the grapes, and performed other tasks in the winery that were usually done by men (in addition to taking care of families and volunteering in hospitals to care for the wounded).

Ironically, 1914 turned out to be an excellent vintage, and production of Champagne continued throughout the war years, though in drastically reduced amounts.

If the vines took a beating, the people fared much worse, especially in Reims. Thousands of Champenois were killed or seriously injured (overall the war would result in a staggering sixteen million deaths and twenty million injuries), and the proud city was mercilessly pummeled by enemy artillery until close to 90 percent of its buildings were destroyed. Even more devastating, its glorious cathedral, where Clovis was converted to Christianity, where Joan of Arc launched the liberation of France from English invaders, and where French kings had traditionally been crowned for over one thousand years, was reduced to a hollow smoking shell.

The cathedral would eventually be painstakingly restored, but other things could not.[26] If the outbreak of World War I can be said to signal the historical end of the Belle Époque, the bombing of the Reims cathedral can be seen as its psychological end, an all-too-visible confirmation that the "Beautiful Epoch" was indeed over and a new and decidedly less beautiful world had taken its place.

While the era of celebration was finished, the celebratory aura surrounding Champagne lived on—though the wanton abandon of the previous period was replaced by a touch of nostalgia and, perhaps, an even greater hope for better times to come.

Paul Krug managed to steer his family business through the perilous waters of the first two crises by lobbying for decisive action against phylloxera early on and, recognizing the barely contained desperation of the growers (with whom he had spent much time as a child), advocating for stricter regulations on the provenance of grapes and controls to ensure fair pricing. But dying as he did in 1910, he was spared the grief of the Champagne Riots of 1911 and the horrors of World War I.

Of Paul's ten children, Joseph II, born 1869, was the one earmarked to carry on the family business. Though very different from his father—Joseph II was frailer, more sensitive, and reserved, not unlike his namesake grandfather—he was the one who clearly showed the greatest aptitude for the Champagne business and, as quickly became clear once he began participating in the winemaking activities, the one who had inherited the family knack for blending.

Notwithstanding his natural ability, Joseph II was rather unambitious when it came to business and was perfectly happy to travel around the world and pursue his other pastimes up until 1903, when he was compelled to officially join the business.

The following year, Joseph married Jeanne Hollier Larousse (great-niece of the famed lexicographer Pierre Larousse), and upon his father's death six years after that, he assumed full control of the firm. In 1912 Jeanne gave birth to the couple's first and only child, a boy, whom they named Paul.

When war broke out, Joseph was called into action and sent to the front lines of battle, and the following year he was captured and sent to a prisoner-of-war camp. While he was away Jeanne managed the business as best she could, given the sorry state of the vineyards, the absence of workers, and the lack of materials. It was Jeanne, in fact, who rose to the occasion (much as Barbe-Nicole Ponsardin had done a century before) and took charge of blending the 1915 Champagne herself, with the help of cellar master M. Payen.

Besides managing the business and looking after her child, Jeanne volunteered as a nurse and eventually created a wartime hospital and a chapel in the cellars beneath Rue Coquebert. The Great War ended on November 11, 1918, but Jeanne's nursing didn't: she created an organization called Retour à Reims to aid returning citizens and soldiers and paid particular attention to her husband, who, having contracted double pneumonia in prison camp, returned home frailer than ever. As it seemed he would not last very long and Paul II was only a young child, Jeanne's nephew, Jean Seydoux, was appointed interim managing director of the firm and would prove to be a loyal and valuable asset to the house for decades to come.

Joseph II, however, surprised everybody and made a brilliant comeback. In addition to getting the firm's production back on its feet (with a little help from Jean Seydoux), he also carried on the family tradition of blending Champagne—some two hundred thousand bottles' worth in 1919—for other houses. Paul II became increasingly active in the business (he officially joined the company in 1933), while Jeanne was awarded the Croix de Guerre and the Médaille de la Reconnaissance, and made a Chevalier of the Legion of Honor for her wartime activities. Everybody at Krug—like most everyone else in the region—did their part to pick up the pieces and get back on track. But the future would not always be smooth sailing.

∽◉∽

WITH the *vins clairs*, the intensity and focus of the tasting routine ratchets up yet another notch. All of the 2013 wines that were previewed last fall by drawing a sample from a single barrel of each pyramid are tasted again now that all the barrels of each separate parcel have been racked and blended together in one stainless-steel vat. And, as we dive in, what Eric said to me before the holiday break, that the wines after *soutirage* are entirely different from what we tasted the first time around, is immediately confirmed: the wines now taste more complete, more balanced, and even more compelling. Part of it has to do with the subtle complexity and equilibrium that comes with the combination of wines made from grapes of the same parcel fermented in different individual containers; another factor is that the wine has had an opportunity to sit and mellow out for several months; and yet another factor has to do with the burst of oxygen the wines get during the *soutirage*, which wakes them up.

Compared to the "newborn babies" of the first round and the mature reserve wines of the second, these wines are full of energy and verve, and eager to show what they've got to offer.

By this time I am fairly comfortable with both the procedure and the participants: my French has improved, especially my descriptive adjectives. I've even picked up some of the typically Champenois descriptors like *racé* (elegant, polished), *vif* (lively), *pain grillé* (toasty), *brioche* (buttery pastry), *croquante* (crunchy), *amertume* (bitter), *ver-deur* (green, as in astringent), and *bonbon* (hard candy). I make a quick assessment of each wine without thinking about it too much and automatically offer my numerical score, even though I'm still not entirely sure what purpose it serves.

But aside from being more comfortable, I also realize that the very way I approach and evaluate the wines is different. I can't quite put my finger on it until one day when a woman from the Krug market-ing department sits in on a tasting session and Eric gives her a brief introduction: "What we are looking for here is not so much a de-scription of the wine as a vision of what it may become; we're not interested so much in the individual wine itself as in the particular characteristics it possesses that might make a significant contribu-tion to the blend."

This helps me comprehend intellectually what I have already be-gun to understand intuitively and what struck me as so odd about these tastings from the very beginning.

In all the other tasting situations I experienced previously, what you are evaluating is *the wine*. It might be very new or very young; it might need time to soften, develop, and evolve to reach its full po-tential. But it's all there; the only question is how it will evolve and when it will reach its peak. In these Krug tastings, on the other hand, the wines are never perceived as complete in and of themselves but rather as components or ingredients that will be at some point be used, along with many others, to create a greater whole (the *assem-blage*). It's this greater whole that ultimately matters, and the contri-bution each individual piece will make to it.

What makes it even trickier, however, is that this "greater whole" of the blend is not itself the final product. After all the pieces are put together, the assembled wine will undergo another major trans-formation, the *prise de mousse*, the taking-on of bubbles, followed by yet another, an extended maturation period of six years or more. This means that in order to accurately taste and evaluate these wines,

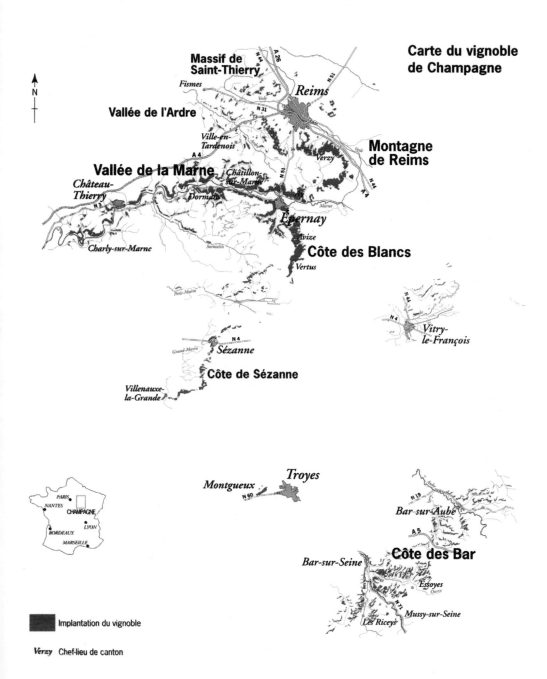

The vineyards of Champagne. *Copyright Comité Champagne.*

During *le tirage,* the wine is transferred from barrel to bottle for the second fermentation.

During the r*emuage,* bottles are hand-twisted to gradually move the sediment from the second fermentation down to the mouth for disgorgement.

Workmen tap the underside of champagne bottles to loosen sediment; traditionally, this was done by candlelight to better see the sediment through the thick glass. The workers wore protective goggles due to the possibility that the bottles might explode.

All images this page: Henry Vizetelly, A History of Champagne, *1882.*

A contemporary image of the Champagne Riots of 1911. *Alfredo Dagli Orti/Art Archive at Art Resource, New York.*

Although the story of Dom Pérignon's happy discovery of Champagne's bubbliness turns out to be popular myth, he did lay the critical foundation for winemaking in Champagne that facilitated the development of the *méthode champenoise,* and thus can rightly be called the Father of Champagne. *Kharbine-Tapabor/Art Archive at Art Resource, New York.*

The original widow of Champagne, Barbe-Nicole Clicquot-Ponsardin, sits in front of the Château de Boursault with her great-granddaughter, Anne de Rochechouart-Mortemart, at her feet. Painting by Léon Cogniet, 1859. *Gianni Dagli Orti/Art Archive at Art Resource, New York.*

Un bar aux Folies Bergère, by Édouard Manet, 1882. *Courtauld Gallery, London.*

Louise Weber, better known by her *nom d'artiste* "La Goulue," in a photograph by Louis Victor Paul Bacard, circa 1885. *Alfredo Dugli Orti/Art Archive at Art Resource, New York.*

Music hall star "Champagne Charlie," aka George Leybourne, promoted Champagne—specifically that of Moët & Chandon—in a popular song with music by Alfred Lee. Leybourne should not be confused with the other original Champagne Charlie, Charles-Camille Heidsieck, who intrepidly promoted his own brand of Champagne in America.

Barrels are lined up in the Krug courtyard, Rue Coquebert, in anticipation of harvest. *Alan Tardi, 2013.*

The traditional Coquard press at Clos du Mesnil, fully charged, just before the lid is lowered and pressing begins. *Alan Tardi, 2013.*

An old plaque set into the wall surrounding the Clos du Mesnil reads: "This wall was constructed in 1698 by Claude Jannin and Pierre Dehee, and the vineyard was planted in the same year by Gaspard Jannin, son of Claude." *Alan Tardi, 2013.*

Pinot noir grapes undergoing *veraison,* the gradual changing of color from green to red, in the Montagne de Reims area of Champagne. Based on this photo, the color transformation is just over 70 percent complete. *Alan Tardi, 2013.*

Barrels sit in the courtyard of Clos d'Ambonnay during harvest. *Alan Tardi, 2013.*

one must do so with an innate understanding of this entire process. Vision indeed!

We dive in to the Côte des Blancs with wines from Avize, Oger, and Mesnil, including a Clos du Mesnil made of the grapes I watched being harvested and pressed, the creamy pale-yellow juice falling into the well and steadily filling it up. I give it seventeen points, and Julie is so excited by this wine that she coins a new adjective at the end of her comments: "The raciness, the elegance . . . it's, well, it's very *Clos du Mesnil*."

Rémi Krug sits in on one of the tastings, and Étienne Bâtonnet joins us for another that consists of wines from the Montagne de Reims, including Ambonnay pinot noirs from his press. Étienne is characteristically soft-spoken but more serious this time and a tough judge of his own wines, which are solid and well balanced, even elegant, with a nice edge of earthiness and rusticity. At the end he thanks Eric and says what a pleasure it was to be able to come and sample the actual wines made from his grapes, since they haven't been indecipherably mixed together with others, which is what usually happens.

Eric tells me later that he regularly invites suppliers to come and taste the wines made from the grapes they supplied, either in formal tastings or a casual cellar visit. "They love to see what becomes of their grapes; it gives them great pride. And they appreciate the way we respect the integrity of each individual parcel, which further strengthens their connection to us. But it's not always that simple." He goes on to tell me about a longtime supplier who had passed away; while his wife was determined to carry on the family business, the grapes were not nearly as good as they had been when he was alive. When the widow came and tasted the wines, she immediately noticed the difference. It made her very upset, but it also helped her rectify the problem and get the quality back up to a level that was acceptable to Krug and that her husband would have been proud of.

This tasting of *vin clairs* goes on for about four weeks, during which Eric assiduously fills the pages of his notebook with comments and scores on each and every one of the more than two hundred 2013 wines in his small precise script.

I don't know if it's just my imagination, but as the tastings in this final phase progress, I begin to sense the weight of the impending assemblage hanging in the air.

"Are you already beginning to think about the Grande Cuvée blend and which wines might play a principal role?" I ask Eric.

"Oh no," he replies, "it is too early for that. Right now I'm just tasting the wines to see what we've got." A few days later, however, excited after an especially good tasting, he lets slip *"Il y a un bon truc ici. Peut être il y aura un vintage!"* ("There's some good stuff here. Perhaps we might have a vintage!")

As the tasting process starts to wind down, I detect a new light-ness and playfulness in the tasting room. People tell more jokes than usual and laugh a bit more freely. At the end of one session, they even go around the table comparing the songs their parents sang to them as children, and Julie gives some examples of the songs she now sings to her own daughters. While Laurent and Jérôme pour the left-over wine into beakers for disposal, Julie blurts out, *"Oh la la!* It sounds like we're in a *pissoir!"* This causes someone to mention the fly designs inside the urinals in the train stations, and someone else begins singing "Tous les Hommes Sont des Cochons" ("All Men Are Pigs"), a French rendition of a recent hit by a European electro-pop group of fictional characters called the Studio Killers.

Just before we all get up to leave, Eric turns to me with a playful grin and says in a tone of faux remorse, "I'm sorry, but you see how it is at the end; we sing, we joke, we relax a bit. *C'est normal, n'est-ce pas?"*

"Yes," I reply, "it most certainly is."

CHAPTER 7

❧ ❧

ASSEMBLAGE

In November 1918, the war finally ended. People buried their dead and began picking up the pieces of their shattered lives: trenches were filled in, vineyards were replanted, and, little by little, the rhythms of Champagne began to return to (almost) normal.

But something was different. Fundamental beliefs had been put to the test, new priorities had taken root, a new sense of national and regional identity had been born and along with it a stronger realization of mutual interdependence. The quarrels of Champenois against Champenois, grower against producer, north against south, were less important now than the necessity of coming together for the well-being—perhaps even the survival—of all concerned.

The recognition of mutual interdependence had finally come to a majority of Champenois and the desire for collaboration was finally there, but creating a real framework for it would take some more time.

The first major step was taken on July 22, 1927, when a decree was made that clearly defined the authorized grape-growing and production areas of Champagne. In order to do this, each village submitted proposals of the precise territories in their township they felt should be included in the zone, based on evidence that the site was being used for viticulture at the present time of the decree, or, if not currently under vine, had been before the arrival of the phyllox-era epidemic. While this system was far from perfect, it was certainly better than nothing.

An interdisciplinary committee then evaluated the validity of these claims and made their determination. At the end of the exam-ination process, a detailed and clearly delimited zone was established consisting of little more than half of the sixty thousand hectares of vines that existed in Champagne before phylloxera.

Besides delineating the boundaries of the zone, these regulations also stipulated the grape varieties that could be used—pinot noir, meunier, chardonnay, pinot blanc, and pinot gris, as well as two an-cient varieties, arbane and petit meslier—and, by default, those that couldn't, particularly gamay, which had been widely planted through-out the southern department of the Aube.

Most importantly, the 1927 edict annulled the previously estab-lished second-class status of the Aube, making all authorized sub-zones full and equal partners of the *Champagne viticole*, though not necessarily of equal monetary value (the Échelle des Crus was still in full force and grapes from the south generally received a lower price than those of the north). A few years later, these regulations were expanded to include more stringent quality-control measures such as maximum yield of grapes per hectare, maximum yield of juice from grapes at pressing, minimum alcohol content, and minimum aging requirements, and a regulating body called the Commission de Châlons was established to enforce them.

While the problems facing the Champagne district did not imme-diately disappear, the 1927 decree officially laid claim to the exclu-sive use of the name *Champagne*, established clear boundaries of the zone, set legal parameters for the production and commercialization of Champagne, and established a regulatory body to enforce compli-ance and take action if necessary (which it often was). With this, the Champagne appellation—the legal connection of the name of the wine, the grapes used to make it, and its method of production to a clearly defined area—was officially born. And it happened just in time.

Having these laws in place, and the increased spirit of cooperation between growers and producers that led to the creation of them, helped the industry survive the would-be devastating effects of events that took place in the first thirty years of the twentieth century: the huge loss of sales to Russia in the aftermath of the Russian Revolution; Prohibition in the United States, which began in 1920 (and would last thirteen years); and the stock market crash of 1929, which led to the Great Depression. In 1935, France instituted a cohesive nationwide regulatory and labeling system called the Appellation d'Origine Contrôlée (AOC), which set the standard for regulatory systems in wine areas throughout the world, and Champagne was one of the original regions (along with Burgundy, Bordeaux, and the Rhône Valley) to fall under its protective aegis.[1]

This was a good thing, because Champagne was soon going to need all the help it could get.

※

WORLD War I had been dubbed "the war to end all wars." But, unfortunately, it wasn't. Twenty years later, yet another major conflict broke out in Europe that caused both massive destruction and loss of life and sent shock waves throughout the entire world. Once again Germany was one of the principal instigators, and once again Champagne found itself right in the middle of the action. But this time was different.

This time there was no prolonged standoff of opposing entrenchments along the Western Front or incessant, devastating bombings by the aggressors. There was, in fact, little resistance whatsoever to the overwhelming onslaught of the Third Reich: in no time at all France capitulated and, with very few casualties and minimal damage, the Nazis took control of Paris and occupied Reims.

People throughout the northern territory of the Marne knew this was coming, and many had taken precautions such as hiding stocks of Champagne behind false walls deep within their cavernous cellars. But even they were surprised at the swiftness with which the German occupation took place, as well as a bit relieved to have been spared the relentless artillery barrage of the previous war. The apparent clemency, however, was deceptive.

The Nazis operated with surgical precision and clear strategic intent. They spared Reims and admonished their conquering soldiers not to loot the wine cellars (which did not, however, prevent millions of bottles of Champagne from disappearing in the first several weeks). They understood the monetary and aesthetic value of the art treasures of each of the European countries they conquered, and they knew the economic importance and symbolic prestige of Champagne. They were also quite fond of drinking it.

As German forces occupied areas of France and Italy, Field Marshall General Hermann Göring put individuals, usually those with some degree of expertise in the field, in charge of managing the acquisition of the conquered territories' assets. And in the principal wine areas of France, these officials were dubbed *weinführers* ("wine leaders").

When the Champenois learned who the weinführer of Champagne was going to be, they breathed a sigh of relief: Otto Klaebisch had been born and raised in France, where his parents were Cognac merchants. And later, in Germany, he worked for an importing company that distributed Lanson Champagne, so he was quite familiar with both the wine and the region.

Klaebisch, it appeared, was practically one of them. But this feeling of kinship didn't last long. The new Champagne weinführer wasted no time: shortly after his arrival in Reims, he went before the organization of growers and producers known as the Bureau de Répartition du Champagne and told them what he expected.[2]

It began with a weekly quota of 350,000 bottles for Nazi forces, to be labeled "Produced for the Wehrmacht," but the number quickly increased to around 500,000 (a very difficult demand to meet after a series of terrible vintages and during a time when materials and man-power were in critically short supply). Nazi-controlled establishments in France were to receive first priority for Champagne; anything that might be left after that could be sold to other Nazi-approved customers. All the wine would be paid for, Klaebisch assured them. But with the French franc greatly devalued and the German Reichsmark hugely inflated by the occupiers, whatever payment they might possibly receive would hardly cover the cost of production.

The Champanois were, quite literally, over a barrel: they needed to find some way of effectively dealing with the Champagne wein-führer in order for their industry to have even a slim chance of surviving. The only way they could possibly hope to do that was by all sticking together and speaking with a united voice. But someone still needed to do the talking. On this at least the farmers and producers were of one mind: there was only one person with the diplomatic skill and force of character to stand up to Klaebisch.

Comte Robert-Jean de Vogüé was a descendant of one of France's oldest noble families and a highly respected member of the Champagne community. He had taken the helm of Moët & Chandon in 1930 during the difficult period of the Great Depression and Prohibition in America, and he came from an illustrious family full of winemakers.[3]

From the very beginning, Klaebisch, who came from humble merchant stock and, unlike most of the other weinführers, made a point of always wearing his military uniform, seemed enamored of de Vogüé's title and noble pedigree. Robert-Jean was genteel and aristocratic, both in manner and bearing, but he was also tough as nails. As their working relationship unfolded, the two played a delicate game of cat and mouse, with the roles often changing back and forth. While the weinführer ostensibly had the upper hand, de Vogüé repeatedly devised ways of gaining some leverage without appearing to be overly aggressive.

Right off the bat he did something no one had ever quite succeeded in doing before in Champagne: he brought the growers and the houses together in one organization that spoke for the entire industry. The Comité Interprofessionnel du Vin de Champagne (CIVC), now known simply as the Comité Champagne, was created on April 12, 1941, with a co-presidency consisting of a representative of the maisons (the first to occupy the post was de Vogüé himself) and a representative of the vignerons (Maurice Doyard).

There was not much the CIVC could do about the big quotas, but de Vogüé and Doyard bargained hard for reasonable prices and won many concessions from the weinführer for materials and labor, even gaining the release of some sequestered Champenois, arguing that it would not be possible to produce the amount of Champagne Klaebisch demanded if they had no one to do the work. At the same time the Champenois did whatever they could to subtly sabotage the shipments for the Nazis—intentionally misaddressing shipments, adding rebêche to the wine, and doing anything else they could to make sure the wine was of the lowest quality possible—while appearing to be complacently industrious.

Klaebisch and de Vogüé had a complicated relationship. They were enemies, to be sure, but there was also an air of courtesy and mutual respect—one might even say amicability—to their rapport. Their interaction came to a head on November 24, 1943, when de Vogüé and Claude Fourmon, a manager at Moët, were in the weinführer's office. The phone rang; Klaebisch answered, listened attentively, then snapped "*Jawohl! Heil Hitler!*" and hung up. "Excuse me," he then said softly. "That was the Gestapo. It appears that you are under arrest for crimes against the Third Reich." At that moment, the door flew open and Gestapo agents with drawn pistols burst in and took the two into custody.

Fourmon was sent to the Bergen-Belsen concentration camp while Comte de Vogüé, who, it turns out, was the political head of the Résistance movement in northeastern France, was sentenced to death. When word of the sentence got out, the Champenois—growers and bottlers alike—were incensed and a general strike was called; everything came to a complete stop and people were determined to keep it that way until de Vogüé was spared.

Klaebisch's own position was, in fact, tenuous. He might well have been the big cheese of Champagne, but he had a number of *führers* above him (including Göring and Hitler) who did not like to be without their Champagne,[4] and if production did not resume soon, the consequences for him could be grave.

The death sentence was rescinded and on June 27, 1944, de Vogüé was deported to Germany, where he was confined in the Karlsruhe, Rheinbach, Ziegenhain, and Rheinberg prison camps. Conditions were terrible; he contracted gangrene in his finger and, in the absence of medical attention, cut it off himself with a sharpened piece of glass. But he survived. Nearly eighteen months passed before the Rheinberg camp was liberated on May 3, 1945.

The German Instrument of Surrender was signed in Reims at 2:41 a.m. on May 7, 1945, by representatives of the *Wehrmacht* High Command, the Allied Expeditionary Force, and the Soviet High Command, and witnessed by a French representative, officially ending World War II. Champagne corks certainly popped that night, but it was more out of relief than celebration, for it would take a long time to come to terms with the horrors that were committed during this conflict.

Following a period of convalescence, de Vogüé returned to Champagne and resumed his duties at Moët & Chandon, and so did Claude Fourmon.

After the war Otto Klaebisch was put on trial for economic war crimes. When Comte Robert-Jean de Vogüé was called as a witness for the prosecution, he stunned everyone by defending the former weinführer of Champagne: "He was in a difficult situation," de Vogüé testified. "I don't believe for a minute that he would have ever ordered my arrest or those of my colleagues. It was the Gestapo."[5]

Klaebisch was found not guilty and Robert-Jean de Vogüé was awarded the Médaille de la Résistance. De Vogüé, who died in 1976, remains one of the most respected figures of Champagne, admired by growers and producers alike, and the organization he was instrumental in creating, the Comité Champagne, lives on as a lasting legacy of the critical importance of collaboration among everyone involved in the making of Champagne.

De Vogüé's unwavering resistance to the Germans—especially the weinführer—clearly demonstrates that he was an exceptional individual. But he was not alone. Many Champenois did whatever they possibly could to oppose the Nazis, and the Krugs were among them. Paul II was commissioned into the French intelligence agency while both Joseph and Jeanne Krug were active in the Résistance, particularly in hiding fallen Allied airmen and helping them escape out of France. Both were arrested by the Gestapo and eventually released for lack of evidence. Jeanne, however, was arrested yet again and this time sent to Fort de Romainville near Paris, which functioned as transit hub for deportation to concentration camps in Germany. During her time at Romainville Jeanne became so ill that she was left there to die. But she didn't.

After the war finally ended, Jeanne returned to Reims, resumed her work at the Retour à Reims (which she continued until her death in 1954), and added yet another medal, the Médaille de la Résistance, to her already abundant collection.

∽◡◠

BY the beginning of March, the exhaustive tasting of the *vins clairs*—236 different wines from the 2013 harvest, plus the 150 or so different wines in reserve—is finished, and Eric's black notebook is packed with copious notes and numerical scores on each and every one of them. Compared to the buoyant jollity of the tasting room, the chef de cave now has an air of focus and seriousness about him, like an athlete warming up for a big competition or a musician waiting to go onstage. This is understandable for his most decisive work is about to begin.

"We have everything now," Eric says, gravely holding up his black tome. "We have carefully tasted and critiqued all the wines and we know exactly how much we have of each one. Now all I have to do is figure out what to do with them."

This is, of course, a drastic understatement, and it's clear from the sardonic grin on Eric's face that he knows it.

Creating the blends is the moment of truth in Champagne. While most everything else—the weather, the quality and abundance of the harvest, the character of the wines—is beyond anyone's control, the assemblage is where the chef de cave takes the reins and makes the critical choices and decisions that will have a significant impact on the image and success of the house (not to mention his own reputation) for years to come.

It happens every year in just about every winery in Champagne, and while the basic process of blending is the same, each winemaker does it a little bit differently, based on the material at their disposal and the style and philosophy of the house.

At Krug, blending is the very heart of the firm's existence, its *raison d'être*, one might say, going right back to the founding of the company by Joseph Krug. And, like many of the other things I've encountered thus far, the way they do it is not quite what I expected.

❧

IN the beginning, just about all wine was blended. People collected whatever kinds of grapes they could find, smashed them up, and let them ferment together. When vineyards began to be created, different varieties were often planted side by side, then harvested and vinified together. This is still done in many places today.[5]

In Champagne, however, blending has always been the norm and remains so today, with few exceptions.[6] It originated out of necessity in order to make up for the scarcity of a poor harvest or the shortcomings of a single variety, area, or growing season. Blending grapes and, later, adding wine from reserve stocks, helped make up for these shortcomings as well as provide the quantity of sparkling wine necessary to satisfy market demand while producing a better-balanced, more pleasant product year in and year out.

But at a certain point, not long after the major kinks of producing the wine had been worked out and the basic process of the *méthode champenoise* had been established, something began to change: out of the sometimes desperate attempt to come up with a reasonably palatable and marketable wine, something unexpectedly beautiful and unique began to emerge. An entirely different possibility began to develop: Necessity gave way to discretion, and blending became more of a creative aesthetic activity rather than just a purely compulsory one.[8]

This transition started to happen right around the time Joseph Krug began to envision a house of his own, and it was precisely *this* aspect of Champagne—the possibility of creating a new sort of vinous beauty each and every year through the rigorous selection of materials and careful composition of a blend—that he fell in love with and felt compelled to pursue at all costs. Joseph was widely acknowledged as master blender even before he started his own business, and it was this activity on which the success of his house depended.[9]

For both Joseph and Paul Krug, blending for other houses was a significant part of their livelihood and one on which the solidity of their business relied for many years.[10] Joseph, in fact, left clear instructions on what variations of the basic house blend—variations both in the level of sweetness and the body and intensity of the Champagne—worked best in different countries where their wine was sold.

As the market for Champagne continued to expand and demand continued to increase, savvy producers developed—largely through blending—their own unique and consistent styles that became closely associated with their brand. In time, this house style was often expanded over a range of wines made from different blends of grapes called *cuvées*.[11] While the range of each house's offerings typically forms a hierarchical pyramid, from the basic nonvintage

Champagne at the bottom, made every year in relatively large quantity and sold at the lowest price, to the *tête de cuvées* at the top,[12] the house of Krug, holding fast to the vision of its founder, takes a radically different approach, as we shall soon see. But first let's take a look at some of the types of special cuvées that emerged.

The first prestige cuvée to actually hit the market was Dom Pérignon, which was created by Moët & Chandon in 1921 but not actually released until 1936, and even then only to a limited audience by subscription. According to Tom Stevenson, one of the foremost experts on Champagne, the idea was conceived in 1932 by an English journalist named Lawrence Wren, who suggested it to Robert-Jean de Vogüé. During the Great Depression, when sales were lagging and many houses were struggling to survive, the people at Moët & Chandon felt they needed to come up with something truly special (and not inexpensive) to rekindle interest, which also helps explain why they named it after a legendary monk whom they then promoted as the blind creator of Champagne.[13]

While Dom Pérignon was the first prestige cuvée to be marketed, the prototype of prestige Champagne was created by Louis Roederer for Tsar Alexander II in 1876 but it was not made available to the public until 1945. A special bottle was designed for the tsar's Champagne with clear glass and a flat bottom (so nothing could be concealed inside or underneath the bottle), and for that reason the wine became known as Cristal.

Though it was long thought that Veuve Clicquot was the first to release a rosé Champagne in 1775, documentation recently located by the indefatigable researcher Isabelle Pierre shows that Ruinart actually shipped some rosé Champagne as early as 1764, which would make them the earliest producer of pink Champagne on record.[14] Dom Ruinart was also one of the first to make a *blanc de blancs*, or "white from white grapes," in 1947.[15]

A vintage Champagne is one in which all the grapes used to make it come from a single year, which is indicated on the bottle (the grapes, however, may still be a blended of different varieties from different places within the zone).[16] Moët & Chandon is thought to have initiated this practice in Champagne beginning with the 1840 vintage (which was released in 1842). Some other sources credit Veuve Clicquot with producing the first Champagne with the year on the bottle during the famous comet vintage of 1811, though it is probable that the wine was not made exclusively of grapes from that year. Historian Isabelle Pierre says that Veuve Clicquot's Livre de Tirage of 1810 indicates a cuvée was made only of grapes from that year, but was identified only by a colored ribbon around the bottle's neck. According to the Comité Champagne, vintage bottlings did not begin to become more common until after 1865, and official regulations pertaining to vintage were not added to the Champagne AOC until the decree of October 17, 1952.

Finally, there are the clos.[17] Because all the grapes for a clos must by definition come one specific plot enclosed by a wall or hedge—a plot that is usually planted with a single grape variety—and are usually made from the grapes of one specific vintage, these Champagnes are rare exceptions to the blending rule. The first single-vineyard clos to be bottled commercially on its own was Philipponnat's 1935 Clos des Goisses, and the first single cru wine on record was Le Mesnil-sur-Oger by the tiny house of Salon, in 1911. Notwithstanding a few exceptions, the creation of single-village and single-vineyard wines in Champagne did not really begin to take off until the mid-1980s.

The Krug approach is a bit different from that of most other Champagne houses, and it is based on the principles that were clearly spelled out in Joseph's notebook:

> My opinion on blends [*cuvées de tirage*] and how they should be composed:
>
> 1. It is not possible to make a good wine except from good elements [that is] wines of good growths [crus].

One may obtain a blend of good appearance with mean or mediocre elements and growths [crus], but these are exceptions: one can
never rely on them and they put one's whole method and reputation
at risk.

2. The greatest care must be taken in making the blend completely homogenous, [and in] fining, racking and bottling.

In principle, a good house ought to make two similarly composed
blends: one light [*cuvée légère*] for the north of Europe and the Black
Sea countries, [and] the other full-bodied [*cuvée corsée*] for the Rhine
country, Belgium, England and America.[18]

The exact composition of both blends, he wrote, should change as
necessary according to the year, and the *liqueur d'expédition*, the mixture of wine and sugar that is typically added to the Champagne after
disgorgement, should be adjusted according to the preferences of the
client.[19] In some cases he also advised adding "a small dose of fine
spirit of cognac" to the *liqueur*, which was not unusual at the time.

Over time, the two-*cuvée* concept was extended to two different
kinds of Champagne made, however, in the same vinous style and on
the same level of importance: one a perfectly balanced blend combining both the finesse of the *cuvée légère* and the full-bodied intensity of the *cuvée corsée*, created each year from carefully selected
grapes of the recent vintage as well as older wines from the reserve
cellar; and the other a vintage wine composed of grapes from a single
growing season, made only in certain years and reflecting the particularities of that specific vintage.

This concept of two different but stylistically similar cuvées of
equal quality, envisioned by Joseph Krug and passed down from one
generation to the next, remains the house's operating principle to
this day.

The first of the two cuvées, the one made every year, was given
the name "Private Cuvée" in 1861 (the name was changed to
"Grande Cuvée" in 1978). The house of Krug made its first vintage

Champagne in 1904 (though bottles with a year indicated on the label are said to have been found in the Krug cellars as early as 1880); a rosé Champagne was added to the Krug portfolio in 1983, a single-vineyard blanc de blancs from Clos du Mesnil in 1986, and a single-vineyard blanc de noirs from Clos d'Ambonnay in 2007.

While Krug Grande Cuvée is made every year (and the nonvintage rosé is made almost every year), a vintage Champagne is made only in certain vintages, when, as Eric says, "the year itself has a special story to tell," and the clos are only produced in years in which the particular parcels show exceptionally well. "Krug Grande Cuvée represents breadth and expansiveness," says Maggie, "while Krug Vintage is more precise, as the wine comes from one particular year, and the two clos are about precision and depth because they come not only from one vintage but from one small parcel and one grape variety as well."

What's most unusual is that Krug maintains there is no hierarchy in their portfolio. "All our wines are on the same high level of quality," Eric says. "The price differences between them reflect rarity, *not* quality or importance."

Ironically, the two most expensive wines in the Krug portfolio, Clos du Mesnil and Clos d'Ambonnay, are the most straightforward to make, while the Grande Cuvée requires the greatest amount of time and work and the largest investment of resources.

In fact, Krug Grande Cuvée is the flagship of the entire house, the wine that most clearly reflects the company's origins and identity, and it is on this wine that the future of the house most depends. Because of this, in addition to all the other considerations, Eric must keep a careful eye on the contents of the reserve cellar to make sure that there is a sufficient amount of wine to serve the needs of the house for decades to come.

"It's simple," Eric tells me. "Without a well-stocked cellar of reserve wines there is no Grande Cuvée, and without Grande Cuvée there is no Krug."

"*Alors,*" he continues, "now I must begin to formulate my *plan de tirage*. But before I can begin to think about what to do with the wines, I must have an idea of what we will need in eight or ten years, when these wines will be released. So we have a meeting, Maggie, the house's financial controller, and I. We look at the stock we have in-house and what we will be releasing in the upcoming years, and then we make some projections of what we anticipate we will need in the future. But please understand: I'm not talking about increasing or decreasing our overall production, but about how much Champagne we think we may decide to release onto the market in a given year in the future."[20]

The selection of wines to turn into Champagne is called *tirage*, from the French verb *tirer* ("to pull"), because they are pulled out of the inventory and turned into bottles of Champagne to release onto the market.[21]

"After this meeting," Eric continues, "I tell Marie—though she already knows by now—not to make any appointments for me for the next couple weeks. I take the production forecast and my black notebook into my office, I close the door, and I stay there. I cannot have any distractions; I need calm and quiet. I don't talk to anyone, I don't go anywhere."

"Do you retaste all the wines?" I ask.

"No," he replies. "It would take way too long and is really not necessary. I have already carefully tasted them in the tasting room along with everyone else. This exercise is purely theoretical. I look over what we have; I look at what we need. I make a composite of the scores and carefully review all the notes I took at all the tastings we did over the past five months."

Eureka! When he says that I finally understand the point of the numerical scores. It is not so much a question of grading the wines themselves as about helping to provide a consensus of experience of the tasting panel that he can later use as a guide to zero his attention in on certain wines. The descriptive notes then help him figure out what to do with them.

"Little by little," he continues, "I start to form pictures in my head, and then, slowly, I start to sketch things out."

As he says this, he actually makes a little sketching motion with his hand, which, though he says he can't draw, makes me think of an artist beginning the first tentative sketches of a painting. In this case it's a large canvas with a rather complex composition, a group portrait, and each member needs its due amount of attention. In the center foreground, taking up much of the room and getting lots of detail, is the Grande Cuvée; just off to the side, in a notably different but complementary color palette, is the rosé. Does this composition need a vintage? Given the anomalous character of 2013, with all of its ups and downs and unusually late but brilliant harvest, this vintage certainly seems to fulfill the criteria of a year with an interesting story to tell.

Some of the unique materials from 2013 must be retained in the paint box to add their special luster to future creations. And the clos might well be sketched into the canvas at a later point, in the background perhaps, and smaller in size, but commanding attention nonetheless because of their unusually striking appearance.

This painting gets repainted each year, and while the composition may (and inevitably does) change somewhat from year to year, the basic components and style are always essentially the same.

This metaphor of an artist is apt in some ways and deceptive in others.

It has become fashionable these days to think of the Champagne chef de cave as a sensory artist, an alchemist who magically transforms coarse *vins clairs* into beautifully complex bubbly potions, much as a perfumer creates an exotic new scent or a fashion designer creates a new haute couture line. There is an element of truth to this, to be sure: the blending of different wines (grape varieties, subzones, vintages) together into a harmonious whole and then subjecting this static mix to the mysterious transformation of a second fermentation that makes it sparkle and gives it a whole new life. But the work of the chef de cave is not purely a question of creative whim. Here there are issues of supply and demand, financial projections, inventory control, cash flow and continuity, not to mention other, less tangible but nonetheless critical considerations, such as personal reputation, brand image, and holding true to a long-established house style.

There are artists in some fields who can work in near total creative freedom and spontaneity with little or no interference of practical concerns (perhaps this is more of a postmodern reality).[22] But then there are others—Bach, Michelangelo, Leonardo da Vinci, for example— who created enduring masterpieces within what would appear to impossibly restrictive parameters of tight deadlines, the limitations or special talents of available performers, the preferences of cantankerous patrons, and the base but real necessity of making enough money to put food on the table for themselves and their families.

At first, the idea of assemblage as a "theoretical process" strikes me as a bit odd. But then I remember Eric in the tasting room: one big gulp, hold, spit, done; the wine, and its potential value as a useful ingredient, is microscopically assessed in an instant and his impressions, along with those of his colleagues, jotted down in the notebook, then forgotten about (for the time being) as he moves on to the next one.

Perhaps it is in this critical faculty, honed and developed over a lifetime, of being able to distinguish minute yet significant nuances of sensory impressions and assess the inherent qualities of materials and their potential contribution to the ensemble, to determine how the colors on the palette—and on the palate—can best be combined into a harmonious whole *and* project how it will all come out after the paint dries (in this case, after the second fermentation and long maturation period have taken place), that the true artistry of the Champagne blender lies.

I think back to Eric the previous summer—racking up kilometers all over Champagne visiting vineyards, tasting grapes, and chatting with growers—and see him as a kind of hunter-collector, a Leonardo visiting the mines of Carrara in search of the perfect block of marble or a master chef at market sourcing the very best materials, following Joseph Krug's basic precept, "It is not possible to make good wines without using good elements."

The "good elements" are all here, encapsulated in Eric's black notebook. Now it's time to put them to use.

After nearly two weeks holed up in his office with notebook, projections, scratch pad, and laptop, Eric emerges from the wilderness, so to speak, relieved, triumphant, and demurely smiling, with his *plan de tirage*.

He takes me into the conference room next door and rigs up his laptop to project onto the screen.

"Okay, so now I will explain to you my *plan de tirage* and the methodology behind how I work."

The affable chef de cave, with his computerized tables and measurements of accretion and depletion, now seems like an economics professor about to give a lecture on supply and demand of gross domestic product of a small country for the next two decades.

"By July before harvest I know the total amount of wine we have in our cellars of each of the three grape varieties, so if we're a bit low in any one of them I can contract accordingly when I'm out visiting growers."

Historically, Eric tells me, the Krug Grande Cuvée consists of approximately 30–35 percent chardonnay, 40–45 percent pinot noir, and 20–25 percent meunier, and about 40 percent of the blend is reserve wine; this is not a fixed *recipe* but rather a *tendency*, a rule of thumb based on the past 150 years that provides a working idea. Each year's Grande Cuvée is neither an exact replica nor a totally brand new creation but rather a *re*-creation that is new and different each time yet always stylistically *Krug*.

Once Eric knows exactly what he has at his disposal in the cellar and approximately how many bottles of wine they need to make, he closes himself in his office with his tasting notes and his laptop and starts playing around with his material, like an artist assembling found objects into the perfect composition.

"We began this year with about two hundred individual wines from the 2013 vintage, which became one hundred and seventy-five after we combined some of the smaller parcels together, plus about one hundred and fifty wines in reserve. The oldest wine in reserve right now is 1998.

"Eventually, things fall into place. *Et voilà!*" Eric makes a little drum roll on the table, then hits "enter" on his computer and a new table pops up on the screen. "Here is this year's Grande Cuvée."

I look eagerly over the screen, which displays the basic proportions of the 2013 AK50:

35% chardonnay
22% meunier
43% pinot noir

Sixty percent of the wine is from the 2013 harvest; the remaining 40 percent is from the reserve collection. All in all there are a total of 175 different wines in the blend.

But my eyes keep going, for this is not the only assemblage on the page. The chef de cave has prepared three additional variations . . . [23]

The next morning, we're back in the conference room, where Eric presents his *Tableau du Tirage 2013* to Maggie and Olivier, and I realize then that what he gave me yesterday was a sort of dry run for this annual presentation. Then we stroll over to the tasting room, where Laurent, Julie, and Jérôme are waiting for us. While the outward ambience is amiable, there is a palpable undercurrent of professional reserve and purpose. It's time to get down to business.

Julie begins with a recap of 2013, noting the cool rainy spring and the presence of *millerandage*, especially in the Côte des Blancs. She also discusses the unusually late ripening, the early start of picking in Clos du Mesnil, and the longer-than-usual harvest period in which the grapes of Clos du Mesnil were finishing fermentation before those of Clos d'Ambonnay were even picked. Eric mentions the disparity of the vintage: "For us it was a very good year, though one cannot say it was an excellent vintage overall. The grapes in some parts of Champagne were really great and a bit disappointing in others."

Then we begin to taste.

Eric and team have arranged a truly fascinating tasting that clearly shows all of the basic building blocks used to construct the Grande Cuvée.

We begin by tasting the 2013 subblends by grape variety: The chardonnay blend has a tropical fruit aroma, ripe pineapple palate, long flavor arc, and crisp acid finish. The pinot noir blend is lean and muscular but supple, with lively fresh fruit and tart red currant acidity and a long fruit jelly finish, solidly proportioned but restrained and elegant at the same time. And the meunier blend has a ripe cherry nose and rich earthy palate with a touch of spice.

Next we do a similar thing but with the reserve wines, and it is amazing to see the difference between the two. The reserve chardonnay blend contains eleven wines from four different vintages. It has a subtle aroma but is soft and silky in the mouth, with grilled, toasty, nutty flavors and a taut finish. The reserve pinot noir blend, containing eight wines from three vintages, has lots of finesse, with a beautiful aroma of dried rose petals, roasted pear flavors, and a long, long finish. There are three wines, all from 2012, in the reserve meunier blend, which has a smoky scent with a dense, toffee-like texture and a lingering chocolaty finish.

"Okay," says Eric, "now that our palates are warmed up, let's get serious."

We are each given four new glasses, which we rinse with a tiny bit of the 2013 chardonnay blend we sampled. The four bottles are passed around in succession and we pour a bit of each one into our respective glasses. We now have all four contenders for the Grande Cuvée of 2013 before us. Our task is to put the four wines in numerical order according to our preference; the version with the most number ones takes the prize.

It was quiet before, but now an even more profound silence descends as everyone begins carefully examining the wines, a silence articulated by the soft sounds of deep inhalations, airy slurps, throaty gurgles, and liquid being spit into metal sinks.

After about ten minutes (though it seems much longer), pens are placed down, people take a final sniff or sip, then wait: the moment of truth has come.

Eric slowly looks up and over to his right: "Julie, your preferences please."

As he goes around the table receiving and jotting down everybody's order of preference, I am surprised by the absence of a clear consensus. Julie and I both come out in favor of the first blend as our number one. It seems to me the most perfectly balanced, with a tightly knit structure that suggests a thoroughbred fidgeting at the starting gate, a captivating aroma, and a fresh, racy acidity. Being a novice at this, I also try to imagine what would happen after the second fermentation and long maturing on the lees, which, I reason, would give it that creamy yeastiness and layered complexity it lacks right now. Olivier is the only person at the table to give the fourth blend top billing (though both Eric and Maggie give it runner-up). Eric and Maggie both give the third blend first place, and Laurent fluctuates between the first and third but ultimately comes out on the side of the third, which tips the balance.

Once all the votes are in, Maggie enthusiastically proclaims her preference: "Richness without heaviness, and many layers—that is the essence of Krug Grande Cuvée!"

"The first has great acidity and clarity," Eric adds, "but the additional element gives the third blend extra depth and personality, which will blossom even more over time."

With that, the blueprint for the Grande Cuvée of 2013 has been decided, and a lovely one it is indeed. It seems like the perfect compilation of all the multifarious components that have been compiled throughout this lengthy process, and Eric's closing statement— " . . . depth and complexity that will blossom even more over time"— sticks in my head. The first decisive step in the creation of the 2013-based Krug Grande Cuvée has just been taken, but it won't be finished for a long time to come.

After taking care of a few other matters of business (we still have to sample and vote on how exactly much red wine should be added to the base blend for the rosé, and on Eric's proposed blend for the 2013 vintage, should it be deemed worthy of release in ten years or so), notebooks are shut and coats gathered, and we head out for a celebratory lunch at the nearby Brasserie les Halles, where we revel in cool, beautifully effervescent, already finished and released Grande Cuvée that we can swallow without compunction.

Once he passes the exact formulas of the definitive blends off to Laurent and the jump-suited team to execute, the chef de cave's most important work for the year is done—though in a few months it will begin all over again with vineyard visits and contracts. Hanging out the next day in his office with the door open, he seems much more relaxed than I have ever seen him.

"So now you know what I do. This is basically how I have worked since I came here in 1998.[24] I worked very closely with Henri and learned how Krug works. After tasting all the wines with Henri and Rémi and discussing the assemblage, I would make a few different blends, then we would all sit down to taste and see which one they liked best. That's still pretty much what I do now. There's really no recipe or formula. Every year is a bit different, but the vision is always the same. I suppose you could think of it as a journey; the final destination is always the same—the house of Krug, the style of our wine, and the vision of our founder—but each year we take a slightly different path to get there."

Eric pauses for a long moment, as he occasionally did on our long car journeys. "I've spent my whole life in Champagne, but it still seems a bit strange to me, the time," he says quietly, without looking up. "The wine we're preparing now will not come onto the market until 2021; the clos and the vintage, if we make them, in 2025. I'll be retired by then. I hope!"

While Eric and I are talking, Laurent and the jump-suited workers have already begun to execute the *tirage*,[25] starting with the Grande

Cuvée. Following this year's recipe to the milliliter, the exact quantities of all the different wines are pumped into the *cuves de mixtion* where the *liqueur de tirage*, a mixture of sugar and select yeast dissolved in wine (in this case, last year's Grande Cuvée assemblage) calculated precisely according to the principles of the réduction François to produce the desired amount of bubbliness without making the bottles explode,[26] is added and big paddles inside the tank mix it up. From there the wine is sent to the bottling line, where it is pumped into clean sterilized bottles, which are then sealed with a crown cap like the cap on a bottle of soda,[27] except that the inside of this cap is lined with a thin layer of cork and a hollow polyethylene plug called a *bidule*, and a code is stamped on the top of the cap that identifies the contents inside. Someone in a blue jumpsuit at the other end of the line grabs the bottles off the conveyor belt and places them in a wire cage.

When the cage is full it's brought down to the cellar, where each bottle is carefully laid out atop two very long thin strips of wood, with necks pointing toward the wall. When the first row is complete, another is laid on top with necks facing out, then the process repeats. After four double rows have been stacked, two more strips of wood are laid over the top and more rows are stacked on top, until the stack is shoulder high. Then another row begins in front.

The strips of wood are called *lattes* in French. The Grande Cuvée–to-be is now officially *sur lattes*.[28] And it will stay there in the dark, cool cellar, untouched, for six years.

PART III

MATURITY

THE POSTMODERN ERA AND
THE REBIRTH OF CHAMPAGNE

CHAPTER 8

LET THERE BE BUBBLES

AFTER the intense, prolonged period of activity that climaxes in the assemblage and the bustle of *tirage*—the careful blending of wines, the whir of the mixing tanks, the incessant clinking of bottles on the bottling line, the strident beeping of backward-zipping forklifts moving cages full of bottles—another one of those odd, typically Champenois periods of profound quiet after the storm and (apparent) stasis descends.

The bottles have been carefully laid out in the cellar like bones in a catacomb and left to sit there, collecting dust. But there's an important difference: contrary to outward appearances, these bottles are very much alive; a dynamic metamorphosis is taking place inside them that will turn the contents into something else altogether.

Though Champagne might have started out as a still wine (albeit with a natural propensity to fizz), once people started enjoying the bubbles instead of trying to get rid of them, it was precisely this feature that came to define it. And it is precisely the process of making the wine sparkle, *la prise de mousse*, which most clearly distinguishes the *méthode champenoise* and sets this wine apart from every other type of wine there is.

What's going on inside the bottles during the second fermentation is very similar to what happened to the grape juice in the first one—the yeast goes to work on the sugar, transforming it into alcohol and creating carbon dioxide as a by-product—but there are some important differences. There is much less sugar introduced at this stage than there was in the ripe grapes after harvest, so the second fermentation is considerably slower, less intense, and less turbulent than the first one was. An easy barometer of this is alcohol level: the first fermentation generates around nine to ten and a half degrees whereas the second adds only an additional degree or two.[1]

Another and much more significant difference has to do with the vessel in which the fermentation takes place. The tanks or casks used for the first fermentation usually have a portal on top that may be kept open during the process to let the gas escape. For those, like Krug, who use barrels for fermentation, the gas passes through the pores in the wood, albeit more slowly than freely escaping into open air, and the rubber stoppers in the barrels can be removed periodically as necessary to let the gas escape.

The second fermentation, on the other hand, occurs in airtight, heavy-duty glass bottles sealed with a thick cork or metal cap.[2] Instead of escaping, the trapped carbon dioxide takes the form of tiny gaseous molecules distributed throughout the liquid in the bottle. And there they remain, waiting patiently—and sometimes for a very long time indeed—until they are finally released and get their brief moment to rise and shine.

Bubbles give Champagne its crackle and pop, its foamy finesse, its distinctive, brilliant, effervescent personality. When it's poured into a glass you can see them rise up through the liquid like tiny hot-air balloons, and you can even hear them gently bursting on the surface, like the surf breaking softly on a long sandy beach. You can feel them tickling your nose when you tilt the glass, and tingling on your palate when you take a sip.

Bubbles bring a whole other dimension to a beverage, but not all bubbles are created equal. Champagne bubbles are very different than bubbles in beer or bubbles in beverages created through the modern mechanical technique of carbonization.[3] While carbonated bubbles tend to be big and clunky and anonymously standard, Champagne bubbles, known as *mousse* or *perlage*, are fine and elegant. They change from one wine to another, evolve in the glass in front of you, and evolve in the cork-closed bottle over time. *These* bubbles have personality—large or small, aggressive or demure, delicate little fizzles or big gaseous explosions—and they add a notable element of individuality to the wine they inhabit.

Most people like the bubbliness of Champagne: the bubbles lift their spirits and tickle their fancy. But one person, a physicist named Gérard Liger-Belair, became totally entranced by them, setting up a laboratory complete with high-speed microphotographic equipment to delve deeply into how they actually work. And his findings are quite astounding.

"Following the *prise de mousse*," he explains, "the liquid inside the bottle is completely saturated with a tremendous amount of carbonic dioxide gas molecules and the pressure is very high.[4] In a closed bottle, the gas and liquid are in a state of atmospheric equilibrium. But when you *uncork* it, that equilibrium is thrown out of balance, and that's when the bubbles are really born."[5]

With the sudden change of pressure, turbulence is created, the gas is mobilized, and bubbles form, which are pulled by gravity to the surface, where foam is created. This turbulence can be minimized by making sure the bottle is properly chilled, by gently easing out the cork, and by pouring it gently into a slightly tilted glass. But it's still there. And it's in the glass that the really interesting things start to happen.

"There's enough carbon dioxide in an average glass of Champagne to produce about eleven million bubbles," says Liger-Belair. "Most of it escapes as free vapor at the surface; the larger the surface, the quicker the gas escapes. But there's still enough gas left in the glass to produce upwards of a million bubbles."

It was previously thought that the bubbles were created by carbonic gas trapped in tiny pores in the glass itself. But Liger-Belair's powerful equipment helped him determine what actually happens: when the wine is poured into a glass, carbon dioxide molecules in the liquid find their way into air pockets in microscopic tubular fibers on the inner surface of the glass; atmospheric pressure then gradually forces the gas out of ends of the tubes, forming bubbles whose size and circumference is, to some extent, determined by the size of the openings in the fiber.[6] The bubbles then move upwards in lines of quick succession called *bubble trains*, while the viscosity of the liquid creates a drag and slows the ascent. Successive bubbles naturally follow the lead of the ones ahead of them, creating a drafting effect, not unlike what cyclists do in a race. Sometimes the drafting bubbles speed up and bump into the one ahead of them, causing a diversion of the train. As they float upwards, other, smaller free-floating gas particles attach themselves to and merge with the bubbles, making them bigger.[7] For this reason, the greater the distance the bubbles have to travel to get to the surface, the bigger they are by the time they get there.

Besides carbon dioxide gas, the bubbles also contain volatile aromatic molecules. On their upward journey they collect particles that stick on the outside of the bubble wall, creating a sort of shell that helps preserve them, and when they reach the top, they spread out across the surface of the liquid. Some burst, creating an audible crackly sound and releasing their fragrance, while others actually continue up beyond the surface and burst in the air (that's what you feel tickling your face when you tilt the glass to take a sip). When this happens, the aroma and gas go off into the atmosphere while the heavier components fall back into the glass, creating a trampoline effect that bounces them up into the atmosphere again.

"A bursting bubble creates a sort of vacuum on the surface that the surrounding bubbles rush to fill, creating a pattern that resembles the petals of a flower, and the upward trajectory of a bubble jet looks like the Eiffel Tower," says Liger-Belair, flipping through his enlarged photographs of microscopic images with an air of pride and affection, not unlike a father showing photos of his children.

Indeed, most people looking at these pictures and listening to the impassioned physicist explain them would be quite amazed to know what's actually going on in their glass of Champagne, and this magnified insight would significantly enhance their appreciation and enjoyment of its contents. It might even induce a lucky winner to pause a moment before spraying the precious contents of a bottle (and its billions of tiny bubbles) over everyone within reach.[8]

Which brings us to the glass itself.

Just as the individual bottle (with its evolution into thick lead glass and pressure-resistant cork) had a major impact on the development of Champagne, the vessel in which it is ingested had—and continues to have—a significant impact on its consumption.

Part of this significance is symbolic—think of the significance the Holy Grail had on Western civilization—and part of it is practical.

In the early 1400s, the island of Murano in the Venetian Lagoon became the capital of glassmaking in the Western world thanks to the exceedingly high level of craftsmanship that developed there, stimulated by a powerful guild system and the support of the Venetian doges, as well as by the special characteristics of the natural materials that were used in the manufacture. By the 1600s, a small glass called the *tazza* ("cup"), with a flared bowl that was specially designed for the consumption of wine, was being widely produced on the island and sold throughout Europe.

Murano maintained its uncontested supremacy as the world's most important glass center up until the late seventeenth century, when George Ravenscroft discovered that adding flint and lead oxide to molten glass made it easier to work with, as well as giving the finished product more durability and a higher refractive index, resulting in a brilliant shine and the characteristic "ping" of crystal when tapped.[9]

After returning to England in 1666, Ravenscroft set up a glassworks of his own specializing in the manufacture of drinking glasses, where he renamed the Italian *tazza* the English *cup*, which later became the French *coupe*. He received a patent on his glassmaking process in 1674, making him the exclusive producer of lead crystal in England. When the patent expired in 1681, the technique spread quickly throughout the country and England became a major rival to Murano's domination of the glass industry. From there the production of lead crystal coupes spread far and wide, suggesting that once again the Brits must be given credit for the popularization of something the French hold very close to their hearts—very close indeed, as it turns out.

People must drink in order to survive. While human beings can cup water in their hands to get it into their mouths if they have to, drinking it out of a vessel gives the object a special significance from the get-go. And if the contents happen to be some kind of enhanced water, such as wine (or wine with bubbles), the significance becomes even greater.

In addition to (perhaps even stemming from) this aspect of its life-giving sustenance, there is a built-in intimacy to the act of drinking. The glass is, in some sense, a replacement for a mother's breast or a baby's bottle. (Is it merely coincidental that the names of parts of the glass—foot, shoulders, lip, mouth—are human features? Maybe, but it's an interesting coincidence nonetheless.)

Over time, specific types of glasses were developed in different places for specific types of wine. And, given the special nature of sparkling wine, the type of glass in which its consumed has, as Liger-Belair's work on the behavior of Champagne bubbles has clearly shown, a major impact on our experience of drinking it.

The earliest—and certainly most infamous—type of glass used specifically for the consumption of Champagne is the *coupe de Cham-*

pagne, a glass with a relatively short stem and very wide, shallow bowl. It became popular in the dance halls of Paris and music halls of London, and gained additional notoriety with the widespread allegation that the shape of the glass was modeled on the breast of Marie Antoinette.[10] As enticing as this idea might be—and evidently was—it is thoroughly fictitious.

Louis XVI did indeed give his wife, Marie Antoinette, a *bol sein* (that is, a bowl in the shape of a breast) in 1787—actually he gave her a set of four—but it was not modeled on her breast. The bowls were commissioned from the royal porcelain manufacturer in Sèvres as part of a dairy the king built for her at an estate he acquired in Rambouillet so that, while he was out hunting, she could amuse herself by pretending to be a milkmaid. (A wistful "return to the simple life" of the country peasant was all the rage among the aristocracy at the time, as was a campaign by the royal physician to promote breast-feeding.) The cup, which does look remarkably like a breast—flesh-colored with a pink nipple at the bottom, sitting on a tripod of three goat heads—was intended for milk, not wine.

In fact, the cups Louis gave his wife were nothing new but rather a Sèvres version of a drinking vessel of ancient Greek origin called a *mastos* ("breast").[11]

With all this heavily loaded symbolism attached to the idea of drinking something—especially Champagne—out of a breast, it's easy to understand why the coupe became so popular in the sexually charged party atmosphere of the Belle Époque. And this holds true in our own time as well.

In 2008, Karl Lagerfeld created a glass for Dom Pérignon Champagne inspired by the breasts of model Claudia Schiffer that echoed the design of the Louis XVI cup down to the white bowl and red nipple sitting atop three little porcelain pillar bottles of Dom Pérignon. And in 2014, British artist Jane McAdam Freud designed a classic Champagne coupe with base and stem (but no nipple) supposedly made from a mold of Kate Moss's left breast, which would hardly have caused the artist's great-grandfather Sigmund to bat an eye.[12]

While the idea of drinking bubbly wine out of a glass molded on the breast of a beautiful woman might be kind of fun to some people (as well as just a little bit naughty), the fact is that the coupe is not really the best glass with which to fully enjoy the qualities of a fine Champagne. Because the bowl is so shallow, the bubbles have less distance to travel, meaning that you don't get to watch the delicate bubble trains rising to the surface and the bubbles themselves don't have a chance to develop much volume. What's more, because the surface area is so extensive and the lip wide open, the aromas are much less focused, the carbon dioxide vaporizes more quickly, and so do the bubbles. These faults do not, however, discourage newlyweds from using the glass to create Champagne tower fountains at wedding receptions, or even the Champenois themselves from steadfastly insisting to use the term *coupe de Champagne* instead of *verre* ("glass") regardless of what shape the glass they're using might actually be.

Another type of glass that became popular for Champagne in the early part of the twentieth century was the flute, which has a long stem and an even longer narrow cylindrical bowl, hence its name. It allows you to watch the entire journey of the bubble trains from the very bottom all the way up to the top, increasing in size along the way as they pick up carbon passengers, packing themselves into the narrow circumference at the top, and patiently waiting their turn to break through the surface into the atmosphere to release their aroma and create microscopic Eiffel Towers.

But there's a problem with flutes: the narrowness of the bowl doesn't permit enough air to get into the wine to aerate it, which, in the case of a complex, full-bodied Champagne like the Krug Grande Cuvée, is desirable (almost necessary, in fact) in order to allow its full richness of flavor and intensity of perfume to develop, and to be able to fully enjoy it once it does. It can be a bit difficult to get your nose inside the narrow mouth of the glass to smell what's going on in there, and the flurry of upwardly propelled bubbles can lay assault to the nostrils.

For all these reasons, many people prefer the tulip, which has a slightly wider, slightly shorter bowl that tapers in slightly at the top. Though all the numerous factors of the drinking vessel (including feel of the stem, thinness of the glass, and shape of the bowl) do affect the sensory experience of the wine that is consumed out of it, in most cases a good white-wine glass with a medium-sized bowl and slight taper at the mouth works perfectly fine.[13]

CHAPTER 9

※✦ ✦※

MATURATION AND
DISGORGEMENT

RE-FERMENTATION in the sealed bottles takes about two to three months, depending on a variety of factors, such as the ambient temperature in the cellar, the density and pH of the wine, and the characteristics of the specific strains of yeast that were used to induce it.

After consuming all the available sugar (a process that produces, along with the carbon dioxide, an additional degree or so of alcohol), the yeast molecules begin to self-destruct as the cell walls are broken down by enzymes in the yeast itself, throwing off particles that float through the liquid like celestial debris through outer space and gradually settle on the bottom of the horizontally laying bottle. This process is known as *autolysis*, from the Greek words for "self" (*auto*) and "destruction" or "decomposition" (*lysis*). If the bottles resembled *memento mori* when they were first laid down *sur latte*, now, it would seem, they truly are! But here, too, appearances can be deceiving.

Winemakers have recognized the positive effects of leaving wine in contact with the fine sedimentary lees (*sur lie*) at least since ancient Roman times, though they didn't understand much about why.

This extended maturation period is, in fact, extremely important for the end result of the Champagne, and it is one of the three principle factors that distinguish the *méthode champenoise* from all other ways of making sparkling wine.[1]

During maturation the dead yeast cells continue to break down, releasing important materials into the wine such as nitrogen, polysaccharides, nucleic and fatty acids, vitamins, proteins, and aroma compounds. And, while it may seem a bit odd, this cellular debris of dead yeast makes significant contributions to the finished wine, including enhancing its flavor and aroma, increasing the fineness and persistence of bubbles, contributing to the full, almost creamy mouth feel that is characteristic of fine Champagne, protecting the health and stability of the wine, and even increasing its longevity.[2]

The AOC regulations stipulate nonvintage Champagne must remain on the lees (*sur lie*) for at least fifteen months after *tirage* and vintage Champagne for at least thirty-six months, though many producers choose to go beyond the minimum, especially for their *têtes des cuvées*—sometimes way beyond. Krug leaves the Grande Cuvée *sur lie* for at least six years and vintage Champagnes (as well as the two clos) for ten.

✦

THINGS were different after the Second World War. Champagne now had an appellation, the Institut National des Appellations d'Origine (INAO) was solidly established, and the Comité Champagne, made up of growers, producers, and merchants, was there to mediate disputes and promote the interests of all. Economies were bouncing back, established distribution channels were reopened, and the sparkling wine of Champagne was now known and appreciated all over the world, even by those who never drank it. "Shampain" quickly became a synonym for any expensive bubbly wine, a symbol of luxury, the good life, celebration, and success. The seductive name, the heavy bottle with the shiny foil top, the ritual of service, the distinctive pop—for a great many people throughout the world, these ancillary things became almost as important as the wine itself—for many, in fact, perhaps even more so.

In some ways, Champagne had become a victim of its own popular success.

While wine had been used to christen the maiden voyage of sailing vessels since the time of the ancient Greeks, in the postwar period Champagne became the preferred libation to smash on a new cruise ship's bow before its maiden voyage, both because of the luxury it implied and because the foamy explosion put on a more spectacular show than still wine—at least *when* it exploded (because of the thick glass, the bottle didn't always break on impact, which was taken as a sign of bad luck).

In 1967, Americans Dan Gurney and A.J. Foyt made a surprise upset victory in the twenty-four-hour endurance car race in Le Mans, France, with their Ford GT beating out the Italian Ferrari and the German Porsche. When Gurney stepped up to the winner's pedestal and was handed a magnum of Moët, he was so excited that instead of cradling it for photographers he shook the bottle, popped the cork, and sprayed it all over the startled group of onlookers, including Henry Ford II, unwittingly launching a tradition that would become a ritual in winner's circles and locker rooms at sporting events throughout the world.

This practice is not unlike what the victorious Cossacks did with their sabers, except for one important difference: after brashly slicing off the top (which did cause some of the wine to spray out), they drank it. Many other people during this period preferred to drink Champagne gussied up in a cocktail. And that is precisely how many Americans first tasted it.

"Professor" Jerry (Jeremiah) Thomas's seminal book, *The Bar-Tender's Guide: How to Mix Drinks, or The Bon-Vivant's Companion*, published in 1862, contained recipes for both Champagne cocktail and Champagne punch. By the 1950s the Champagne cocktail—a mix of Champagne, cognac, and Angostura bitters, with a sugar cube, orange slice, and maraschino cherry—had worked its way into American popular culture, and Champagne punch remains a favorite at bridal showers to this day.

In many ways it seemed as if Champagne, the wine adored by kings and monks and cancan girls and gourmands because they liked to drink it, had been taken over by the image of Champagne as a symbol of status and celebration.

Champagne had become a sort of international cliché and the industry rose to the occasion, posting solid gains in production, distribution, and price from the early 1950s on. Having been driven by brand recognition from the very beginning, the established houses now solidified their foothold through the newly emerging practices of mass marketing and mass promotion. Brand names with a pedigree and a nice ring to them became commodities that, when family proprietors died out or could no longer effectively compete, were sold to and carried on by new commercial entities. Some houses developed large amounts of capital and began acquiring interest in other houses, escalating a tradition that had been going on in Champagne since the second wave of the early 1800s, right up to the present day, when independent family-owned and operated companies are becoming increasingly rare.

Krug resisted these tendencies for many years, remaining a strictly family-owned and operated Champagne manufacturer for over a century, with key family members personally creating the cuvées. Its unique style of richly layered, carefully blended Champagne was by now well established, and there were enough people who liked it, mostly in the United Kingdom and America, to keep the company solvent. And things hummed complacently along.

In 1959, Joseph II ceded control of the company to his son, Paul II, but still remained active in the firm. Three years later, Jean

Seydoux died, leaving Paul II sole manager of the house. That same year (1962), Paul's son Henri joined the company, followed by his other son, Rémi, in 1965.

Then, ineluctably necessitated by a changing world, Krug began to change too.

Historically, the house of Krug held firmly to the classic Champagne division between the roles of grower and merchant and had never owned its own vineyards,[3] choosing instead to focus on making wine and building strong and lasting relationships with its vigneron suppliers. But by the early 1960s, ever-stiffer competition for grapes and ever-stricter CIVC regulations regarding allocations was making it increasingly difficult to acquire the high-quality "elements" they needed to make their Champagne. While close relationships with growers were no less important, it was becoming increasingly clear that not having vineyards of their own left both the company and the fulfillment of the founder's mandate dangerously vulnerable. In order to ensure some degree of stability and continuity, they needed to own at least a portion of their own vineyards.

But this raised another issue: In order to be able to acquire vineyards, they needed capital. And in order to raise sufficient capital, they would have to change the structure of the business.

Joseph II died in 1967 at ninety-seven years old, greatly surpassing everybody's expectations. In 1970, Krug established itself as a corporate entity and, with whatever funds they were able to scrape together, began purchasing desirable vineyard parcels that became available, mostly from suppliers with whom they had been dealing for many years.

Though certainly a positive step in terms of sourcing grapes, it was not enough to change the overall situation and did nothing to address the other major problem of distribution, which was becoming increasingly critical. While no one really knew it at the time, this change of corporate structure signaled the end of one era and the beginning of another, a signpost that Paul II, along with his sons

Henri and Rémi, had no choice but to follow, bravely marching the house Joseph Krug created into an entirely new and decidedly different world than the one from which it had come.

∽

IN the 1970s and '80s, many of the seeds that were sowed in the postwar period of the 1950s and '60s began to bear fruit. This was a time of change, both in the world at large and in the world of Champagne. Technology was developing at lightning speed and communication along with it; economies were growing, and businesses were both expanding and consolidating though a flurry of mergers and acquisitions. While this brought many new opportunities for some, it also raised many new challenges for others.

The promotion of brand names and commerce had been an inherent part of Champagne from the very beginning; after all, most of the earliest commercial producers had been textile merchants and/or manufacturers. But these businesses were mostly family-owned and operated concerns, family *houses* as it were, in which the family members played a central role in their activities, often determining the style of the house and creating the blends each year.

During the 1960s and '70s, this model started to change. Champagne was an international commodity: demand from the worldwide market for Champagne was high and so was the demand by bottlers for grapes. Yields, established and enforced by the Comité Champagne, were pushed to the legal limit; garbage was trucked in from Paris and distributed through the vineyards as fertilizer (pieces of garbage from the 1980s still occasionally turn up in the vineyards), blue plastic bags and all, while chemical pesticides and herbicides were widely used to stave off diseases that could interfere with production. Large commercial enterprises continued to run the show as they had done since the beginning, but now they wielded even more power by banding together into liaisons or partnerships, or becoming parts of large corporate conglomerates.

In 1969 two major players in the beverage industry, the huge co-gnac producer Rémy Martin (founded in 1724) and the popular li-queur enterprise founded by brothers Edouard-Jean and Adolphe Cointreau in 1849, joined forces to create a worldwide distribution network for their products. And in 1971, the Champagne house orig-inally founded by Claude Moët in 1743 (which had already acquired Ruinart in 1962 and Mercier in 1970) merged with the other major cognac company, founded by Irishman Richard Hennessy in 1765.

For many small to medium-sized Champagne houses, this was a challenging time in which they had to face the increasing difficulty of successfully competing in the arena of international marketing with the large and well-established brands. The days of Champagne Charlie traveling around the world peddling his product were rapidly coming to an end.

For Krug, this was also an important period of experimentation, exploration, and expansion of the founder's vision. In 1971, a group of some twenty small vineyard parcels in the Côte des Blancs was acquired, one of which was the Clos du Mesnil. Though this vine-yard, like the others, was originally purchased simply to guarantee a supply of excellent grapes for the Grande Cuvée, once the new vines began to reach maturity, another idea began to take shape: "My fa-ther, along with my uncle [Rémi] and my grandfather [Paul II] no-ticed that the grapes from the Clos du Mesnil had very particular characteristics—especially in certain years," Olivier Krug told me, "and they began to vinify the grapes separately and think about the possibility of producing a single-variety single-parcel blanc de blancs in certain years when the unique characteristics of the Clos showed particularly well."[4]

Nineteen seventy-nine was such a vintage.

Nineteen seventy-nine was also the year that Krug first brought in a chef de cave from outside to manage the winemaking operations, though forty-two-year-old Henri was still very much involved in overseeing them and remained largely responsible for key decisions in the winery and tasting room.

Two years earlier, a major organizational change had taken place that was probably inevitable and had probably been envisioned for some time: in 1977, cognac giant Rémy Martin acquired a 33 percent stake in Krug.[5] This provided an essential influx of capital to acquire more vineyards, as well as to renovate and replant properties they already owned and upgrade the winery at Rue Coquebert. Besides cash, the association with Rémy Martin offered Krug a much more efficient and extensive distribution network, permitting the brothers to focus on their chief areas of specialization, Henri overseeing the house's winemaking activities and Rémi its marketing and communication.

While the extended Krug family still owned a majority share of the house and Paul II and sons were left pretty much to operate it as they chose, there was no denying the fact that the once independent family enterprise was now part of a large corporation and an entirely new and different business reality.

***

SOONER or later in the life of a bottle of Champagne, the maturation period comes to an end and the finished (though not yet necessarily fully developed) wine must prepare to leave its underground birthplace and go out into the world, where someone will acquire and consume it or cellar it to let it develop some more.

But before the wine can be considered finished and released, something else of critical importance must happen: the dead yeast particles must be removed from the bottle. *Dégorgement*, as the process to remove them is called, is the third principal factor (after the *prise de mousse* in bottle and the extended maturation on the lees) that defines the *méthode champenoise*, and it remains, essentially, the same technique developed by Widow Clicquot and her cellar master two hundred years ago.

After the obligatory maturation period time has passed and it is determined that it is time for the bottles to be disgorged, they are inserted horizontally into a *pupitre* (a wooden upside-down V with elliptical holes cut into it) and turned a small amount each day, while giving the bottle a little shake and shifting its position slightly upwards in the hole. The initial horizontal position of the bottle collects all the dead yeast particles on the bottom, the sharp back-and-forth twist and shake dislodges the sediment from the glass, and the slight lifting of the bottle shifts all the sediment down towards the neck without causing it to become resuspended, thus leaving the wine in the bottle totally clear.

After six to eight weeks, the bottles are standing nearly vertical in the *pupitre* with the neck pointing down, and all the sediment is collected in the narrow mouth, just inside the cap.[6] This process is known as *remuage*, or "riddling."

An experienced *remueur* can handle forty thousand bottles a day, but this entails a tremendous amount of highly skilled (and costly) labor as well as space. For this reason, today most houses have adopted a mechanical system of *remuage* using a device called a *gyropalette*.[7] The mechanism involves the gradual rotation of a metal wine cage on a wooden pallet and can riddle five hundred bottles at a time in a small amount of space and in a fraction of the time required for hand-riddling. Because the gyropalette can be programmed in different ways and speeds, the technology can be adapted in whatever way a producer considers most useful. Proponents say it produces the same results at a lower cost in less time and with a higher level of consistency.

Krug adopted the use of the gyropalette in 2001.[8] "We proceeded very carefully," Eric told me. "We experimented over a long period and compared the results very closely with hand-riddled bottles. To be perfectly honest, we found no qualitative difference whatsoever. It saves us space and it saves us labor. But as for time, we are not in a hurry: while you can speed up the process with a gyropalette if you want to, we prefer to do a very slow, gradual *remuage*, so for us the time it takes is about the same."

Traditionally, once the *remuage* is finished, the bottles are then carefully arranged between two walls of the cellar with the necks pointing down (*sur pointe*) and subsequent layers stacked on top with the mouth of the upper bottle in the punt of the one below, creating a seemingly precarious wall of upside-down bottles awaiting their moment of disgorgement. But nowadays most of those who use a gyropalette simply leave them *sur pointe* in the metal cage, thus eliminating the possibility of a domino-like collapse.

After resting thus for a few weeks, the bottles are ready for the actual disgorgement. There are basically two ways to do it. In the traditional method known as à la volée, the *dégorgeur* grabs an upside-down bottle and, holding it in his left hand, tilts it upright while carefully watching the rising bubble of gas. Just when the bubble reaches the plug of sediment under the cap, he pops off the cap with a claw-like opener called a *clé* or *la pince à dégorger*, shooting the plug of sediment into the air, and quickly puts his left thumb over the opening to prevent the loss of wine.

Timing here is absolutely critical: if the cap is removed too early—that is, before the gas bubble reaches the sediment—too much wine is lost; if too late, there's a good chance some of the sediment will fall back into the wine.

The other way to remove the sediment is a later refinement of the process called à la glace, which involves quickly freezing the tops of the still upside-down bottles in a brine solution at minus twenty-five degrees Celsius, solidifying the plug of sediment, which can then be easily popped out. This procedure makes the process much easier and more consistent and is adaptable to mechanization, and it's what most houses (including Krug) do today.

Once the sediment has been removed and while the bottle is still open, a final step takes place: a mixture of sugar dissolved in wine called the *liqueur d'expédition* is added to fill the lost space in the bottle and to bring the finished wine up to the desired level of sweetness. Originally this was a corrective step: besides adjusting the sweetness of the Champagne according to different taste preferences, other things besides wine and sugar—cognac, spices, herbal extracts, and a variety of other flavoring elements—were often added to improve the final product, though any such additives are strictly forbidden today.

The addition of sugar at this stage—the third and final time that sugar is added to the wine—is known as *dosage*, and due to changing taste preferences, the desired levels of sweetness are generally much lower today than they were in the past.

∽✑⌣

As animals, we have a natural attraction to sweet things. Sweet is the opposite of bitter, sour, acerbic; sweetness has an immediate gratification and, biologically speaking, something that tastes good—that is, sweet—is less likely to be harmful to us than something that tastes bad.

This explains why babies, once they begin to move beyond the sour though nutritious solution of mother's milk, crave sugar. Gradually, as life goes on, our tastes change and develop as we gain experience and confidence in the world and seek out new and different taste experiences that are not only not harmful but may actually give us pleasure and thus be beneficial to our survival. At some point many of us begin to discover and appreciate other flavor sensations like bitter coffee, salty caviar, pungent anchovies, stinky cheese, the spicy burn of hot peppers, or the peaty smokiness of scotch whiskey.

Over the long evolution of wine in Western society, human beings began, in a sense, like babies. In ancient Greece and ancient Rome, before the ready availability of refined sugar, when peoples' lives were already filled with much bitterness and blandness, the natural sweetness of a wine (which usually indicated a superior grape-growing spot that typically produced extremely ripe, sugar-packed grapes) was highly prized. Many techniques were developed to make less-sweet wines more palatable; ancient Romans, for example, often mixed honey into their wine and developed a process of drying grapes to concentrate their sugar before vinification.

Sweetness remained an irresistible object of desire for a long, long time. Then, something began to change.

Champagne was born as a sweet wine. In the cool northern reaches of the Champagne area, the addition of sugar to the must before fermentation was often necessary, and the practice became key to the survival of winemaking in the region. Sugar also proved to be the answer to the problem of intentionally initiating (and, thanks to Jean-Baptiste François, controlling) the second fermentation in bottle, and the final addition of sugar in the *liqueur d'expédition* made the still rather acidic wine more appealing to peoples' palates. In fact, it appeared that the more sugar was added, the more appealing it became, and Champagne producers were happy to oblige.

The Russians had an extremely sweet tooth when it came to Champagne, typically preferring upwards of fifty grams per liter. The vast majority of Champagne that was consumed in the noble courts of Europe, the dance halls of the Belle Époque, and the brothels of New Orleans was decidedly sweet, and even the enamored idealist Joseph Krug (who was, after all, also a businessman) had no problem sweetening his carefully constructed blends to the preferences of different markets where his Champagne was being sold.

When Louise Pommery tried introducing the first truly and intentionally dry Champagne to the British (who had already developed a taste for dry gin) in 1874, they called it "brutish"—that is, coarse, harsh, or cruel—and promptly sent it back. Then, eventually, in a sort of *déjà vu* of what had happened with the spontaneous appearance of bubbles in the wine of Champagne centuries before, some Brits started to ask for it.

Much of the bubbly that was consumed in America in the 1950s and 1960s was semisweet (demi-sec), and even in France, where many wine drinkers viewed Champagne (indeed, many still do) as an aperitif before a meal or an accompaniment to dessert after, much of the Champagne was technically "sec"—that is, between seventeen and thirty-two grams of sugar per liter.[9]

Then, in the late 1970s and '80s, many more people began discovering the beauty of "brut"—twelve grams or less of sugar per liter. Besides being less cloying and sugary, it makes Champagne more versatile for accompanying savory foods and permits more of the inherent flavor characteristics of the particular grape variety and place of origin to come through.

Today, the majority of Champagne produced is brut. In the past ten to fifteen years a new tendency has emerged of producing extra-brut Champagnes (less than six grams of sugar per liter) or even brut nature, which, with less than three grams of residual sugar per liter, might cause even Mme. Pommery to crinkle up her nose. Indeed, as the name suggests, brut nature—also known as *zero dosage*—has no sugar at all added after the second fermentation, and tasting a brut nature wine right after it's been disgorged à la volée can be a bracing (and immensely intriguing) experience, like shining a spotlight on a naked, bare-bones wine with nothing (or very little, anyway) to cover up or obscure its essential qualities or flaws.

Interestingly, while the tendency seems to be heading towards ever drier Champagnes, there is also an emerging, almost nostalgic backpedaling countertrend towards a sweeter style such as Pol Roger Rich, a demi-sec with thirty-four grams of sugar per liter that was launched in 2001, and Moët & Chandon Nectar Impérial (made in both regular and rosé versions) with enough sugar (forty-five grams per liter) to make a Russian smile.

There's something for everyone in Champagne, and people are free to choose their preferred level of sweetness or brutness according to their taste. For me, while I have a natural aversion towards sweetness in wine, some brut nature can seem a bit rough and raw, while some Champagnes on the higher end of the brut scale (or even, in rare cases, the lower end of extra-sec) can come off seeming not overly sweet. In the end, it's a question of achieving a delicate equilibrium between all the various components in a particular Champagne. There is also the question of ageability: some people argue that a moderate to high level of sugar helps preserve wine over a long stretch of time, which also suggests that a zero dosage Champagne might be less age-worthy, though, as brut nature is a fairly recent phenomenon, we will have to wait a very long time to find out.

For Krug, dosage is a moot point: "All Krug Champagnes have about six grams of sugar per liter," Eric said, "enough to tame the acidity but not enough to make it seem sweet. We want the sugar to be completely invisible. This allows all the special qualities of each Grand Cuvée to come through and, along with the fairly high percentage of reserve wines and long maturation *sur lattes*, contributes to the full-bodied layered quality that is typical of Krug."

After disgorgement and dosage (if it is being done, which is usually is), the bottle is sealed with a cork and the wire cage devised by Adolphe Jacquesson,[10] and allowed to sit for a while—ideally a minimum of six months, though Krug allows it to rest for ten months to one year—before finally getting its foil capsule and label and being sent off into the world.

The act of removing the sediment is the final step in the *méthode champenoise* and the dividing line in the sand between the two lives of Champagne. During the maturation phase following the second fermentation in bottle, the dying yeast particles gradually break down, dispersing all kinds of beneficial materials into the wine that help allow it to mature and develop. This phase can be extended almost indefinitely; even after the yeast molecules have thoroughly decomposed and given off just about everything they have to give (which most people believe happens within about ten to fifteen years or so), the residual sediment in the bottle seems to have a positive effect on protecting and preserving the liquid inside. This has given rise to another category of Champagne, often called *oenothèque* or "recently disgorged," indicating a bottle that has spent extra time in the cellar before being disgorged and released onto the market. Besides the beneficial presence of the decomposed yeast itself, there is also the beneficial impact of maintaining the perfect equilibrium in the closed bottle.[11]

When disgorgement does take place, besides popping out the compacted disk of sediment, it throws the interior equilibrium out of whack, some gas vapor escapes, and oxygen enters into contact with the liquid in the bottle, not to mention the shock of the addition of the *liqueur d'expédition.*

While the Champagne *sur lie* is suspended outside of time in a sort of vinous Shangri-La, once the sediment comes out its real life begins. After a short rest, the Champagne is ready for shipping and consumption. But it doesn't have to be consumed immediately. After disgorgement, the aging period truly begins. And when it comes to Champagne, this can last for a very long time and have a very beneficial outcome, both for the Champagne itself and for the people who have the pleasure of drinking it. Precisely for this reason, knowing when a given Champagne was disgorged can make a big difference in determining when might be the best time to pop it open.

⁕

THROUGHOUT the 1970s and '80s the house of Krug struggled to keep its head above water and retain a sense of its own unique identity within the new corporate reality. Paul II was getting older and, understandably, gradually retiring from day-to-day activities of the business. Henri was something of a recluse, much as his grandfather Joseph II had been, preferring to keep to himself in the cellars and vineyards, while his more extroverted younger brother Rémi traveled the world preaching the merits of the extraordinary Champagne with the un-French sounding name to the adoring choir of converts who had taken to referring to themselves as "Krugistes."

Krug had always cultivated a following for its unique style of Champagne—a Champagne that was more vinous and complex, more layered and fuller-bodied than most, but always loaded with personality rather than mere bubbles. The loyal following continued—in fact, it became something of a cult and the name *Krug* a buzzword of the initiated elite—but it was not enough to keep the business secure in the new fast-paced global marketplace. The house now had vine-yards of its own, guaranteeing a secure supply of at least a portion of the high-quality grapes it needed, and an efficient distribution net-work that made the Champagne available in markets around the world, but people still had to want to buy it.

"There is Champagne, and then there is Krug," Rémi often pro-claimed, attempting to differentiate his Grande Cuvée from all the other less expensive (and less exceptional) non-vintage Champagnes, arguing that "Krug Grande Cuvée is not *non* anything, it's *multi!*" while at the same time steadfastly declining to specify what the "multi" actually consisted of: "Would anyone ask a great chef for his recipe or a great painter the secret behind his palette of colors?"

This lack of information, in addition to the high price and elitist aura surrounding the brand, gave Krug an air of secrecy, aloofness, and exclusivity: the wine was as expensive as other houses' prestige cuvées even though it was not a vintage or a grand cru, and no one knew what was inside it; the house did not receive visitors, and the imposing gate at Rue Coquebert was usually shut tight.

This approach had worked okay in the past—it wasn't like they had millions of bottles to sell anyway—but as the new decade of the 1990s unfolded, it was becoming increasingly difficult to remain commercially viable.

Krug was not the only Champagne house to struggle to adapt it-self to the new global economy, nor was wine the only sector. French fashion was booming and fashion houses, like many other businesses in the luxury market, were jostling to reposition themselves for bet-ter chances at success—and survival.

In 1946, a young visionary designer named Christian Dior launched his own fashion house with the backing of a textile mogul and race-horse breeder named Marcel Boussac, through his company, Boussac Saint-Frères. Dior introduced a whole new take on fashion known as the "New Look" as well as an entirely new approach to vertical brand-ing. Christian Dior Parfums was created in 1947, a New York City boutique followed a year later, and by 1950 the name was slapped on a wide variety of luxury products, from lipstick to lingerie.

In 1968, Christian Dior Parfums was sold off to Moët-Hennessy to raise cash due to Boussac's steadily weakening textile business. When Boussac Saint-Frères filed for bankruptcy in 1978, its assets were snapped up by the Agache-Willot Group, which, besides substantial textile operations, also owned the Le Bon Marché chain of retail shops and an assortment of other enterprises. Three years later Agache-Willot filed for bankruptcy too. With the conglomerate employing over twenty thousand people in France and its businesses accounting for a substantial amount of the French economy, the socialist government could not afford to let it go down, but it wasn't able to find a viable solution either.

Three years later, while the polarized politicians were still debating the pros and cons of a bailout, a young entrepreneur appeared on the scene like a knight in shining armor to save the day. While no one knew it at the time, the knight was about to trade in his shining armor for silken haute couture and make a serious play to become the king of luxury.

Bernard Jean Étienne Arnault was born into a family of entrepreneurs in Roubaix, France, on March 5, 1949. After graduating from the prestigious École Polytechnique in 1971, he joined his father's construction and real estate company as an engineer and, after rapidly demonstrating his business prowess, was promoted to CEO in 1978.

In 1984, just back from three years in America developing condos in southern Florida, Arnault saw what he perceived as an exceptional business opportunity and seized it, putting together a deal with the investment firm Lazard Frères to purchase the Agache-Willot Group (including Boussac Saint-Frères and Christian Dior Couture) for one franc and paying off its substantial debt.

The first thing he did was to sell off all the Agache-Willot subsidiaries except for Bon Marché and Christian Dior Couture and reposition the new company as Christian Dior S.A. With the cash raised from the sales, he began acquiring select luxury properties, including fashion label Christian Lacroix and leather-goods producer Céline. Then, in 1988, another extremely attractive opportunity came his way.

Following the merger of 1987, the corporate marriage of Louis Vuitton and Moët-Hennessy was experiencing some post-honeymoon turbulence, with chairman Alain Chevalier of Moët and vice-chairman Henry Racamier of Vuitton jockeying for position.

In an attempt to gain a firmer foothold, Racamier invited Arnault to invest in LVMH, which he did, forging a deal with Guinness to acquire a 24 percent stake. Additional investments made Arnault the conglomerate's largest shareholder with 35 percent voting rights. Then, after an acrimonious and widely publicized legal battle, Racamier was removed, and in January 1989, the forty-year-old man-who-would-be-king was unanimously elected CEO of LVMH. With undisputed control of LVMH and Christian Dior and all of their numerous high-end subsidiaries, Arnault set about cherry-picking other suitable properties and building the world's biggest holding company of luxury brands.

Paul Krug II passed away in 1997 at the age of eighty-five. In 1998, a new chef de cave named Eric Lebel was recruited from his ten-year stint at Maison de Venoge. And on January 21, 1999, when Champagne-filled New Year's celebrations had just about faded to a distant memory, it was announced that LVMH had made a deal to purchase Krug from Rémy Cointreau for the then unheard-of sum of one billion French francs.

The roaring nineties were going to go out with a bang, though it was not at all clear what was going to take their place in the new millennium.

CHAPTER 10

❧❧ ❧❧

INTO THE WORLD

THE bottles of the 2013-based Grande Cuvée–to-be remain neatly stacked up in the dark, cool, cavernous cellars deep below Rue Coquebert. Occasionally, the muted lights click on and someone passes by on their way to deposit something or to retrieve something else, hardly bothering to give them a look. And why should they? They're not ready yet; nothing needs to be done to them and nothing is happening to them—at least not on the surface.

Inside, the wine is in a state of limbo, quietly developing, imperceptibly pulsating in anticipation of being born. Or rather, *reborn.* Through the autolytic process of self-destruction, something new is being created. But this is not the first instance of reincarnation the liquid inside these bottles has undergone.

All wine could be considered a rebirth of sorts in which grape juice emerges from the transformative process of fermentation as wine, locking the unique characteristics of the grape, along with the imprint of the place and season where it grew and ripened to maturity, into the liquid. But Champagne takes this transformational process much further.

Assemblage, the combining of various wines in a careful, intelligent way, creates an entirely new wine that is much more than the sum of its individual parts. The second fermentation transforms this still wine into yet something else—a transformation the tasting panel takes fully into consideration when evaluating the base wines and creating a blend—and this new bubbly wine develops and evolves over time on the lees.

Disgorgement, when the yeast sediment is finally removed and the wine is given its dosage (if it is going to get one) and prepared to be sent out into the world, signals yet another life cycle of the wine, which thereafter continues to develop and evolve right up until the moment when the cork is popped and the wine is consumed.

While all of this rebirth and transformation is taking its own time deep inside the cellars, outside, time does not stop: things change, life swirls on . . .

♱

FOR most of the past four hundred years, Champagne has pushed relentlessly forward, from its fierce competition for supremacy with Burgundy, through its gradual acceptance of bubbles, development of the *méthode champenoise,* and creation of a defined appellation, to world recognition, all while struggling to overcome challenges such as devastating wars, internal conflict, changing tastes, economic collapse, economic expansion, and an ever-changing and increasingly competitive marketplace.

While change continues its ineluctable march forward, some things begin to double back upon themselves: nascent, long-dormant seeds begin to sprout; out of what appeared to be a static, very predictable landscape, new life blossoms, and it takes on a number of different forms.

Part of this new blossoming was reflected (or stimulated or anticipated) by the transition of taste preferences from sweet to dry: As long as Champagne was packed with sugar, it was a commodity, a manufactured beverage that, while pleasant and immediately gratifying, said less about the particularities of the specific place it came from than about the refined process that was employed to create it. The drier the wine got (both in response to market demand and producer preferences), the more the special character of the grapes from different areas used to make it came out, regardless of whether they were used singly or in a blend. This is precisely the type of Champagne that Joseph Krug envisioned and became obsessed with way back in 1843 (though most of his wines still had what would be considered today a fairly high amount of dosage) and also the kind of wine that Saint-Évremond praised even before it had bubbles.

With a drier wine (with less sugar added to "correct" shortcomings), nuances become more apparent and the vineyard becomes viewed more as the unique birthplace of grapes with individual character, rather than as an open-air incubator to squeeze as much out of the land as possible with the aid of chemical pesticides, herbicides, and fertilizers. This was a profound change: what was once the garbage dump of Paris became reborn as a complex mosaic of diverse terroirs to be respected, celebrated, and well cared for. Beginning in the mid- to late 1980s, some renegade growers began to farm their vineyards in an organic or even biodynamic manner, bucking trends and receiving ridicule. Now more and more growers are implementing environmentally friendly practices, and even the Comité Champagne has gotten on board, encouraging winegrowers to adopt a program of environmentally friendly, sustainable viticultural practices.

The southern department of the Aube, adopted home of Saint Bernard and historic seat of the counts of Champagne, was excluded from the first official map of the *Champagne viticole* in 1908; it had to fight to be included in the revised boundaries and resign itself to second-class citizenship until 1927. Even after receiving full and equal status in the first Champagne AOC of 1936, the Aube continued to be looked down upon as the black sheep of the south and functioned primarily as an important, though largely anonymous, supplier of grapes for the large commercial bottlers of the Marne. Now things have changed.

In recent years the Aube has emerged from the shadows and been strikingly reborn. Whereas the relatively few Champagne producers that existed in the Aube once felt embarrassed by the vinosity of their wine, today they are proud of it. Easier access to channels of marketing and distribution and a growing number of consumers on the lookout for new and interesting wines has brought the region out of the shadows, and it has been receiving a whole slew of attention and even praise for offering a "new" and different face of Champagne. This, in turn, has encouraged more and more Aubois to start making, labeling, and marketing their own wines. Many of these producers are quite small, producing a minuscule amount of wine—as little as ten or twenty thousand bottles a year, compared to millions—but all it takes is an energetic importer or two and good placement in a few chic restaurants in Paris and New York (often at prices commensurate with some of the famous *marques*) to create a successful closet industry. Most of these producers do little or no dosage, and a high percentage of them are committed to organic or biodynamic methods of farming.

This same trend is going on all over the region, even in the commercial center of the Marne, where a whole "new" generation of small grower-producers has emerged. Spurred on by an increasingly curious and open-minded population of consumers, and aided by much more accessible channels of communication and distribution, more and more farmers are starting to make and market their own wine rather than just selling their grapes, and many who owned presses that traditionally sold must to large houses to ferment and turn into Champagne are now doing it themselves.

What has long been a sharp (and often contentious) line of division in Champagne between vignerons who grow grapes and maisons who produce and commercialize Champagne, is becoming increasingly blurred. "Grower-producer" is a category that is growing exponentially and radically changing the profile of Champagne.

Compared to the large, familiar brands that maintain a consistent house style year in and year out, grower-producers focus on diversity and personality, along with a handcrafted artisanal approach and wines that are more localized to a specific area, precisely because they have fewer vineyards to draw from.[1]

The smaller scale of these operations permits grower-producers to explore the implementation of new techniques, such as a solera-type process of adding wine of a new vintage to a *cuve* of wine of past vintages, creating a sort of perpetual reserve. Grower-producers, having a fairly small amount of land to cultivate in the first place and being the ones to both grow their grapes and turn them into wine, are more open to experimenting with alternative methods of working in the vineyards, like organic or even biodynamic viniculture, and in the winery. Many of them also embrace the old practice of fermenting in wooden barrels, which was largely abandoned with the introduction of temperature-controlled stainless-steel tanks. Aside from philosophical and stylistic preference, individual small barrels are often more logistically appropriate to the small scale of these producers, many of whom make small quantities of different wines from tiny individual parcels. This renaissance of wood has radically changed the face of Champagne, helping to create wines that go beyond the previous norm of crisp, clean, and often anonymous bubbliness.

After the rebound from the devastation of World War I and the creation of the CIVC, Champagne consolidated its protocol, focusing solidly on the three principal grapevines, the ones that were most predominant, productive, and versatile: pinot noir, chardonnay, and meunier. While four other varieties—petit meslier, arbane, pinot blanc, and pinot gris (also known as *fromenteau*)—were allowed in the appellation, mostly because they were already there and had been for a long time, they were definitely not encouraged. Even meunier, while totally accepted and widely planted, was looked down upon as somewhat inferior to pinot noir,[2] while gamay—the grape variety used to make fruity beaujolais and which was planted widely throughout the Aube—was unequivocally excluded.

Despite the clear and overwhelmingly strong favoritism towards the big three, some vignerons stubbornly continued to cultivate one or more of the other four varieties even though they had much less market value, and their persistence has paid off. Today the *other* grapes of Champagne are receiving lots of attention—many who never had them before are planting them now or acquiring musts to experiment with—and these obscure varieties have also become something of a battle cry for the counterculture of grower-producers, many of whom are using these previously marginalized grapes to create unusual new signature cuvées, either singly or in a blend.[3]

While no one expects the four once-lost-but-now-found varieties to threaten the entrenched dominance of the big three, restoring their due place on the roster offers the mostly small producers who have gotten behind them new vehicles for expressing their particular terroir and winemaking style, which in turn adds a whole new dimension to the profile of Champagne.

In this age of popular Food TV, shiny exposed kitchens, and hot celebrity chefs, it's hard to believe that not very long ago, cooking was a not very respectable occupation, just one notch above manual labor, and the foremen that ran the kitchens were mostly anonymous. Auguste Escoffier, chef-partner at the Hôtel Ritz, was one of the first to break out of the mold, but it would take close to a century for the rest of the industry to begin to catch up.

The figure of the chef de cave was much like that of the chef de cuisine—the person who did most of the dirty work in the basement while the monsieur upstairs got to give orders, taste wines, and make up the blends.

While chefs de cave have always existed in the larger Champagne houses, they were mostly anonymous workers who oversaw the daily operations of the wineries. But over the past few decades, as many of the houses began to change from family-run businesses to corporate ones and the family members who had traditionally been responsible for the key winemaking decisions were no longer around (or at least not quite as involved), the role of the chef de cave began to change too.

Today, many chefs de cave have emerged from the shadows, and some of them are becoming as famous as rock stars or celebrity chefs—well, almost.

When Eric began working at Krug in 1998, he, like most of his peers, was a largely anonymous (though surely valued and respected) employee, operating in the shadow of his employers, Henri and Rémi; that started changing as Eric settled in, Henri gradually started to step back, and the structure of the house began to change.

Now Eric puts his ten-year tutelage to good use, calling many of the shots, supervising his team, and interacting closely with President and CEO Maggie Henríquez and Director Olivier Krug.[4] Instead of being kept strictly behind the scenes, he, like many of the other top chefs de cave today, is very visible indeed, both in Champagne and at special events around the world.

This has many positive aspects, for it puts a human face on the person who is chiefly responsible for the creation of the wine behind the glitzy brand name and offers a direct link to the complex activity of winemaking that no salesperson or promotional material can. This trend towards increased visibility and recognition of the chef de cave will likely continue to grow along with peoples' interest in who made (or, rather was chiefly responsible for the making of) their wine and how they did it. One can only hope it will not go so far as to spawn reality shows along the lines of *Cellars of Hell*.

Curiously, the 170-year-old house of Krug is at the center of many of these twenty-first-century trends in Champagne. Their steadfast adherence to the use of wooden barrels has set the wood barrel standard and provided a reference point for the revival by a whole new generation of converts. The house's early forging of close and lasting relationships with its vigneron suppliers (remember that Joseph had his young son Paul spend time with a family of vignerons for a period in order to gain a better appreciation of their life) foreshadowed today's spirit of interdependence and mutual respect between growers and producers. Moreover, the house's parcel-by-parcel approach, whereby grower suppliers can come to the winery after fermentation to taste their own individual wine, has made Krug the grande marque of vignerons. All of the suppliers I encountered on my many visits with Eric were extremely proud to supply Krug, and it is precisely this sense of pride and validation of the individual that has induced a whole new generation of grape growers to become grower-producers of Champagne. Finally, not withstanding Krug's allegiance to its standard-bearer, Grande Cuvée, it was among the first of the established houses to champion the concept of terroir in Champagne, which has now been widely embraced throughout the region.

∾◗∼

CHAMPAGNE has always been the go-to beverage of elite trendsetters—discerning gourmands like Saint-Évremond and his Coteaux buddies, kings, emperors, courtesans, rich industrialists, cancan dancers, fashion designers, and race car drivers. It has added its elegant effervescence to festivities in a multifarious array of places, from ornate palaces to raunchy dance halls, sedate salons to brothels, formal ballrooms to hot-air balloons, contributing to the celebration of good fortune (or, sometimes, the mollification of misfortune), success, rites of passage, and simply the joy of being alive.

Because of its high prestige and elaborate method of production, Champagne is not cheap and never has been, which has made it something of a status symbol from the very beginning. But Champagne does not discriminate: it is available to anyone who wants it and can pay for it—or has friends who can.

In recent years, one of the most significant groups of trendsetters to emerge has been rap and hip-hop stars, and the huge popularity of the genre has brought material success to many of its chief proponents, mostly young black men, who, in addition to their musical skill and knack for rhythmic rhyming, have demonstrated an impressive ability to develop their high-profile personas into corporate-style profit-generating brands.

Many of these performers gravitate towards what are generally perceived as the finer things of life, visible symbols of their attainment of fame and wealth: heavy gold jewelry, designer clothes, luxurious cars, big homes, expensive watches, and fancy brand-name wines and liquors. One of the first alcoholic beverages rappers latched on to was cognac. In 2002, Busta Rhymes and P. Diddy came out with a big hit called "Pass the Courvoisier." After sales jumped nearly 20 percent, the spirit's parent company, Allied Domecq, happily made a lucrative deal with the artists' management company for the continued promotion of their products, much as Moët & Chandon and Veuve Clicquot did more than a century earlier with music hall stars Champagne Charlie and the Great Vance.

Many other luxury products and brands have been coveted by rappers and mentioned in their songs, with a corresponding impact on sales. And it was not long before they turned their attention to Champagne. Just as Madame de Pompadour advised Louis XV on matters of taste and had a huge impact on the wines and brands that graced the royal table, rappers had an adviser on Champagne known as Branson B. (aka Branson Belchie). Though not himself a musician—he had a candy shop in Harlem that was a neighborhood fixture—Branson B. knew most everyone on the New York hip-hop scene and, having himself developed a keen interest in and appreciation of Champagne in the 1970s, would often bring some of his favorite bottles to recording sessions to share. And it wasn't long before the artists, enjoying both the cool bubbles and the aura of high-brow exclusivity, began to mention the wine in their songs.

Brands such as Piper-Heidsieck and Taittinger were early favorites of performers such as LL Cool J and Notorious B.I.G. But the Champagne that made the biggest splash on the hip-hop scene was the special cuvée Louis Roederer originally created for Tsar Alexander II in 1876 that became known as Cristal: it is expensive, it has a clear bottle with a gold label, and its name easily lends itself to rhyming lyrics.

Affectionately known as "Cris" or "Crissi" among rappers (much as Bollinger was known as "the Boy" and Veuve Clicquot as "the Widow" by other groups of Champagne guzzlers in times past), Cristal became the most popular bubbly in top hip-hop clubs throughout America, where bottles costing upwards of several hundred dollars (considerably more for a magnum or jeroboam) were popped and passed around with abandon. And one of the most vocal fans (and thus promoters) of Cristal was one of the most famous rappers of all, Jay Z, who called out the name of the Champagne frequently in his song lyrics and included it in his music videos, right up to the moment he had a public falling-out with the brand.

In May 2006, the "Intelligent Life" insert of *The Economist* ran a story on prestige Champagnes in which Roederer's managing director Frédéric Rouzaud said he observed the popularity of Cristal among hip-hop artists and rappers with "curiosity and serenity." Asked whether the association might hurt the brand, Rouzaud replied: "That's a good question, but what can we do? We can't forbid people from buying it. I'm sure Dom Pérignon or Krug would be delighted to have their business."

When Jay Z learned of these statements, he promptly exorcised the name from all his song lyrics and videos, removed Cristal from his chain of clubs, and, happily taking Rouzaud up on his suggestion, replaced it with Krug and Dom Pérignon. But he didn't stop there: Five months after the falling-out, Jay Z released a music video for "Show Me What You Got" that was set in Monaco and replete with fast cars, sleek speedboats, and beautiful women. When, at a fancy casino, a waiter presents him with a bottle of Cristal, it is dismissively waved away in favor of a bottle (presented in a silver briefcase that Jay Z himself was earlier shown carrying) completely encased in shiny golden armor and emblazoned with an embossed ace of spades logo. The video, ending with a cigar-smoking Jay Z making the symbol of a spade with his hands, immediately thrust the unknown Champagne into the hip-hop limelight.

The name on the back of the golden bottle is Armand de Brignac, which is not a producer but rather a second label of a company called Cattier in Chigny-les-Roses. Before Jay Z "discovered" Armand de Brignac, the Champagne was known as Cattier Antique Gold, which came in the same gold bottle (encased in a golden cage, no less) and cost about seventy dollars. The Armand de Brignac "Ace of Spades" (which costs more than three times what the Antique Gold did) was actually born in 2006, the same year as Jay Z's falling-out with Cristal, which makes the timing of the incident rather propitious. was the rap star just looking for a convenient way to remove himself from an association in which he had no vested interest in favor of one in which he did? In the fall of 2014, Jay Z (who is rumored to have had a stake in the Ace from the get-go) bought the Armand de Brignac brand from its American parent company, which makes sense, for though the bottle might have been gold before, it was the Midas touch of the rapper that actually made it worth its weight.

While Jay Z may well have perceived Rouzaud's comments as racist, it appears that the Champagne producer was only stating the obvious: he has no more control of who buys his product than Jay Z has over who buys his. And if the successful rapper is going to be promoting any Champagne, it might as well be his own brand. After all, as one rap song says, it's a dog-eat-dog world.

In acquiring a Champagne label of his own, it would seem that Jay Z was once again following in the footsteps of his bubbly mentor, for a year before the appearance of Armand de Brignac, Branson B. had taken the plunge and traveled to Le Mesnil-sur-Oger to trudge through the vineyards and cellars of maison Guy Charlemagne and assemble his own line of cuvées to import to America. While his wines have a lower price tag than those usually favored by the high-flying hip-hop set, Branson B. seems content: "[My wines are] really good wines, really top quality wines. The grapes come from a village with very chalky soil. The whites tend to be very mineraly, with almost a hint of sea salt, very crisp. For the people in the Champagne world who want to experience these things, it's a unique experience. . . . You know, I think what makes a Champagne great is that you enjoy it."[5]

∽⚬∼

THE Roman Empire began as a small but ambitious tribe in central Italy that expanded quickly throughout the peninsula, then radiated outwards in all directions, until by the early centuries of what would become known as the Christian era, it dominated most of the Western and Near Eastern world.

One of the reasons ancient Romans were able to build and maintain such an extensive empire had to do with their tactics of conquest. Once they set their eye on a desirable target, the Roman legions marched in, bringing sophisticated social structures, advanced technology, and productive systems of agriculture and viticulture. Most importantly, whenever possible they conquered peacefully, leaving the existing local leadership and culture intact, which usually resulted in less destruction, less turmoil, less expense, and thus more value for the empire.

In expanding his own empire of luxury brands, Bernard Arnault employed a similar strategy: As a savvy businessman, Arnault knows that, especially in the image-driven world of luxury, much of the value of a company lies in the brand itself and in the individuality—the people, story, and tradition—behind it.

When LVMH acquired Krug in 1999, its motives were, one would imagine, more about prestige than profit: Krug, with its comparatively low volume and relatively high costs of production, is a mere drop in the *cuve* compared to other giants that were already part of the company. Yet the incomparable sparkle of Krug added a priceless luster to the large and star-studded LVMH crown.

When the news broke in January of 1999, many in the clique of loyal Krugistes immediately began dusting off their mourning attire, but not much really changed after the transaction: Olivier, who had taken a position outside the house in 1997, was brought home to help integrate Krug with its new parent company; Rémi, who had been acting as managing director of Krug since 1973, continued to travel the world promoting the brand; and Henri continued to oversee activities at home while his new chef de cave (Eric Lebel) settled in and did most of the heavy lifting.

But Paul II's death several years earlier, combined with the changing world that had necessitated the creation of a corporate alliance in the first place, was beginning to have an effect. The old model didn't quite work anymore, but a new one that did hadn't turned up yet. When Krug became part of LVMH, the internal workings remained the same—the long-standing relationships with growers remained close, production volume remained the same, the fermentation continued to be done in wood, the elaborate process of tasting the wines and determining the Grande Cuvée blend remained essentially unchanged—but the fuel tank was starting to run low.

In 2002, Henri officially retired, leaving the day-to-day operations of the Krug cellars squarely in the hands of Chef de Cave Eric Lebel, and Rémi became president. Shortly thereafter, LVMH appointed a corporate CEO to oversee Krug's operation for the parent company.

The first non-Krug (and non-French) manager of the house was a Brit named Mark Cornell, who came onboard in 2003 after Hine Cognac, of which he had been CEO, was sold to a UK-based conglomerate. When Cornell left Krug in 2006 to become CEO of Moët-Hennessy USA, he was replaced by thirty-eight-year-old Panos Sarantopoulos, who held the post for two years.

After this series of chief executives and in the midst of a tough economic crisis, the house found itself in a more challenging situation than ever: sales were down, morale was low, and prospects for the future did not look especially promising.

Yet another new CEO was announced in January 2009.

But this chief executive was different.

Margareth (or Maggie, as she prefers to be called) Henríquez was born in Venezuela and says she was meek and reserved as a child, though that might seem hard to believe today.

After receiving a degree in systems engineering, she entered the workforce, and her first serious position came in 1989 as executive vice president at a Venezuelan spirits company called Licorerias Unidas, where she set about turning the struggling company around. Three years later, when Licorerias Unidas merged with three other major liquor companies as Seagram's of Venezuela, Henríquez was made CEO, and she restructured the distribution network, launched several new products, and led what was one of South America's largest spirits companies through a difficult period of recession, inflation, and regulation.

As president and CEO of Nabisco, Mexico, she helped turn the company from break-even to profitable, before returning to wine and spirits in 2001 to take the president and CEO title at Bodegas Chandon in Argentina, a subsidiary of Moët & Chandon and LVMH. Under her guidance, despite an economic collapse and devaluation of the currency, the company launched a number of successful new products and worked out a favorable tax deal with the embattled Argentine government.

Throughout her career, Henríquez had proven herself to be a visionary leader with a knack for reorganizing beleaguered businesses and recreating "lost" corporate identities to make the companies both functional and profitable. But she had never encountered anything quite like Krug.

"When M. Navarre first offered me the position I didn't want to take it," Maggie admitted.[6] "I mean, I loved Grande Cuvée and the other Krug Champagnes—I knew them because we distributed them in South America—but the company seemed way too arrogant for me! But I was ready for a new challenge and this was too good an opportunity to pass up; plus my fiancé was in Paris."[7]

"When I got here in 2009," she continued, "Krug had been badly hit by the economic crisis. Everyone seemed disillusioned and, well, lost, like a tram that had run off its rails and lost its power. I used the same approach that I had used in all the other successful turnarounds I had orchestrated previously, but after a year the results were not good. Even M. Navarre was disappointed with my performance."

She paused for a moment, a slight hint of distress on her face revealing a woman who does not like not to disappoint; then it passed and she continued.

"Then I realized that a luxury house with an unknown story must be developed in a totally different way. But before I could begin to figure out exactly what that way was, I had to learn about the house from the inside out. I told Eric I wanted to sit in on everything he did. And I asked Fabienne for all of the background information she could give me on Krug.[8] Then, gradually, things started to come into focus.

"Spending time with Eric, I began to appreciate the meticulousness of the grape sourcing and the importance of the relationships with the suppliers, how all the wines are kept separate, and the laborious process of determining the blend for the Grande Cuvée each year; I discovered the absolute necessity of the long maturation period and the reason for using the wooden barrels. At the same time, I started learning about Joseph Krug and the radical principles on which the very creation of this house was based: most importantly, I learned about his 'lost' notebook. And then I got it! That was what was missing: this unbroken link to the past. We were doing all these elaborate things to create this marvelously unique yet quintessential Champagne, but no one really knew *why*."

"I was a bit skeptical at first," said Eric. "But Maggie put herself in the middle of everything and asked many questions. Most of all I was encouraged by her curiosity and enthusiasm. 'Finally,' I said to myself, 'we have someone at the top who really cares about wine.'"

"Maggie was a drastic move," Olivier told me, "like a big breath of fresh air. The only problem was it seemed like she never slept; she often e-mailed me in the middle of the night, like when she found out about the notebook! Yes, I knew my great-great-grandfather had left a notebook, but it was tucked away somewhere and I had forgotten all about it. Sometimes it takes someone from outside to understand the true value of what you have and how to articulate it."

Besides putting the figurehead of Joseph Krug front and center (along with his "rediscovered" notebook, whose maroon color became the official color of the house), Henríquez instituted some other radical changes.

"Okay, so we have this great story, this unbroken legacy of quality and passion for excellence passed down through the generations. But what good does it do if no one knows about it? Everything was such a big secret, as if we had something to hide instead of something wonderful to celebrate and share. People were almost made to feel unworthy, as if our wine was too precious to be enjoyed. All of that had to change."

And much of it did.

Veils were lifted and doors were thrown open.[9] Journalists and writers and sommeliers were invited to visit the winery and cellars and vineyards, as well as participate in blending exercises like the one I attended in 2012, in order to better understand what goes on chez Krug and how the Grande Cuvée is created. At the end of the blending workshop, the composition of that year's Grande Cuvée and the provenance of the principal wines used is freely revealed.

But this still left a big gap of information for consumers regarding the individual bottle. Because there is no set recipe for the Grande Cuvée, the proportions of the different grape varieties and reserve wines changes each year, so how then can you know what the one you have is made of or how it might be different from another? On a certain level, Rémi was right: people should simply enjoy the wine without worrying about the details. But often, especially when something is really enjoyable, people want to know more about it, especially now, when people are used to an abundance of readily accessible information. And when it comes to serious collectors who like to store Champagne in their cellars for many years in order to enjoy it at its peak, knowing what year the wine was composed, what the oldest reserve wine in the blend is, and when the bottle was disgorged, becomes essential.

How to retain the mysterious allure, the "different-yet-same" paradox, and the multivintage timelessness of the Grande Cuvée, allowing people to simply savor it without the intrusion of vintage or composition data, and yet make the information available to those that desire it?

Maggie had an idea.

Beginning in 2011, each bottle of Krug Champagne carries an inconspicuous bottle-specific six-digit number on the back label called the Krug ID. The first number indicates the quarter in which the bottle was disgorged, the second two the year, and the last three the lot. By entering the full ID number into the Krug website, one can find detailed information on the wine, such as the year of the oldest reserve wine in the blend (as well as the year of the youngest, or base vintage) and the percentages of each of the three grape varieties used to make the assemblage. The page also offers tasting notes from Eric (as well as a space for consumers to post their own comments on the wine, which could be particularly interesting as time passes and the wines evolve), food-pairing suggestions, and even a suggested musical pairing.

"Times have changed," Maggie said. "People want information, so why not let them have it?"

Needless to say, the idea was very controversial. "I was not in favor of the ID initially," said Eric. "I thought it would trivialize our work. But now I think it is great. Far from undermining what we do, it showcases it." Olivier too is a convert: "At first I said, 'Oh no, we cannot do that! That information is nobody's business but our own.' I had been indoctrinated into this whole air of proprietary secrecy." Now Olivier—who is seldom without his iPad in hand—is one of the ID's biggest fans, punching in the bottle numbers at dinners and tastings to provide details of the specific wines to the guests.

Far from merely climbing the luxury corporate ladder, it would appear that CEO Henríquez has fallen in love with the house and is fiercely defensive of its well-being. While Krug is no longer a family company, her management has validated and empowered Eric in his leading role as chef de cave, taking him out of the cellar and into the limelight, and has also given Olivier back his legacy, while providing a link with the past and a family figurehead for the company, even if it is no longer his.

Many things have certainly changed, but one thing hasn't: an uncompromising commitment to quality. And being a prized part of a hugely profitable corporate entity has some advantages: Eric doesn't have to pinch pennies when searching for the best grapes and negotiating with suppliers, the winery doesn't have to make economic compromises to keep its head above water, and no one from LVMH is crying for higher production or lower costs. Rather than being a threat to the integrity of Krug, Henríquez has turned out to be something of a protective mother hen, supporting and justifying critical decisions that may sometimes result in lower revenue, such as not releasing a 2012 vintage in order to replenish waning reserve stocks, declassifying the 1999 Clos du Mesnil (after years of aging in the cellar) because it did not seem quite exceptional enough, and increasing the time between disgorgement and release from six months to one year.

"The house of Krug will never be compromised!" she frequently proclaims, and one believes that it will not, at least as long as she is watching over it.

This does not, however, prevent some people from decrying the loss of the beloved family winery to a big luxury conglomerate and claiming that the wine has suffered for it. Some lament, "Krug is not what it once was." And that may well be true, but then nothing is. Change is inevitable, especially for a producer of wine, who must deal with changing seasons, climate, tastes, markets, and technology. Not everyone will always like all of the changes that result. But in the case of Krug, it seems clear that the motives behind any changes that have occurred (and which may occur in the future) do not stem from an abandonment of the principles on which the house was founded or a compromise of the commitment to quality.

Wine writer Michael Edwards sums it up quite nicely: "Those armchair critics who claim that Krug Grande Cuvée is not what it was have only a tiny grain of truth on their side. Great wine is not a monolith of fixed composition and character. It changes and evolves, like all great things created by perfectionists. Krug today may lay more stress on freshness and finesse than when I first tasted it forty years ago. But surely, with Champagne that should not be seen as a fault but as a dynamic virtue, mirroring the changing taste preferences of the discerning modern consumer."[10]

EPILOGUE

THE FUTURE OF CHAMPAGNE

WHILE the 2013-based Grande Cuvée continues its slow undisturbed maturation in the individual glass cocoons stacked within the larger cocoon of the dark, cool cellar deep beneath Rue Coquebert, activity at street level swirls frenetically all around it. Both life and Grande Cuvée move unremittingly forward, dragging their past along behind them, though at markedly different paces. And, while we have a fairly good idea what to expect of the Grande Cuvée when it finally emerges—as it surely will, different from yet stylistically similar to its predecessors—we have no idea what to expect of the world it will emerge into.

Champagne, despite its staid provincial ambience, has always been an area of constant (and often tumultuous) change, just as Champagne has always been a high-profile wine in a constant state of evolution. And that has never been truer than it is at this very moment.

Some changes come from outside: While global warming affects the entire planet, it could have an especially challenging impact on Champagne, a wine that was born in part in response to the predominantly cool temperatures of its region. Now, instead of dealing with problems related to underripeness, growers and producers must find ways to avert overripeness and respond rapidly when the grapes reach their optimum maturity, which tends to happen earlier than it did a generation or two ago.[1]

Just when the long battle to link the name of Champagne to the specific area it comes from has been largely won, other bubbly upstarts have appeared on the scene to chip away at its dominance. While some traditionally strong markets for Champagne have declined a bit, others have reemerged (like Russia, after a long hiatus under Communism) and yet other new ones have appeared (like China). And just as the change in preference from sweet to dry had a major impact on production, so new interests in organic and biodynamic approaches to viticulture, "lost" grape varieties, and small grower-producers are also having a significant effect on the region.

Because Champagne has always been an international product—remember the huge impact the English had on its early development—there has always been close synergy with outside influences, and that is likely to continue. But there are also big changes coming from within Champagne that are bound to have a major impact on its future.

One of them has to do with the very thing that prevents the wine from prematurely spilling out of the bottle. The development of the characteristic mushroom-like cork (along with the wire cage for holding it in place) represented a major advancement in both the quality and the marketability of Champagne. It was vastly superior to the rags and wood that preceded it. But cork is not perfect.

Being a natural organic substance, the bark of the *Quercus suber* (cork oak) sometimes contains a chemical compound called 2,4,6-*trichloroanisole* (TCA), which can also be found in wood, water, fruit, and vegetables. Harvested cork bark or cork stoppers may also be infected with TCA through chlorinated substances in agricultural products or chlorine bleach. While it poses no health threat, TCA in the finished cork can give wine an unpleasant aroma—sometimes very pronounced, sometimes quite subtle—of moldy rags, wet dogs, or damp basements. Sometimes the corky smell is not readily discernible, but TCA destroys the wine's flavor and aroma, which might be even worse because it is much more difficult to attribute it to a bad cork.

Though the percentage of infected corks appears to have dropped due to greater knowledge and better detection methods, no way has yet been found to completely avoid TCA contamination of cork stoppers or remove it from tainted cork. This is a big problem for wine in general, but it is especially big for Champagne.

First there is the issue of carbon dioxide: because of the high pressure inside the bottle, the closure must be tight and secure, and cork alternatives made of glass or metal could pose dangerous risks. Then there is the aspect of aging: many Champagnes are capable of evolving in the bottle for a long time after they are released, so the closure must be one that can permit some slow transference between the wine inside the bottle and the air outside, allowing it to breathe during its extended life span. Finally, and perhaps most importantly, over centuries the act of peeling off the colorful foil, untwisting the metal *muselet* (perhaps saving the metal cap as a souvenir), and popping the mushroom cork—or, better yet, easing it off to make an appealing sigh—has become a ritual of celebration that is practically inseparable from the pleasure of drinking the wine itself.

Rituals of celebration are not easily tinkered with. But, because nothing puts more of a damper on celebratory buildup than a spoiled wine, producers of Champagne will continue to struggle to find a satisfactory way to surmount this problem, and one day in the near future they might well find it, just as they have overcome major technical challenges in the past.

Another issue that is being discussed in Champagne is quality. *Sur lattes* refers to the bottles of wine stacked up horizontally on wooden strips during *prise de mousse* and maturation. But buying Champagne *sur latte* refers to a Champagne bottler's practice of purchasing finished wine that someone else made to label and sell as his own. This is perfectly legal (as long as it meets the minimum legal requirements) and not uncommon. In fact, it has been done since the very early days of Champagne, when the relatively few merchants lacked either the expertise or the resources to produce enough Champagne to satisfy the growing demand.

In today's more discriminating marketplace, however, there is the assumption—reasonable or not—that the wine in the bottle was produced by the company whose name is on the label. But the more important issue is that much of the Champagne sold *sur latte* today is of a mediocre quality.

In the 1990s, as other, less-expensive types of sparkling wine began gathering steam (and at a time when many consumers still thought *Champagne* was just a generic name for bubbly wine), some merchants began marketing low-priced Champagne made in large part from inexpensive wine someone else made that was purchased *sur latte*.

Unlike counterfeits of the past, this is genuine Champagne that meets all the legal requirements to use the name—but just barely. The regulations of the appellation were created to ensure a minimal level of quality and transparency, which the overwhelming majority of producers choose to go beyond—sometimes well beyond—in order to make a product of superior quality. But it is also possible for less-scrupulous merchants to do the very minimum necessary by law, flooding the market with mediocre, relatively cheap Champagne. And many conscientious producers, some of whom have demonstrated a commitment to exceptionally high standards of quality for generations, are concerned about it, not so much out of fear of any economic undercutting of their business as of the damage they think it could do to the reputation of Champagne.

In 1992, Christian Bizot, head of Bollinger and nephew of legendary Lily Bollinger, spoke out about the "credibility gap" in Champagne and produced a "Charter of Ethics and Quality," thereby making a public written commitment to high standards of quality and raising the bar for others to do the same. Several did, including Krug.

In 2013 the Union des Maisons de Champagne (UMC) published a list of ten practices that all member houses should abide by, though it included nothing about Champagne *sur latte*. In fact, the real issue here is not so much *sur latte* per se as quality in general, and the fear that allowing it to slip in today's global market could seriously damage the image and value Champagne worked so hard to create.

At the beginning of 2014, a new initiative called Projet 2030 was unveiled, which seeks to guide the future of Champagne for the next fifteen years and beyond. Echoing the creation of the Comité Champagne a half century earlier, the project unites the commercial maisons of the UMC and the vine growers of the Syndicat Général des Vignerons de la Champagne (SGV) in an attempt to close some of the quality gaps in the Champagne AOC regulations, as well as promote a wider adherence to higher levels of environmental sustainability, and thus maintain Champagne's reputation as the most prestigious sparkling wine appellation in the world.

But the biggest change Champagne will be undergoing in the near future is the revision of the AOC map.

As we have seen, the wine-growing area of Champagne, produced by a complex series of geologic and climatic events over millions of years, was defined and articulated by a long succession of vine growers and winemakers, from the ancient Romans through the monks and vignerons to the textile merchants turned sparkling wine manufacturers and other ambitious entrepreneurs. When the first official map of the *Champagne viticole* was drawn up in 1927, it was a good— as well as absolutely necessary—first step to protect Champagne from outside counterfeits and quell internal strife. But it was far from perfect.

The first pass for inclusion in the growing region was done at village level, so much depended on the motivation of the individual mayors: if the mayor owned vineyards (or had influential constituents that did), he would fight harder for the town's vineyards to be included in the zone; if the mayor was less interested and could not be motivated by any of the townspeople, good vineyard areas could be easily omitted, and many were—especially if they happened to be in what was considered to be a less prestigious area, like the Aube. It must be remembered that at the time the current map was created, the price of wine grapes in Champagne was much lower than it is today, and therefore so were land values.

Because the price of the grapes was, in fact, a major point of contention, some system of price regulation was also necessary, and given the tremendous diversity of growing areas in the Champagne region, it is understandable that one fixed price would not have made sense. The Échelle des Crus was about as good a system as one could hope for, especially under the duress of the moment. But it too was not without its flaws. Though many grumbled about the system from its inception (except, of course, for those in grand cru villages), it was implemented and served its purpose for a long time. Then it started to lose relevance.

In recent years the grumblings increased, on both sides of the fence. Then, at a general meeting of the SGV on April 9, 2003, the issue of revising the map of Champagne was raised and put to a vote. After it passed by an overwhelming majority, 393 to 25, a formal request was made to the governing body of the INAO, and it too was accepted. (As mentioned earlier, the Échelle des Crus was officially discontinued in 2010.)

"The idea here is not to *enlarge* the *Champagne viticole*," Thibaut Le Mailloux of the Comité Champagne emphasized, "but rather to reevaluate and possibly revise it. There's a big difference. The overall boundaries of the zone that were mapped out in 1927 will not be expanded. The plan is only to examine the possibility of including some perfectly good vine-growing areas within those boundaries that had been planted with vines before and were excluded."

Once the proposal to "reevaluate and possibly revise" the map of Champagne was accepted, the first step was to invite nominations of specific areas for possible inclusion in the zone. The basic criterion was that any new plots for possible inclusion had to be as good as or

better than the median level of quality within the existing appellation and had to have been previously planted with grapevines. A
group consisting of five experts in the fields of soil science, geology,
history, geography, and agronomy, plus one technical adviser from
the Comité, was formed to conduct a preliminary investigation of
the existing situation and evaluate the proposed additions. But in
order to be truly fair and accurate, besides evaluating new prospects,
they would also have to reevaluate areas currently within the zone
that might fall *below* that same median level of quality.

A detailed and exhaustive investigation of the two main subzones
of Champagne—the *Zone d'Élaboration*, in which all the activities of
winemaking and Champagne production can take place, and the
Zone de Production, a more restricted area where vines may be grown—
began in 2004. On June 26, 2007, the first preview of their findings
was presented to the INAO in a secret meeting (news of which came
out in a story by Sophie Claeys-Pergament in the newspaper *L'Union*
on October 10), and the INAO made its preliminary findings public
in March of 2008.[2]

Essentially, the panel of experts recommended the inclusion of
forty-odd "new" villages and suggested that two towns that are currently within the *Champagne viticole* be removed. After that, the proposal entered a period of public inquiry during which concerned
individuals could voice their opinions about areas that should (or
should not) be included.

Currently, the panel is engaged in the painstaking process of
closely examining each of the individual parcels to determine their
suitability for viticulture. Based on rough estimates, it is possible that
eight to twelve thousand hectares (about twenty to thirty thousand
acres) could be added to the *Zone de Production*, but no final decision
is expected before at least 2018, and it could well go beyond that.[3]

While just about everyone in Champagne feels the weight of impending change looming, no one is really in a hurry. There is a tremendous amount at stake on all fronts, both in terms of money (land

within the appellation generally goes for upwards of a million euros per hectare while land just outside the boundaries is worth considerably less) and the image of Champagne, so people are being extremely cautious (which does not, however, preclude rampant speculation) and the INAO is not saying a word until it has made its determinations.

The Champenois, though quick to adopt something new once they've been convinced of its value, cherish their long-standing traditions and don't let go of them easily. They, along with officials of the INAO, are also very aware that wine lovers throughout the world are watching closely, so they want to get it right. So, while it is clear that something major is going to take place, for the time being, the best answer to questions of exactly what will happen to the map of Champagne and when is "*on verra*" ("we'll see").

❧

WHILE all this uncertainty and anticipation and speculation swirls around up on the surface, the 2013-based Grande Cuvée continues its slow but steady progress in the cellar below, clutching the past and stretching forward into the future.

It is appropriate that this narrative come to a close much where it began: with the unique territory of Champagne, which, as it turns out, is still very much in the midst of an ongoing transition and re-definition. There are many such occurrences with Champagne, in which the end and the beginning seem to merge together, overlapping in an ongoing process of transformation in which the death of one thing gives birth to another. This is especially prone to happen with a classic Champagne like the Grande Cuvée, which incorporates many different vintages from many different areas and has a long threshold of aging, first in the Krug cellars prior to release and then in peoples' personal cellars afterwards. In such cases, the passage of time is often warped, taken out of its normal context, a contrast that is oddly highlighted by the prominent clock on the courtyard façade of the building on rue Coquebert and the activity that is taking place within it.

There is a temporal counterpoint going on here of two time frames interweaving and playing off one another. But, like two continuous voices in a Bach invention, this does not generate a conflict: the two seem to exist in some sort of strange harmony that, though suspended in the wine, is still very much alive, like the millions of tiny bubbles suspended in the liquid. Krug Grande Cuvée is a blending of individual places and times, but not a dissolving of them. In a sense, this could also be said of Champagne in general.

Champagne is always in a continuous state of becoming, with one phase leading into another, like the unfolding steps of a moving staircase. In a bottle, the past—sometimes the quite distant past—can be conjured into the present and actually brought to life, like a genie, with the pop of a cork. Through the "death" of autolysis that takes place during the process of becoming sparkling, Champagne is given not just a new lease on life but also the magical opportunity to actually defy the passage of time. The 1961 magnum of Krug I tasted in the courtyard of Clos du Mesnil in the spring of 2012 is one example. Another is the Champagne that was recovered in the summer of 2010 from the bottom of the Baltic Sea off the coast of Åland, Finland, from a sunken ship that was probably bringing cargo to the tsar of Russia when it went down. Ninety-five of the recovered bottles were produced by a defunct house named Juglar that was assimilated by Jacquesson in 1829, five years before Joseph Krug started working there. Forty-six bottles turned out to be from the house of the Widow Clicquot: when a few of them were sent to the winery for authentication, one of the investigators who got to taste the wine said it had "a toasted, zesty nose with hints of coffee, and a very agreeable taste with accents of flowers and lime-tree."[4] Not bad for a wine made more than 170 years earlier.

The Champenois carry the past behind them and look forward. "One must live in the present," Eric told me, "but always plan for the future, especially when it comes to the Grande Cuvée."

Chef de Cave Eric Lebel learned the "Krug way" from Henri, who learned it from his father, Paul II, who learned it from Joseph II (and his mother, Jeanne), who had learned from Paul I, who had worked side by side with his father, Joseph, son of a German butcher, who came to France to seek his fortune and wound up falling in love with a wine (or rather, as often happens, with his vision of it). All of them had an inherent knack for blending and an intuitive understanding of the house style, along with an unshakable commitment to quality. And each made their mark, carrying the house forward under their watch while the world of Champagne continued to revolve and evolve around them.

Eric was a pivotal character in the transition from a classic family-driven enterprise to a modern corporate one, and the first chef de cave to take on the primary responsibility of creating the blends who was not a Krug, yet the mission remains intact. Lebel has assembled a young, vibrant team and is grooming them to carry on long after he is gone. Perhaps this is yet one more reason behind the importance of the reserve cellar: Eric inherited a large library of reserve wines when he began at Krug, and when he departs he will leave a large library of reserve wines that will bring the past alive in the present and provide a bridge of continuity for a long time to come.

Time marches on, and the daily activities of life along with it. While the 2013-based Grande Cuvée sits in the cellar, the process repeats and the cycle continues, always the same yet always different. Subsequent harvests occur; new wines (always kept separate) finish fermentation in their individual barrels and are meticulously tasted; decisions are taken, assemblages are made to sparkle and laid down in vacated corners of the cellar to carry out their long gestation, while "new" wines (they are already seven to ten years old) are finished and released into the world.

In the winter of 2014 in New York, I meet Eric and Olivier, who are there promoting the just-announced release of Krug Vintage 2003. A pop-up place called the Krug House has been created in an inconspicuous brownstone in Greenwich Village, where journalists, sommeliers, and members of the importer's sales force are invited to come and taste the wine. Actually there are three: Besides the just-released 2003 vintage (which has a tightly wound, focused energy and racy mineral freshness with a touch of spice, despite the exceptionally hot year), we taste a special re-release of the more expansive, more effusive 2003-based Grande Cuvée, composed of 120 different wines and 10 different vintages, the oldest of which is 1988. These two Champagnes side by side provide a perfect demonstration of the Krug mantra that there is no hierarchy among their wines, only a difference of personality, "like a soloist compared to a full orchestra," an analogy that Henri and Rémi Krug used often and Eric does too. Then we taste a third wine, the Vintage 2000, which is completely different from the Vintage 2003: intensely lemon-creamy, with rich, toasty, nutty-caramel flavors and a hint of tobacco. The year 2000, Eric tells us, was unique for its exceedingly early August harvest, something that had not happened in Champagne since 1882. And this demonstrates another longstanding Krug axiom, that the decision of whether to produce a vintage or not is determined by whether the year itself has an interesting story to tell, which both of these clearly do. Two very different vintages, three distinctly different wines, yet all stylistically the same, all stylistically Krug.

When the 2013-based Grande Cuvée finally leaves the cellar in 2021 or 2022 and enters the world, it will receive it baptismal certificate of the Krug label, with "169ème Edition" proudly on the front, and the unique ID that will reveal (for anyone who wants to know) the story of its composition.[5] The oldest wine in the bottle will be already be about twenty years old, but the Grande Cuvée itself will be a baby, bringing the past into the present and carrying it forward into the future.

What will the world be like? Will the map of the Champagne production area have changed (again)? Will small grower-producers have overshadowed the prominence of the grande marques? Will taste preferences have changed (yet again) and, if so, to what? Will the lost grape varieties and the once-excluded area of the Aube have taken center stage?

Nobody knows what the future will actually bring, but two things seem fairly certain: Once the Grande Cuvée of 2013 does come out into the world, it will be around for a very long time, giving pleasure and marking milestones in the lives of those who consume it for many years to come. And, whatever might be going on in Champagne or in the world at large, the house built by Joseph Krug, always the same yet always different, will be quietly at the center of the tumult, doing in some way what it always has done, continuously re-creating the dream of its founder. *Amor vincit omnia.*

❧

FOR me, the journey deep into the house of Krug and into the world of Champagne was a thoroughly fascinating one. Spending time with Eric and team, trudging through the vineyards and seeing the grapes at various stages of development as the strange season unfolded, meeting all the different vignerons, harvesting the grapes, watching François work the press, seeing the must cascading into the *belon* and later bubbling into fermentation in the barrels, sitting in on tasting after tasting and then watching as the assemblage of 2013 slowly came together and was then laid down to undergo the slow process of becoming Champagne—all these experiences, along with bits of research I did on my own, were like collecting clues to a mystery or key pieces of a giant puzzle. While the collected pieces mostly fit together, many are still missing. But I know that even if all the pieces should one day be accumulated and the image complete, some things would still remain mysterious: how the essence of a place can be encapsulated in a grape; how juice can become wine and how a multitude of wines can blend together into a perfectly harmonious whole in which each of the components still plays a crucial part; the birth of a bubble out of the self-destruction of something else; and the inexplicable warping of time in a bottle.

In the end, I learned, however many pieces of the puzzle one might have, the genie can never be entirely explained or completely understood, much less willfully conjured into being. And that's okay: it is enough to thoroughly savor it when it does appear, clink glasses, and toast our good fortune for being alive to enjoy it.

Needless to say, when the Grande Cuvée of 2013 finally makes its way up out of the cellar and into the real world, I'll be there to welcome it and bid it *bon voyage* on its new adventure.

ACKNOWLEDGMENTS

Thanks to Margareth Henríquez for giving me extraordinary access to the house of Krug, to its personnel, and to all the many stages in the creation of a Krug Grande Cuvée, without which this book could not—and indeed, would not—have been written. Thanks to Chef de Cave Eric Lebel for his great generosity and patience in exposing me to his world, for taking the time to explain it to me, and for allowing me to be his *petit ombre* during 2013–2014. Thanks to the Krug enology team. Similarly, I thank all the many people I encountered in Champagne during the course of my extensive research in the field—workers, vignerons, *chefs de pressoir*, producers, forklift and tractor drivers, and many others—who, by helping me understand their role in the making of Champagne, gave me a better understanding of the wine itself. Thanks to Thibaut Le Mailloux of the Comité Champagne for helping me navigate and better understand the complex regulations and procedures of the Champagne appellation as well as the reasons behind them, and a very special thanks to Brigitte Batonnet, also of the Comité, who went way beyond the call of duty to answer and clarify numerous technical and historical questions and even read extensive portions of the text to make sure I got it all right.

In America, I am very grateful for the support of my agent, Meg Thompson of Thompson Literary Agency, who found a home for the book in a remarkably short time. It might never have become a reality, however, were it not for unwavering conviction of my editor, Colleen Lawrie. Five months after acquiring the book, she moved on from the publishing house she had acquired it for; after it was orphaned two more times, Colleen stepped up and proposed bringing it to her new house. Once we got back on track, Colleen made valuable contributions by helping shape the material into the most comprehensible and appealing form, nudging me to be both clear and concise and acting as a constant watchwoman to help me avoid slipping into the mire of wine-geekism.

I could not have asked for a better home for *Champagne, Uncorked* than PublicAffairs/Perseus. Publisher Clive Priddle was readily available, genuinely interested, and thoroughly supportive from the get-go, and, more importantly, he remained so even in the face of potential adversity when many (if not most) others would simply have backed down to the path of least resistance.

Words are one thing, but turning them into a book is another, and kudos (along with my sincere appreciation) are due to the entire production team, especially Pete Garceau, who created a distinctive, intriguing, and beautiful cover; copyeditor Erin Granville, who did an incredible job helping ensure that all the accents and commas were in the right place, that the right words were being used (and were spelled correctly), and generally safeguarding both clarity and accuracy; and Production Manager Sandra Beris, for keeping the entire process organized and on time. Thanks also to Associate Publisher and Director of Publicity Jaime Leifer and her team.

On a personal note, thanks to all the friends and colleagues who read portions of the manuscript and advised on various related issues. Most of all, thank you, Fernanda Franco, for your unwavering support and encouragement, for your help with the book's interior design, and for gracefully tolerating my not infrequent absences, whether I was away in France or Italy or simply fully immersed in front of a computer.

APPENDIX I

Here are all of the different categories of wine operations in Champagne and their definitions, compliments of the Comité Champagne (http://www.champagne .fr/en/comite-champagne/champagne growers-and houses/champagne-growers -and-houses).

The two letters representing the category of production must be listed on the label of every bottle of Champagne.

NM: Négociant manipulant A person or legal entity that buys grapes, grape must, or wine to make Champagne on their own premises and market it under their own label. All of the big Champagne Houses belong in this category.

RM: Récoltant manipulant A grower who makes and markets Champagne under their own label, from grapes exclusively sourced from their own vineyards and processed on their own premises.

RC: Récoltant-coopérateur A cooperative-grower who markets co-op produced Champagne under their own label.

CM: Coopérative de manipulation A wine co-op that markets Champagne made from members' grapes.

SR: Société de Récoltants A family firm of growers that makes and markets Champagne under its own label, using grapes sourced from family vineyards.

ND: Négociant distributeur A distributor who buys in finished bottles of Champagne for labeling on their own premises.

MA: Marque auxiliaire An "own brand" wine label produced exclusively for one client (supermarket, celebrity, or other).

APPENDIX II

According to the Comité Champagne, there are currently thirty-one registered clos in Champagne.

Here is a list of the primary clos that are currently in production:

1. Clos du Mesnil (Mesnil-sur-Oger) Krug, Reims
2. Clos d'Ambonnay (Ambonnay) Krug, Reims
3. Clos l'Abbé (Cramant) Champagne Hubert Soreau, Cramant
4. Clos de l'Aurore (Ville-Dommange) Champagne Bergeronneau-Marion, Ville-Dommange
5. Clos Cazals (Oger) Champagne Claude Cazals, Le Mesnil-sur-Oger
6. Clos des Champions (Cumières) Champagne Leclerc Briant, Épernay
7. Clos des Chaulins (Pargny-lès-Reims) Champagne Médot, Reims
8. Clos des Faubourgs de Notre Dame (Vertus) Champagne Veuve Fourny, Vertus
9. Clos des Goisses (Mareuil-sur-Aÿ) Philipponnat, Mareuil-sur-Aÿ
10. Clos Jacquesson (Dizy) Jacquesson, Dizy
11. Clos du Moulin (Chigny-les-Roses) Cattier, Chigny-les-Roses
12. Le Petit Clos (Bouzy) Champagne Jean Vesselle, Bouzy
13. Clos des Plants de Chênes (Moussy) Champagne José Michel & Fils, Moussy
14. Clos Saint-Hilaire (Mareuil-sur-Aÿ) Billecart Salmon, Mareuil-sur-Aÿ
15. Clos Sainte-Sophie (Montgueux) Champagne Lassaigne, Montgueux
16. Clos Virgile (Beaumont-sur-Vesle) Champagne Portier, Beaumont-sur-Vesle

17. Clos Saint-Jacques and
18. Clos Chaudes (Mareuil-sur-Aÿ) Bollinger, Aÿ (The two clos, which
    are planted with ungrafted vines planted in the old system called
    en folle as opposed to trellised rows, are combined to produce the
    Champagne Vieilles Vignes Françaises.)

APPENDIX III:
EXCERPTS FROM
JOSEPH KRUG'S NOTEBOOK

Here are additional excerpts regarding the composition of cuvées from the notebook of Joseph Krug, as quoted in John Arlott, *Krug, House of Champagne*, and Henri and Rémi Krug, *L'Art du Champagne*.

CUVÉE N. 1—LIGHT-BODIED BLEND:

-1/3 Cramant, Avize, Le Mesnil, etc.

-1/6 Vertus and Pierry

-1/3 Ay, Dizy, and Bouzy

-1/6 Montagne de Reims

This composition may be modified according to the year. If the wines are full-bodied, one must use more light wines such as those of Cramant, Avize, or Le Mesnil, and do the opposite if the if the wines are too light like, for instance, those of 1848.

CUVÉE N. 2—FULL-BODIED BLEND:

-1/5 Cramant

-1/5 Vertus and Pierry

-2/5 Ay and Bouzy

-1/5 Montagne de Reims

Changes may be made according to the year, as for Cuvée N. 1, and according to the circumstances. The two types of wine require two different sorts of liqueur [that is, liqueur d'expédition also kown as dosage]; one without any addition of alcohol or spirit composed of:

-1/6 Vertus, Pierry

-1/3 Cramant, Avize

-1/3 Ay, Dizy or Champillon

-1/6 Verzenay

This will be used to liquor the wines of Europe, the Black Sea and the Rhine countries. The other liquor should be made with the same kinds of wine but select more full-bodied grape varieties, and add a small dose of fine spirit of cognac at least two years old but not too old.

The second liquor would be composed roughly as follows:

-1/6 Vertus, Pierry, etc.

-1/6 Cremant, Avize

-1/3 Ay, Dizy

-1/3 Montagne de Reims

-The above-mentioned spirit

The dosage should be 18 liters or 18 bottles per cask of liquor, to sweeten the wine for England and Belgium.

So far as wine exported to America is concerned, one could blend the two liquors together using 1/3 of one and 2/3 of the other, depending on circumstances.

For the Rhine countries one would take some of the full-bodied blend with the light liquor or the light-bodied blend with the full-bodied liquor. This would meet the demand there for slightly more full-bodied wine than in Saxony and the north of Germany, as well as Poland, Russia and Sweden.

In Hamburg, the demand is for a moderately full-bodied wine, for example a light blend with a full-bodied liquor.

It is always a wise precaution to send samples in advance with various doses to ascertain the taste of customers in each country.

NOTES

PROLOGUE

1. The name *Grande Cuvée* is the proprietary name of a Champagne produced solely and exclusively by the house of Krug and is often referred to as Krug Grande Cuvée.

CHAPTER ONE: WHAT LIES BENEATH

1. Mostly, but not entirely. See sections on the creation of the Champagne AOC region on pages 10–11 and plans to revise the map on page 221–224.

2. The French term *terroir* ("territory") was originally applied to typical regional costumes and dishes that displayed *goût de terroir*, the taste of a particular place. Gradually, the term began to be applied to wines and was adapted by the wine-drinking community at large to refer to the many natural factors—including altitude, exposition, steepness, soil, wind patterns, geographic surroundings, etc.—that together add up to a unique wine-growing environment.

3. James E. Wilson, *Terroir: The Role of Geology, Climate, and Culture in the Making of French Wines* (Berkeley: University of California Press, 1999), 65.

4. While this has historically been the case, viticultural boundaries are changing in response to a warming climate.

5. There are an average of 1,650 hours of sunshine per year in Champagne, compared with 2,069 in Bordeaux and 1,910 in Burgundy.

6. The Marne has the largest surface area of *la Champagne viticole* at 66 percent; the Aube has about 23 percent, and the Aisne 10 percent. The Haute-Marne, with only two communes in the zone, and the Seine-et-Marne, with three towns, make up the rest.

7. See more about the Champagne AOC on page 145.

8. An exception is the little town of Montgueux in the north of the Aube, whose soil consists mostly of chalk.

9. Long known as *pinot meunier*, the variety is now referred to simply as *meunier* in the Champagne area. Meunier, whose name means "miller" in French, is a mutation of the pinot genotype and gets its name from the flourlike white dust on the undersides of the leaves.

10. But they're staging a comeback. See more about the lost varieties of Champagne on pages 201–202.

11. While each of the three primary grape varieties is thought to do best in a particular subzone, all three varieties are grown throughout the subzones of the Marne and the rest of the Champagne area.

12. Initially, wine in Champagne (as in many other wine-producing areas) was intended for immediate consumption and was often quite volatile, frequently spoiling before the next vintage was produced. In years with an abundant harvest of good-quality grapes, a large quantity of good-quality wine was produced, which often exceeded demand and was able to last longer than usual. Such "leftover" wine was typically mixed in with the wine of the following vintage. Only later, during the first half of the nineteenth century, when farming and winemaking methods had advanced and when strong glass bottles and close-fitting corks had been developed to hold it in a way that better preserved it, did wine begin to be *intentionally* held back in reserve for future use in blends, offering a greater level of quality and consistency of style. We will touch upon this topic again later on.

CHAPTER TWO: INTO THE VINEYARDS

1. The verb *gagner* can also be translated as "earn," "gain," or "acquire."

2. It's hard to talk about "normal" when speaking of the weather, but for the past thirty years harvest has usually taken place much earlier than it did in the "olden" days.

3. Oidium, also known as powdery mildew, is a fungal disease (*Uncinula necator*) that often affects grapevines.

4. While wild grapevines were present in Champagne before the ancient Romans arrived, the Romans brought some of their own domesticated grape varieties as well as more sophisticated methods of cultivation and vinification. Besides being a central part of Roman culture and mythology, viticulture was also one of their most successful colonizing tools.

5. *The Rules of Saint Benedict*, which formed the basis for many of the monastic movements that originated in the Middle Ages, outlines the role of the monastic wine cellarer in Chapter 31:

> As cellarer of the monastery let there be chosen from the community one who
> is wise, of mature character, sober, not a great eater, not haughty, not excit-

able, not offensive, not slow, not wasteful, but a God-fearing man who may be like a father to the whole community.

Let him have charge of everything. He shall do nothing without the Abbot's orders, but keep to his instructions. Let him not vex the brethren. If any brother happens to make some unreasonable demand of him, instead of vexing the brother with a contemptuous refusal he should humbly give the reason for denying the improper request.

Let him keep guard over his own soul, mindful always of the Apostle's saying that "he who has ministered well acquires for himself a good standing."

Let him take the greatest care of the sick, of children, of guests and of the poor, knowing without doubt that he will have to render an account for all these on the Day of Judgment.

Let him regard all the utensils of the monastery and its whole property as if they were the sacred vessels of the altar. Let him not think that he may neglect anything. He should be neither a miser nor a prodigal and squanderer of the monastery's substance, but should do all things with measure and in accordance with the Abbot's instructions. (Benedict of Nursia, *St. Benedict's Rule for Monasteries*, trans. Leonard J. Doyle [Collegeville, MN: The Liturgical Press, 2001], e-book.]

6. In 1718, Canon Godinot published a book on winemaking that appeared to be based on the practices of Dom Pérignon, and in 1724 Frère Pierre, who had worked as Pérignon's assistant and succeeded him after his death, recorded his master's viticultural principles in *Traité de la Culture des Vignes de Champagne*.

7. Factors such as excessively high yields of grapes with low natural sugar, poor sanitary conditions in the winery, and inadequate storage containers and closures made wine highly susceptible to spoilage.

8. The first Dom Pérignon (Champagne) was made from the 1921 vintage but released in 1936. See the section on prestige cuvées on page 153.

9. The earliest documented sparkling wine in France to be intentionally made bubbly was produced at the Benedictine Abbey of Saint-Hilaire, near the Languedoc town of Limoux, around 1531. The wine, now known as Blanquette de Limoux, is made by a process called *méthode ancestrale*, which involves adding sugar to corked flasks of wine that induces a second fermentation and makes it sparkle. The sediment, however, is not removed.

10. Jean Oudart (1654–1742) was actually a lay brother; that is, a monk who did not take priestly orders. Châlons-sur-Marne was renamed Châlons-en-Champagne in 1998.

11. While there is no solid proof, Oudart is generally credited with reinstating the use of a cork as bottle stopper in the Champagne area and initiating the use of *liqueur de tirage*, and he was also among the earliest to develop more-organized systems of export.

12. The Taittinger family set up shop as a Champagne producer in 1932 when it purchased the estate of Forester-Fourneaux, based at Château de la

Marquetterie in Pierry, along with the neighboring vineyards developed by Frère Jean Oudart.

13. In the eighteenth century, doctors from medical schools in Reims and Beaune sparred with one another in medical treatises claiming that their wine was better for health than the other. While less antagonistic, the discussion of the health merits of the two wines continues to this day.

14. Though a prolific writer, Saint-Évremond did not intend his work to be published during his lifetime but rather simply shared among friends. One of the most interesting pieces that survives is the following, titled "Portrait of Saint-Évremond, made by Himself," which was written in 1696 to follow an epitaph Saint-Évremond composed for his friend, the celebrated Comte de Grammont, who was then gravely ill.

> He is a philosopher, equally distant from superstition and impiety; a hedonist who has no less aversion to debauchery as he has inclination for pleasure; a man who has never known poverty nor given in to overabundance; he lives in a condition that is despised by those who have everything, envied by those who have nothing, and appreciated by those who find their well-being through their reason. As a young man, he hated dissipation, convinced that is was necessary to acquire wealth in order to enjoy the amenities of a long life. As an old man, he finds it difficult to economize, believing that there is little to fear of being without when one has little time to be miserable. He praises his good nature; he does not complain about his fortune; he detests crime; he tolerates short-comings and laments the unfortunate; he does not look for what is bad about men in order to denounce it, but finds what is laughable in order to take plea-sure in it; he makes himself a secret pleasure to know, but would have made a much greater disclosure of himself to others if discretion had not prevented it.
>
> Life is too short, in his opinion, to read all sorts of books and fill his memory with an infinity of things at the expense of his judgment; he does not attach weight to writings of the most knowledgeable to acquire knowledge, but to the most sensible to fortify his reason; sometimes he looks for the most delicate to give delicacy to his taste, sometimes for the most agreeable to give credit to his genius. It rests for me to portray to you that which concerns friendship and religion: In friendship he is more constant than a philosopher, and more sin-cere than a good-natured young man without experience. And as to religion,
>
>> Of justice and charity,
>> Much more than penitence,
>> He composes his piety.
>> Putting his trust in God,
>> Hoping by all his goodness,
>> In the bosom of Providence
>> He finds his repose and happiness.

[Charles de Marguetel de Saint-Denis Saint-Évremond, "Portrait de Saint-Évremond Fait Par Lui-Même," in *Oeuvres Mêlées de Mr. De Saint-Évremond, Tome Second* (Paris: J. L. Techener Fils, 1865). Translated from the French by Alan Tardi.]

15. Quoted in Patrick Forbes, *Champagne: The Wine, the Land and the People* (London, UK: Victor Gollancz, 1967), 95.

16. The Ordre des Coteaux fizzled out just before the French Revolution but was revived in 1956 by a handful of Champenois, including François Taittinger, and remains active to this day. Under the auspices of the Société Ernest Irroy, Taittinger produces a Champagne in honor of the cofounder of the original Coteaux called "Saint-Évremond," though the wine its namesake drank was most likely still.

17. Ortensia Mancini (born in Rome on June 6, 1646), favorite niece of the Cardinal Mazarin (Saint-Évremond's powerful former boss), is a quite remarkable character. She was married off at fifteen to one of Europe's wealthiest men, Armand-Charles de La Porte, Duc de La Meilleraye, who unfortunately also turned out to be one of its most jealous. His bizarre behavior apparently included knocking out the teeth of his female servants in order to make them unappealing, having exposed body parts in his family's extensive art collection painted over, and sending his adolescent wife and her sixteen-year-old girlfriend, Marie-Sidonie de Lenoncourt (the two young women were probably lovers), to a convent, from which they escaped through a chimney. Ortensia returned to her husband and had four children in rapid succession before fleeing in 1668. Under the protection of a former suitor, Charles-Emmanuel II, Duc de Savoie, she made her way to France, where Louis XIV also offered her his protection. In 1675, after the demise of the duke, Ortensia traveled to London disguised as man and settled in, going on to have a long series of of high-profile love affairs with both rich and powerful men and beautiful women. A steamy relationship between Ortensia and Anne, Countess of Sussex, culminated one evening in St. James's Park with a sword fight between the two women, who were both clad in nightgowns. One can only imagine what her salon was like! Saint-Évremond and Ortensia Mancini became close friends soon after her arrival in England and remained practically inseparable until her death in 1699.

18. Charles de Marguetel de Saint-Denis Saint-Évremond, "A Letter to Count d'Olonne," in *The Works of Monsieur St Évremond, Made English from the French Original*, vol. II, trans. Pierre des Maizeaux (London, 1714), 5.

CHAPTER THREE:
GROWERS, SUPPLIERS, PRESSES

1. Verzy is a grand cru commune for both chardonnay and pinot noir. See page 34 and note 13 on the next page for a description of the Échelle des Crus.

2. I moved to the Barolo wine area of Piedmont, Italy, in 2003, about two years after closing my restaurant in New York. There I immersed myself in the surrounding vineyards and wineries, which provided me with a firsthand, in-depth experience of the process of growing grapes and making wine as it is done in that area. This, naturally, formed the basis of my comparison with other wine areas I visited thereafter, and Champagne presented a sharp contrast with Barolo. Compared to the sedate, well-ordered vineyards of Champagne, the hills of Barolo seem like a crazy hodgepodge of vines, with different degrees of steep-ness and expositions going every which way. Unlike the grapes of Champagne, the principal grapes of Barolo (dolcetto, barbera, and nebbiolo) are predomi-nantly red and the wines are predominantly monovarietal, meaning that most of them consist of a single grape variety rather than a blend of several. Because the color of a red wine comes from the grape skins, all red wines must undergo mac-eration—the practice of leaving the grape juice in contact with the skins for a period of time in order to extract the pigment—as part of the vinification pro-cess. And, since most wines of Barolo are intended to age for an extended period of time, the skins and seeds also contribute tannin, which has an important impact on the structure and longevity of the wines. For these reasons, when people in Barolo evaluate ripeness of grapes in the field, they also take into ac-count the skin and the seeds. This, I would quickly learn, was only the tip of the iceberg that differentiates these two extraordinary wine-growing areas.

3. For a list of the different kinds of wine operations in Champagne, see Appendix I.

4. Phenols are the numerous chemical compounds located in different parts of the grape (skin, pulp, and seeds) that contribute unique flavor and aroma components to the wine made from them.

5. See the discussion of rosé saignée on page 255, note 14, and rosé des Riceys and Coteaux Champenois on page 245, note 17.

6. As I later discovered, there is a good reason for the rather odd-seeming figure of 2,050 liters.

7. The word comes from the French *tailler*, to cut. A division of *premier* and *deuxieme taille* used to be used to differentiate the first and second half of the *taille*, but the practice was officially discontinued in 1994. Note: The word *taille* is also used to indicate the various pruning systems employed in Champagne.

8. The term comes from the French word *rebêcher* ("to re-dig") and refers to the final re-pressing to extract the last remaining juice from the grapes.

9. While the *Zone de Production*, where grapevines for Champagne can grow, consists of 320 villages (at the present time), the *Zone d'Elaboration*, where the grapes can be turned into wine, consists of 635 villages.

10. Read more about phylloxera on pages 128–131.

11. *Métayage* refers to a once widespread system of sharecropping whereby people worked land owned by someone else in return for keeping a portion (usually 50 percent) of the harvest.

12. A *pièce champenoise* is the traditional wooden barrel of Champagne and holds 205 liters.

13. The Échelle des Crus ("ladder of growths or villages") was originally established in 1911 as a pricing structure in which each village in the Champagne AOC appellation was given a numerical rating between 80 and 100. Originally, this number referred to price: grand cru villages are rated at 100 and therefore receive 100 percent of the benchmark price for their grapes, must, or wine; premier cru villages are rated between 90 and 99, and everything else between 80 and 89.

There were originally twelve grand cru villages: Ambonnay, Avize, Aÿ, Beaumont-sur-Vesle, Bouzy, Cramant, Louvois, Mailly-Champagne, Puisieulx, Sillery, Tours-sur-Marne, and Verzenay. In 1985 five more were added: Chouilly, Le Mesnil-sur-Oger, Oger, Oiry, and Verzy.

While the Échelle des Crus system was officially abolished in 2010, the terms *grand cru* and *premier cru* are still used.

14. When the system was first established, it functioned as a price index to ensure fair and consistent pricing based on quality of origin. Today, while the no-longer-official Échelle is still a reference point, growers and producers are free to negotiate their own price.

15. Also known as *tête de cuvées*, prestige cuvées are the very best, most exceptional, and usually most expensive Champagnes that a given house produces.

16. The Comité Champagne sets a legal maximum each year on the amount of grapes that can be harvested.

17. Up until the 1960s Krug owned no vineyards at all; the sites we are now visiting, which amount to about fifteen hectares, were acquired in the mid-1970s. Today Krug owns about twenty hectares of vineyards in grand cru villages, which account for about 24 percent of its annual needs.

18. *Lutte raisonnée*, "reasoned struggle," refers to a viticultural approach somewhere between conventional and organic or biodynamic that, while not officially certified or defined, seeks to be environmentally friendly, avoiding the use of chemicals except in extreme circumstances.

19. Sulfites, also spelled *sulphites*, are chemical compounds that naturally occur in wine grapes to some extent and are used in various stages of the winemaking process—such as during the pressing—to prevent oxidation. Their use in winemaking is thought to date back to the ancient Romans. It is important, however, to use high-quality sulfites in the proper amount—enough to prevent oxidation but not enough to leave a residual flavor or smell on the wine.

20. Growers have three weeks from the official start date to pick the grapes. And there's another time limitation: each year there is an official closing date of the presses, three weeks after the last harvest commencement date, after which no more grapes can be pressed (thus no more wine made). In 2013 the closing date was October 27.

21. In 1663, Samuel Butler used the term *brisk* in reference to bubbly Champagne in his poem "Hudibras":

> I'll carve your name on barks of trees,
> With true love knots and flourishes;
> That shall infuse eternal spring,
> And everlasting flourishing:
> Drink every letter on't in stum,
> And make it brisk champaign become. (Canto I, part II, lines 565–570)

And George Farquhar, a hot young writer of Irish descent, included a scene in his 1698 play *Love and a Bottle* in which one character hands a glass of wine to another, exclaiming, "How it puns and quibbles in the glass!"

Another early English mention of "sparkling Champagne" is in the drinking song in George Etherege's 1676 comedy *The Man of Mode, or Sir Fopling Flutter*:

> The pleasures of love and the joys of good wine
> To perfect our happiness wisely we join.
> We to beauty all day
> Give the sovereign sway,
> And her favourite nymphs devoutly obey.
> At the plays we are constantly making our court,
> And when they are ended we follow the sport,
> To the Mall and the Park,
> Where we love till 'tis dark;
> Then sparkling champagne
> Puts an end to their reign;
> It quickly recovers
> Poor languishing lovers,
> Makes us frolic and gay, and drowns all our sorrow;
> But, alas! we relapse again on the morrow.
> Let ev'ry man stand
> With his glass in his hand,
> And briskly discharge at the word of command.
> Here's a health
> to all those
> Whom to-night we depose:
> Wine and beauty by turns great souls should inspire.
> Present altogether, and now, boys, give fire! (Act IV, Scene 1)

22. While it does appear that the English were the first to show an appreciation for the "brisk" wine from Champagne and that merchants began adding a bit of sugar to encourage the bubbles (at a time when French wine makers were trying

hard to keep them out), one cannot infer from this that the British invented Champagne. The Champenois deserve full credit for creating Champagne and developing the method of producing it, once all the pieces fell together.

23. The presence of corks in bottles was obviously quite familiar to English theatergoers, as suggested in *As You Like It* (first produced in 1698) when Celia says to Rosalind: "I would thou couldst stammer, that thou mightst pour this concealed man out of thy mouth, as wine comes out of a narrow-mouthed bottle, either too much at once, or none at all. I prithee, take the cork out of thy mouth that I may drink thy tidings" (Act III, Scene 2).

CHAPTER FOUR: VENDANGE

1. Actually, there are seven varieties that are permitted under the Champagne AOC, but because the four "lost" varieties (pinot blanc, pinot gris, arbanne, and petit meslier) represent a tiny fraction of the vines planted, starting dates are only announced for the three primary varieties: chardonnay, pinot noir, and meunier.

2. According to a decree of August 19, 1921, issued by the president of the French republic under advice of the minister of agriculture, a clos is "a plot of vines surrounded by a wall, hedge or fence such that it may not be crossed by a horseman on his mount." There are currently thirty-one clos in Champagne. They tend to be quite small (one of the smallest, Clos des Faubourgs de Notre Dame, is less than three-quarters of an acre!), and each one is owned entirely by one house. In order to carry the word *clos* on the label, all the grapes must come exclusively from that one plot, which must be registered with and approved by the Comité Champagne. Moreover, clos are always vintage-dated wines. See a list of the primary clos currently in production in Appendix II.

3. The estate, in fact, previously belonged to a well-to-do Champenois family named Tarin, from whom Krug purchased grapes long before they decided to sell the property.

4. Some people also make a further distinction called the *coeur de cuvée*, which refers to the juice of the middle of the pressing, after the free-run juice and before the taille.

5. The honor of the oldest commercial (still) wine producer of Champagne, however, goes to Pierre Gosset, who, documentation attests, was a wine producer and wine merchant as early as 1584, as well as the mayor of Aÿ, where the house of Gosset was located. Gosset remained a family business for more than four centuries, until 1994, when the Renaud-Cointreau group acquired the brand.

6. A hundred years later, Pierre Taittinger, head of an old Paris-based family of wine merchants, bought Fourneaux's estate, the Château de la Marquetterie, where he had convalesced from battle injuries during World War I, to start up the Taittinger Champagne house.

7. There were rumors that he actually committed suicide out of remorse at the failure of his wine business, but they have not been substantiated.

8. Tsar Alexander II had his own preferences. See the discussion of Cristal in the section on prestige cuvées on page 153.

9. De Müller would eventually marry into the Ruinart family (thus becoming a distant relative of Barbe-Nicole) and start his own Champagne house called Müeller-Ruinart in 1821. While Müeller-Ruinart no longer exists, a house created by one of Müeller's first employees, Joseph-Jacob (Jacques) Bollinger, most certainly does.

10. The name *Brumaire*, the second month (October 22 to November 20) of the French Revolutionary calendar that was in place from 1793 to 1805, comes from the word *brume* ("fog"), which is typical in France at that time of year. (The preceding month, Vendémiaire, refers to the grape harvest.) The coup took place November 9–10, 1799—or 18–19 Brumaire of the year VII—and was given the name of the month in which it occurred.

11. After reorganizing the military and raising conscripts, Napoleon took the offensive and quickly defeated the Austrian, Russian, and English aggressors. The Treaty of Lunéville (1801) restored the terms of the Campo Formio agreement, which, among other things, extended the sovereignty of France up to the east bank of the Rhine. Shortly thereafter, Napoleon created the new French department of Mont-Tonnerre with the city of Mayence (formerly Mainz), Joseph Krug's birthplace, as its capital.

12. Residual sugar is the amount of sugar that is left in a wine after fermentation is complete.

13. While both Chaptal and François made important advances in winemaking, particularly concerning the first and second fermentations, a thorough understanding of the fermentation process would have to wait for the discoveries of Louis Pasteur, scientist and wine lover, who gave a presentation of his research to the Société des Sciences de Lille in 1857 demonstrating that it is the yeast on grape skins interacting with sugar that produces fermentation, rather than the previously held theory of spontaneous generation. Besides studying wine, he also liked to drink it. Pasteur is quoted as saying, "Wine is the most healthful and most hygienic of beverages," and "A bottle of wine contains more philosophy than all the books in the world."

14. The Romani (of which there are many subgroups in different areas, such as Manouche, Tsiganes, and Roms) originally came from northern India. In the ninth century they arrived in Greece, where a number of tribes reunited, and from there fanned out throughout Europe and, eventually, the New World. They arrived in France at the beginning of the fifteenth century and initially settled on large feudal estates until Louis XIV's persecution under the 1682 *Déclaration du Roy Contre les Bohèmes* (many had come to France from Eastern Europe and so were known as Bohemians) forced them to hide and move around, finding refuge and seasonal work wherever they could. Today French

law gives Roms to the right to pursue ambulatory economic activities and provides them with a *livret de circulation* in the absence of a fixed home or permanent residence. Officially, there are about 250,000 Roms in France, but the actual number is likely closer to twice that.

15. The practice of cutting off the top of the bottle of Champagne with a saber is thought to have originated with Napoleon's light cavalry division, known as the Hussars, for whom it was the most expedient way to get the bottle open. Sabering is sometimes still done today, mostly as a spectacle at festive celebrations. Nowadays a short blade called a *Champagne sword* is used in place of a saber. The technique has more to do with the pressure in the bottle than the sharpness of the blade. The back of the instrument (not the sharp edge of the blade) is slid along the side of the bottle on top of the seam in the glass, gathering force and speed as it meets the lip at the top. The pressure inside, combined with the weak spot in the glass and the force on the lip, causes a clean crack in the top of the neck, shooting the lip of the bottle, cork and all, into the air.

16. The Champagne chosen for the occasion was that of Jacquesson & Fils.

CHAPTER FIVE: FERMENTATION

1. Some of the barrels will undergo a spontaneous second fermentation called *malo-lactic*, during which the harsher malic acid is transformed to a softer lactic acid. Some wineries encourage this secondary fermentation by putting the wine in a warmer place, while others prevent it by keeping the wine cool. Krug says it does neither, simply allowing wine in each of the barrels to undergo malo-lactic fermentation or not.

2. The name *Krug* is of German and/or Ashkenazi Jewish origin. From the Middle High German *kruoc* (meaning "jug" or "drinking vessel"), the name probably originated as the metonymic title of a person who made or sold mugs or jugs. In southern and eastern Germany, *Krug* was used as a nickname for a heavy drinker, while in northern Germany the name was used to indicate a tavern- or innkeeper.

3. Representatives from some two hundred states and city-states, as well as other organizations and special-interest groups, attended the congress, making it the first general summit of its kind in Europe. Besides the Big Four, Portugal, Sweden, and, naturally, France signed the agreement. Spain did not sign but ratified it in a treaty in 1817.

4. While it is possible that Krug had met Herr Daumer in Germany before coming to Paris, there is no documentation of this, and it is just as possible—and, I believe, more likely—that Krug encountered the fellow German only after coming to Paris. Though Mainz was a center of commerce for the Rheinpfalz wine region, there is nothing to indicate that Joseph Krug was ever involved with it. There is a notation of *"Weinhandler"* next to Krug's name in the Mainz

birth registry, but it appears to have been added at a later time (once having begun working in Champagne, he undoubtedly used his Mainz connections to good advantage). Other facts bolster the case that he had no experience with wine before arriving in Paris: As his father had a successful butcher shop, it is likely that he helped out in the business as a young man rather than engaging in something like wine. Because he left home at twenty-four, it is unlikely he would have had much involvement in the world of wine before leaving. His first passport listed his occupation as traveling salesman; had he been a wine merchant it would surely have said so. Finally, if Joseph had been involved or even interested in the wine trade, he would surely have stayed in Mainz rather than moving to Hanau, fifty miles from the Rheinpfalz wine area.

5. Quoted in John Arlott, *Krug, House of Champagne*, 62.

6. The practice of adding selected yeasts to the must to induce fermentation is known as *inoculation*.

7. While the lower level of the cellar, well below ground level and with a maze of chambers extending for what seems like miles, is much cooler and best used for storing wine, the more temperate upper level offers the best conditions for fermentation.

8. Emma's letters are in the Krug archives. I have chosen to quote the translated letter in Arlott, *Krug, House of Champagne*, 68–69.

9. Ibid., 69–70.

10. Ibid., 70–71.

11. In fact, Joseph Krug would continue blending wines for other houses even after the new business was established, as would two successive generations of Krugs who came after him. The house of Krug did not blend for any other houses after 1937.

12. The house of Jacquesson continued to operate as a family business up until the late 1800s; after the death of Adolfe's two sons in the 1860s, the company dwindled. In 1974 the Chiquet family purchased the business, and brothers Laurent and Jean-Hervé continue to produce Champagne under the Jacquesson name.

CHAPTER SIX: TASTING, TASTING, TASTING

1. Pruning the dormant vine is the first step of the annual growing cycle, and one of the most critical. In the Champagne AOC only four specific methods of pruning are permitted: chablis (cane pruning, leaving a number of short bud-bearing branches), cordon (spur pruning on a permanent branch, or *cordon*), guyot (single or double cane pruning, leaving one to two canes and one to two spurs per vine), and vallée de la marne (two cane pruning similar to guyot, used only for meunier).

2. Unfortunately, despite other popular hits, including "Cool Burgundy Ben" and "The Daring Young Man on the Flying Trapeze," the music hall in-

carnation of Champagne Charlie died penniless and largely forgotten on September 15, 1884, at the age of forty-two.

3. Born Élisabeth-Céleste Veinard in Paris in 1824, she too lost her father when she was six and had a negligent mother. She made her debut as a dancer at the Cirque Olympique when she was sixteen and, adopting the stage name Céleste Mogador, became a star at the Bal Mabille helping develop what were to become wildly popular dances like the quadrille and the cancan. Here, among many glamorous and admiring patrons, Céleste met the Comte de Chabrillan, who, much to the chagrin of his family, fell madly in love the dancer and married her in 1854. Her husband became the French consul to Australia and died there in 1858.

4. Boum-Boum the clown, alias Geronimo Medrano, would take over the circus, located at 63 boulevard de Rochechouart in Montmartre, when Fernando left in 1897. While the building was torn down in 1973, the Cirque Medrano still exists today as a traveling circus.

5. Louise-Joséphine Weber died in 1929 and was buried in the cemetery of Pantin outside Paris in an unceremonious ceremony attended by only a few people. In 1992, at the request of her great-grandson Michel Souvais and with the assistance of then mayor Jacques Chirac, her remains were transferred to their proper resting place in Montmartre Cemetery. Céleste Mogador, Comtesse de Chabrillan, fared much better. After retiring from the dance halls of Paris, she built herself a grand country house in the town of Vésinet and named it Chalet Lionel after her husband. In the aftermath of the Franco-Prussian War, however, feeling the house was too large, the solitary comtesse gave it to the Société de Secours aux Alsaciens-Lorrains, which turned it into an orphanage, and moved into a smaller house called the Chalet des Fleurs, where she died in 1909. After La Goulue set off on her own, Valentin le Désossé slipped back into anonymity, contenting himself, one imagines, in the affairs of his wine shop. He did, however, make one last brief reappearance on December 28, 1902, along with Jane Avril, Grille d'Égoût, and la Môme Fromage, at the last dance of the Moulin Rouge, before it was transformed into a theater/concert venue. Perpetually polite, he left these words: "Today is not an ordinary day. I would like to thank all the personnel, employees and guests and, above all, all the women who have chased after me during these long years." ("*Paris, Entre Montmartre et la Place Blanche,*" Moulin Rouge, http://www.moulinrouge.fr/histoire/grandes-periodes. Translated from the French by Alan Tardi.)

6. After the fair, the cask was brought back to Épernay and used for blending until 1947. It is still on display in the winery.

7. Besides the Mercier incident at the Universal Exposition, there is another story concerning Champagne and hot air balloons: During one of the earlier test rides, a balloon was blown off-course and landed in a field. When the terrified peasants saw it coming down, they thought it was some kind of monster and went at it with pitchforks. The only way the occupants could

pacify them and prove they intended no harm was by offering them a glass of Champagne. In any event, it has become a common ritual among balloonists to open a bottle of Champagne upon landing, reciting the Balloonist's Prayer:

> The winds have welcomed you with softness
> The sun has blessed you with its warm hands
> You have flown so high and so well
> That God has joined you in your laughter
> and set you gently back into the loving arms of Mother Earth.

There's another, more succinct toast that may be used on either takeoff or landing: "To soft winds and gentle landings."

8. Known as "La Quarante" after its location at 40 boulevard Lundy, the mansion was demolished in 1971 and a row of townhouses was put in its place. But the cellars under the building were retained, and the Krug family continued to live in quarters on the property for three subsequent generations.

9. The Syndicat du Commerce des Vins de Champagne was created in 1882 and continues to play an important role today as the Union des Maisons de Champagne (UMC).

10. The term was used in 1996 by then Federal Reserve Board chairman Alan Greenspan.

11. Up until 1960, all reserve wines were kept in magnums under cork, but after careful experimentation and examination, they found that stainless-steel tanks offered a better opportunity for reserve wines to mature longer and reach their full potential. In the 1970s, special stainless-steel vats normally used to hold milk were adopted to store reserve wines. And the winery is now in the process of installing a whole new battery of high-tech vats in a variety of sizes that minimize oxidation while still letting the wines breathe.

12. The fridge in the tasting room is stocked with bottles that the enology team must sample and evaluate for some reason or other, such as a slight flaw in the glass bottle, a Champagne that is about ready to be released, or stock that was returned from an importer's overseas warehouse.

13. Eric mentioned that while 2012 was a very difficult year due to excessive rain and hail, the red varieties generally fared better than the white.

14. Working in restaurants for many years, often until very late at night, I developed the habit of eating little or nothing during the day (tasting food as necessary while standing up and on the run) and having a decent meal only after service was over and I could actually sit down. For better or worse, the habit has stuck.

15. Built in 1929, the market, along with the neighborhood, had slipped into seedy decay until being renovated and reopened in 2012.

16. The place is now occupied by another excellent restaurant called Brasserie Les Halles.

17. When I asked restaurateurs why they had no Coteaux Champenois or Rosé des Riceys on their list, they often said it was because they are overpriced and that Burgundy and Provence offer better wines for much less. It may well be true that these wines are a bit expensive, but they are totally unique expressions of the unique territory of Champagne and are completely different from wines of any other area. Whether they are worth the price, however, is up to each individual consumer. I felt they were worth every penny.

18. While Jefferson's experiments with *Vitis vinifera* were largely unsuccessful in his lifetime, one can say that he anticipated and even laid a foundation for future developments of winemaking using European grape varieties in America.

19. The aphid was first officially identified as the cause of the problem in 1868 by a botanist from University of Montpellier named Jules-Emile Planchon, along with his colleagues Felix Sahut and Gaston Bazille, and his findings were confirmed two years later by an American entomologist named Charles Valentine Riley.

20. It is difficult to say who first came up with the idea of grafting as the solution to phylloxera, though a Bordeaux wine grower named Leo Laliman insisted that he was the first to proclaim it publically in 1869 and was therefore entitled to the reward of over three hundred thousand francs offered by the French government. Another early advocate of grafting was Jules-Emile Planchon. In any event, Laliman did not receive the money because, according to the government, he had not invented the technique and because it did not eradicate the insect but merely made the vine more resistant.

21. Some people maintain that there is a subtle but perceptible difference in flavor between wine from grapevines grafted onto American rootstock and wine from vines on ungrafted roots, and they are probably right. There are, in fact, pockets where, for one reason or another, phylloxera was not able to install itself and wreak havoc (such as areas with loose sandy soil or at extremely high altitudes). Bollinger's Champagne called Vieilles Vignes Françaises was originally made from three small vineyards of ungrafted vines, until the Croix Rouge vineyard in Bouzy succumbed to phylloxera in 2004. (Two small ungrafted enclosed vineyards, the Clos des Chaudes Terres and the Clos Saint-Jacques, are still used to make the Champagne.)

22. A group called the Syndicat Antiphylloxerique, funded by the cities of Reims and Épernay and composed of both Champagne merchants and vine growers, was created in 1891 specifically to address the phylloxera problem, but many vine growers refused to join, citing expensive fees and intrusive inspections. The farmers had a fundamental distrust of the government and felt that the wealthy merchants were trying to swindle them. After its first term of five years, the Syndicat was not renewed.

Another group, the Association Viticole Champenoise (AVC), formed in 1898 by twenty-four houses that owned vineyards, made carbon disulfide available to vignerons at little or no cost, but many of them refused to use it.

23. However, these numbers are changing as more grape farmers begin to produce and commercialize their own wine and more houses seek to acquire vineyards of their own. The Comité Champagne currently lists 16,000 vignerons and 320 maisons.

24. The Syndicat du Commerce des Vins de Champagne (today known as the Union des Maisons de Champagnes, or UMC) was created in 1882 by a group of influential houses (including Krug) to protect Champagne and prevent the name from being used—that is, misused—by anyone outside the zone. And in 1904, a similar group called the Fédération des Syndicats de la Champagne was formed, uniting numerous small local groups of farmers into one, to better represent their interests.

25. The attempts of the opposing forces to outflank one another that lead to the creation of the Western Front became known as the "Race to the Sea."

26. Following the end of the war in 1919, restoration of the Reims cathedral began thanks to the financial support of the Rockefeller family, and it's still going on to this day. The cathedral was declared a UNESCO World Heritage Site in 1991.

CHAPTER SEVEN: ASSEMBLAGE

1. The Institut National des Appellations d'Origine (INAO) was created in 1935 by a wine producer of the Rhône Valley named Baron Pierre Le Roy de Boiseaumarié and the French minister of agriculture to regulate and protect the names of well-known wines, which naturally involved defining their area of production and other distinguishing characteristics. The name of the organization was later changed to the Institut National de l'Origine et de la Qualité, but the abbreviation commonly used to refer to it remains "INAO."

2. At the beginning of the German occupation, the Vichy government created a system of Bureaux de Répartition in agricultural areas throughout France to satisfy German demands for food and wine while also meeting the needs of the French population. Champenois growers and producers requested, however, that a special bureau be created for Champagne and the request was granted, essentially turning the Châlons Commission into the Bureau de Répartition du Champagne with the two former heads of the Commission, Robert Jean de Vogüé for the houses and Maurice Doyard for the growers, as its leaders. The Bureau de Répartition du Champagne became the CIVC in 1941.

3. Comte Robert-Jean de Vogüé was Bertrand de Vogüé's brother and a distant cousin of a prominent Burgundian producer named Comte Georges de Vogüé, proprietor of the famed Domaine de la Romanée-Conti estate.

4. While Hitler was a teetotaler, he nonetheless insisted on having ample supplies of Champagne around as a sort of war trophy and to serve to his top generals or other individuals he wanted to impress.

5. Don and Petie Kladstrup, *Wine and War: The French, the Nazis, and the Battle for France's Greatest Treasure* (New York, NY: Broadway Books, 2002), 237.

6. A blend that takes place in the vineyard at harvest rather than in the winery is known as a *field blend*.

7. The prevalence of single-variety, single-vintage, and single-vineyard Champagnes is increasing with the emergence of a new generation of small grower-producers, as we shall see later on.

8. Something similar happened with the practice of creating elaborate sauces, a cornerstone of French cuisine that started from the need to cover the unpleasantness of spoiled meat, and the creation of beautiful perfumes, which began as a way to cover up unpleasant body orders, all of which suggests an special aptitude in the French psyche for turning an unpleasant shortcoming into an appealing art.

9. Dom Pierre Pérignon was considered a master blender, too, but the blends he composed were of grapes going into the press rather than a blend of finished wines, which is a different kind of blending altogether.

10. Krug blended Champagne for other houses up until 1937, when it stopped under the reign of Joseph II. The reason, one imagines, is simply that it was no longer necessary.

11. The word *cuvée* comes from the word for the vat (*cuve*) in which the wines were blended.

12. *Tête de cuvées*, or prestige cuvées, also known as *cuvées spéciales*, are usually aged for an extended time before release, and many of them are made only in certain exceptional years. Made from special blends of the very best grapes from the very best vineyards or *crus*, *tête de cuvées* are the very best, most special, and most expensive wines a house produces.

13. Moët & Chandon had acquired the Abbey of Saint-Pierre in the town of Hautvillers, Dom Pérignon's old stomping grounds, in 1921. According to Richard Juhlin, one of the foremost experts on Champagne, up until 1943, the Dom Pérignon wine was produced from the regular Moët vintage blend that had been aged for an extended period, but from 1947 on it was made from its own special blend.

14. According to Isabelle Pierre, early rosé producers made the wine pink by adding a coloring agent made from elderberries. Mme. Clicquot is thought to have created the *rosé d'assemblage* method of simply adding a bit of red wine to the white wine in 1818, which became the method typically employed in Champagne by those who made rosé. The technique used in most other areas known as *saignée* (from the past tense form of the verb "to bleed") involves bleeding off some of the juice of macerating red grapes after only 24 to 72 hours, resulting in a pale pinkish color. This latter process has historically been used in the production of Rosé des Riceys and has been gaining popularity in other areas of Champagne in recent years.

Despite having been produced quite early on, Champagne rosé really didn't start to catch on until the 1950s and was still considered something of a black (or, shall we say, *pink*) sheep in the region for long after that: "The firms that do make pink Champagne seldom serve it to their guests," wrote Patrick Forbes in

1967. "Indeed, pink Champagne, in the Champagne district, is considered somewhat of a *question délicate*, and is best avoided." Forbes goes on to explain the reason for the delicacy:

> The twentieth-century Champenois is intensely aware, and proud, of his inheritance. He knows that immense efforts were expended by his forebears to build up the smooth-running businesses with which he is connected today. And, being a realist, he knows perfectly well that the Rock of Gibraltar on which his inheritance rests is a golden sparkling wine. To him there is something unreal about pink champagne. . . . He considers it alien to the mainstream of his destiny; he makes it because many of his own countrymen and many foreigners like it; but he would not consider that the end of the world had come if not another drop was ever made again. [*Champagne: The Wine, the Land and the People*, 377–378.]

15. The Côte des Bar has become quite well known for its *blanc de blancs* made from pinot blanc, which is locally referred to as *vrai blanc*, and a number of mostly smaller producers in the Marne have been experimenting with making a Champagne from one or a combination of the four lost white varieties.

16. Under AOC regulations, a vintage-labeled Champagne must mature in the cellar for at least three years, instead of the fifteen months for a nonvintage one.

17. See note 2 on page 247 for a definition of a Champagne clos. For a list of the primary clos currently in production, see Appendix II.

18. John Arlott, *Krug, House of Champagne*, 103–105. Arlott includes a photo of the text in Joseph Krug's notebook on page 104. The same material from Joseph Krug's notebook is quoted in French by Henri and Rémi Krug in *L'Art du Champagne*, 76–78.

19. In his notebook, Krug indicated the basic composition of the two blends, including the specific crus and percentages to be used, along with their respective *liqueurs de tirage*, which are listed in both of the above-mentioned sources.

20. Because Champagne houses typically maintain large stocks of reserve wines, they are able to decide how much wine to release in any given year and how much to hold for future use. (This is very different from other wine-producing areas, whose production is closely based on what they are able to harvest in any given year.) While some vintages might yield a bit more or less, the cardinal rules here are that what is released onto the market must be in line with actual demand and that what goes out of the cellar must be replaced with new wine coming in. Most medium to large Champagne houses keep stocks equivalent to about three years of normal sales Krug maintains about eight years of stock.

21. Just as each Champagne producer can respond strategically to the demand for their wines, the entire region can also respond to overall market

demand by such bureaucratic measures as raising or lowering the maximum yield of grapes per hectare or allowing for release of wine from each supplier's personal reserve. Each grower in Champagne is allowed a personal reserve of up to eight thousand kilos of grapes (or its equivalent in still wine) compiled from excess over the maximum yield per hectare to be used as a buffer against less-abundant harvests. This reserve is referred to as a *blockage*. A grower must request and receive an official permission of *déblocage* in order to draw from this reserve.

22. When Marcel Duchamp entered a urinal in an exhibition of the Society of Independent Artists in 1917, he declared that anything an artist calls art is art, and Andy Warhol took this concept to new heights of popular awareness by suggesting that anyone who calls himself an artist is (as long as he can get other people to think so too).

23. The three variations on the primary blend subtly employ other available "elements" from the Krug cellars, but I was asked not to reveal what they are.

24. Before coming to Krug, Eric was the chef de cave for ten years at the house of de Venoge in Épernay, founded in 1837 by Swiss-born Henri-Marc de Venoge.

25. Tirage, which essentially refers to the bottling of wines for the *prise de mousse*, cannot legally take place before January 1 following the harvest, though Krug typically waits until mid- to late March.

26. Twenty-four grams of sugar per liter of wine will produce around 6 kg/cm^2 of pressure by the end of the second alcoholic fermentation.

27. The crown cap, invented by a Baltimore-based mechanical engineer of Irish descent named William Painter in 1889 (patented in 1892), was not widely adopted in Champagne for the second fermentation until around 1960. Prior to that a temporary cork was used that was held in place by a metal clip (called an *agrafe* in French), which also required a squared-off lip on the mouth of the bottle (*bague carré*) to hold it. While the majority of Champagne houses switched to crown caps, some continue to use *tirage sur liège* (cork) for certain cuvées, while other, very small producers continued to use it for their entire production. Today the practice of using cork instead of crown caps for the *prise de mousse* and subsequent maturation period is experiencing something of a comeback, especially on the part of small grower-producers. According to Henri Krug, the risk of corkiness and oxidation was extremely high: "We made numerous tastings to compare wines closed with corks and those closed with metal capsules, and after five or six years of experimentation, it became clear to us that there was no distinguishable qualitative difference between the two. So why then continue to run these very high risks?" (Henri and Rémi Krug, *L'Art du Champagne*, 56.) Translated from the French by Alan Tardi.

28. "*Latte*" may also be used in the plural form, with an *s* at the end, but the meaning is the same.

CHAPTER EIGHT: LET THERE BE BUBBLES

1. Though the process of making a wine sparkle is generally referred to as the *second fermentation* (second, that is, to the first, or alcoholic, fermentation) or re-fermentation, it is, in cases where a malo-lactic fermentation has taken place, actually the third. Though sugar is often added (chaptalization) to boost alcohol during the first (alcoholic) fermentation, it is minimal; most of the sugar involved in the fermentation is that which is already present in the grapes.

2. Actually, the thin cork lining and slightly porous material of the polyethylene *bidule* do permit a minuscule transference of oxygen to occur during the extended maturation period, but the microscopic pores in the material are too small to permit the escape of carbon dioxide.

3. Joseph Priestly (1733–1804), an English theologian, scientist, natural philosopher, and liberal political theorist, discovered how to infuse liquid with carbon dioxide gas in 1767. Five years later he published a pamphlet called "Directions for Impregnating Water with Fixed Air." While Priestly did not exploit his discovery commercially, many others did, such as J. J. Schweppe, who founded a factory in Geneva in 1783 to produce bubbly water based on Priestly's process. While Priestly discovered a method to make water bubbly, it can also emerge from the earth already "carbonized" by essentially undergoing the same process naturally on its long journey from deep below the earth to the surface, though naturally sparkling mineral waters are a definite minority.

As a footnote to a footnote, due to his unorthodox religious and political beliefs (and his outspokenness at voicing them), Joseph Priestly was forced to flee England after his house and church were burned down by an angry mob and eventually made his way to Northumberland County, Pennsylvania, where he spent the last ten years of his life.

4. There are about 3.375 ml of dissolved carbon dioxide in a standard 750 ml bottle of Champagne.

5. In a closed bottle under pressure, the liquid is supercharged with carbonic gas molecules dispersed throughout, but because the environment is one of total equilibrium, there are no bubbles. In another environment of total atmospheric equilibrium, such as outer space, with zero gravity, there would not be any bubbles either.

6. Though other factors, such as the age of the wine and the amount of sugar added for the *prise de mousse*, certainly have an impact.

7. This is a phenomenon known as *Ostwald ripening*.

8. Much of the information in this section was extracted from Gérard Liger-Belair's book, *Uncorked: The Science of Champagne*, which also contains many of his high-speed macroscopic bubble photos.

9. Ravenscroft, who had developed a thriving London-based import-export business, lived in Venice between 1651 and 1666, where he was involved in

the glass trade, and it is likely that he learned about the advantages of lead oxide in Murano.

10. Other legends say the *coupe* was modeled on the breast of Madame de Pompadour, or Madame du Barry, who followed her as mistress to Louis XV, or Napoleon's wife, Empress Joséphine, or Diane de Poitiers, mistress of Henry II, or even Helen of Troy.

11. In ancient Greek, Roman, and Etruscan traditions, *mastoi* were probably used in rituals and as votive offerings. An elderly person drinking milk out of a *mastos* may have symbolized rebirth in the afterlife and represented a reenactment of the goddess Hera (Juno in Roman mythology) giving her breast to the infant Hercules, thus making him immortal.

Yet one more thing to suggest that the association between Marie Antoinette's breast cup and the Champagne coupe is pure fancy is the fact that they don't even look alike. While the *mastos* has a deep parabolic curve with no stem or attached base and a nipple on the bottom, the coupe bowl is wide and shallow and nippleless. In fact, its shape resembles more closely another ancient Greek drinking vessel called a *kylix*, which typically had a wide shallow bowl with a short stem and a base and was used specifically for the consumption of wine at *symposia* (drinking parties, which often got a bit raucous). The saucerlike interior was often painted with sexually suggestive scenes that only became visible after the wine was drunk; the shallow shape enabled the participants to drink while reclining, as they usually were at *symposia*, and also facilitated playing a game called *kottabos*, which consisted of flinging the sediment left in the cup at targets, all of which would probably have made the *kylix* a big hit at the dance halls and brothels of Belle Époque Paris.

12. Sigmund Freud might find more interesting fetish fodder in the crystal slipper glass that high-fashion shoe designer Christian Louboutin did for Piper-Heidsieck in 2009, though even he might be a bit perplexed about how to actually drink from it.

13. In 2012 Krug resolved the glass issue by commissioning a glass called "Le Joseph," designed especially for the Grande Cuvée (and other Krug wines) by the Bavarian manufacturer Riedel. The company, founded in 1756, has been specializing in variety specific wineglasses since the 1950s and is now custom-designing glasses to reflect the particular styles of select producers.

CHAPTER NINE:
MATURATON AND DISGORGEMENT

1. Those factors: (1) second fermentation in an individual bottle, (2) extended maturation on the lees, and (3) disgorgement. As for *autolysis* (p. 179), wine tasters sometimes use the term "autolytic" as an adjective to describe pronounced sensory characteristics of the decomposed yeast particles in a Champagne.

2. Yeast is a particularly good scavenger of oxygen, which helps create a reductive atmosphere, thus limiting oxidation and prolonging the life of the wine.

3. During the golden years of Paul I, there was a period when he acquired some vineyards, mostly to help out a friend who needed to sell them, but he sold them off several years later to finance the wedding of his son, Joseph II.

4. While producing a single-vintage single-variety *blanc de blancs* Champagne from the Clos du Mesnil might not have been the intention when they acquired the vineyard, the Krugs were surely familiar with the *blanc de blancs* of Le Mesnil-sur-Oger first produced by Eugène Aimé Salon in 1921 and thereafter only in exceptional vintages, as well as the Clos des Goisses that Philipponnat began bottling in 1935.

5. When I posed a question about the Rémy Martin acquisition, Olivier Krug stressed that "this was not a sudden purchase by external investors but rather a progressive alliance between two families united by the same quest for excellence and with the same strategic issues for their businesses."

6. Most producers today use a hollow polyurethane plug called a *bidule*, which helps collect the sediment.

7. The gyropallete was created by Champagne producers Claude Cazals and Jacques Ducoin in 1968.

8. Special sizes, small lots, and half bottles are still riddled by hand.

9. There are seven officially recognized levels of sweetness in Champagne (measured in grams per liter):

     -Brut Nature (Pas Dosé, Zéro Dosage): less than 3 g/l
     -Extra Brut: less than 6 g/l
     -Brut: less than 12 g/l
     -Extra Sec/Extra Dry: 12–17 g/l
     -Sec/Dry: 17–32 g/l
     -Demi-sec: 32–50 g/l
     -Doux/Sweet: 50+ g/l

10. Cork became the preferred closure for wine due to its porous structure, which not only prevents the liquid from escaping the bottle prematurely but also permits a slow exchange of oxygen, which can be beneficial for wines that are meant to age over a long period of time. While cork stoppers can be made from a single piece of cork bark, due to the extremely high pressure inside a bottle of Champagne, an especially wide (thirty-one-millimeter) cork was required. Because it would be nearly impossibly to cut such a large cork out of a single piece, a special agglomerated cork was developed for Champagne composed of small particles of cork compressed into a large cylindrical plug with several discs of natural cork glued onto the bottom, which is the part that actually comes into contact with the wine. The characteristic mushroom-like

shape that emerges from an opened bottle comes from the bottom half of the agglomerated cork having been squeezed into the narrow mouth of the bottle.

The small disc of metal that is placed on top of the cork to prevent the metal wires from digging into it is called the *plaque de muselet* and, because at usually bears the name and/or logo of the producer, is often kept as a souvenir of the bottle and the occasion on which it was consumed.

11. One of the earliest Champagnes to receive extended lees aging was Dom Pérignon, which was created in 1921 but not released until 1936. In 1963, Bollinger, in association with its US agent, released a limited amount of re-cently disgorged Champagne from 1947, before initiating the Bollinger R.D. in 1967 with three recently disgorged vintages—1952, 1953, and 1955.

CHAPTER TEN: INTO THE WORLD

1. A winemaker named Anselme Selosse jump-started this revolution in 1980 when he took over his family winery in the town of Avize and focused intensely on the expression of terroir in his wines, encouraging a whole new generation of other small grower producers to emerge.

2. While Krug has thus far not shown any interest in the four other grape varieties, it has historically been a big supporter of meunier, typically using an unusually higher percentage of it in its wines than most other houses.

3. Three examples are: L'Original from Pierre Gerbais in the Aube, made from 100 percent pinot vrai blanc; BAM! from Tarlant, which combines pinot blanc, arbane, and petit meslier; and Les 7 from Laherte Frères, which com-bines all seven approved grape varieties.

4. Lebel was the one to raise concern about the shortage of reserve stocks in 2012, which resulted in the decision to not make a vintage that year, and also advocated for the declassification of a would-be Clos du Mesnil 1999 be-cause he and his team did not consider it quite up to snuff.

5. Zack O'Malley Greenburg, "Hip-Hop's Unofficial Sommelier," *Forbes*, August 17, 2010, http://www.forbes.com/2010/08/17/branson-b-champagne -business-entertainment-hip-hop-cash-kings-sommelier.html.

6. V. Christophe Navarre is chief executive officer of wines and spirits at LVMH.

7. Henríquez is now married to that fiancé, Canadian-born Gérard Sibourd-Baudry.

8. Fabienne Moreau has been head of the Patrimony Department of MHCS (Moët Hennessy Champagne Services, a division that oversees all LVMH Cham-pagne brands) since 2003. Isabelle Pierre is her colleague in the department.

9. "Thrown open" figuratively speaking: because Krug is a small house without facilities or personnel to readily accommodate the public, visits are limited and available only by reservation.

10. Michael Edwards, *The Finest Wines of Champagne: A Guide to the Best Cuvées, Houses, and Growers* (Berkeley: University of California Press, 2009), 57.

EPILOGUE

1. While this poses potential problems for traditional wine-growing regions like Champagne, it opens up opportunities for other areas that were previously unable to grow wine grapes, such as the United Kingdom, whose inability to produce wine had a significant impact on the development of Champagne.

2. Journalist, author, and sparkling wine authority Tom Stevenson was largely responsible for bringing detailed information about these goings-on to the world outside Champagne.

3. Authorization to plant new plots will be gradually phased in so as not to exceed 1–2 percent of the current vineyard, in order to avoid any sudden increase in production (this on top of the fact that it takes seven to eight years for a new vineyard to reach full productivity), and the farming of any declassified vineyard areas will be gradually phased out.

4. Louise Nordstrom, "After 200 Years, Champagne Lost Fizz, Not Flavor," Associated Press, November 17, 2010.

5. Beginning in 2016, Krug will begin a new program of Grande Cuvée labeling whereby, in addition to the bottle ID number on the back, each label will bear an edition number which corresponds to the years since Joseph Krug first began releasing the special Champagne he envisioned. As Krug & Cie. began operations in 1843, the first edition of his wine was released the following year (edition number one) and every year thereafter. The 2013-based Grande Cuvée will thus be the 169th edition.

RESOURCES

BOOKS

There are many excellent books on Champagne, as befits a wine of such widespread appeal and immense cultural significance. Here are a few that were especially useful to me in writing this book:

John Arlott, Krug, *House of Champagne* (London, UK: Davis-Poynter Ltd., 1976).

Henri and Rémi Krug *L'Art du Champagne* (Paris: R. Laffont, 1979).

Michael Edwards, *The Finest Wines of Champagne: A Guide to the Best Cuvées, Houses and Growers* (London: Aurum Press Ltd., 2009).

Patrick Forbes, *Champagne: The Wine, the Land and the People* (London: Gollancz, 1983).

Richard Juhlin, *A Scent of Champagne* (New York: Skyhorse Publishing, 2013).

Petie and Don Kladstrup, *Champagne: How the World's Most Glamorous Wine Triumphed Over War and Hard Times* (New York: Harper Perennial, 2006).

Gérard Liger-Belair, *Uncorked: The Science of Champagne* (Princeton University Press, 2004).

Tilar J. Mazzeo, *The Widow Clicquot* (New York: Harper Business, 2009).

Tom Stevenson and Essi Avellan, *Christie's World Encyclopedia of Champagne & Sparkling Wine* (New York: Sterling Epicure, 2014).

Henry Vizetelly, *A History of Champagne* (London: Vizetelly & Co. and New York: Scribner & Welford, 1882).

WEB

Of the bounty of Champagne information on the Internet, I found these websites particularly informative:

www.champagne.fr is the official site of the Comité Champagne (CIVC).

www.sgv-champagne.fr The Syndicat General des Vignerons and www.champagnesdevignerons.com Les Champagnes des Vignerons, are websites of Champagne grower organizations.

www.maisons-champagne.com is the site of the Union des Maisons de Champagne (UMC) and Syndicat des Grandes Marques de Champagne

www.champagneguide.net is an excellent and informative website by American Peter Liem.

Pasquale Catanzariti

ALAN TARDI is an award-winning writer specializing in wine and food. He has worked as a chef, restaurateur, sommelier, and consultant in some of New York City's finest restaurants and has written numerous stories for publications including the *New York Times*, *Wine Spectator*, *Wine & Spirits*, *Decanter*, and *Food Arts*. He is the author of *Romancing the Vine: Life, Love and Transformation in the Vineyards of Barolo*, which won the James Beard Award for Best Wine and Spirits Book in 2006. He divides his time between New York and Castiglione Falletto, Italy.

PublicAffairs is a publishing house founded in 1997. It is a tribute to the standards, values, and flair of three persons who have served as mentors to countless reporters, writers, editors, and book people of all kinds, including me.

I. F. STONE, proprietor of *I. F. Stone's Weekly*, combined a commitment to the First Amendment with entrepreneurial zeal and reporting skill and became one of the great independent journalists in American history. At the age of eighty, Izzy published *The Trial of Socrates*, which was a national bestseller. He wrote the book after he taught himself ancient Greek.

BENJAMIN C. BRADLEE was for nearly thirty years the charismatic editorial leader of *The Washington Post*. It was Ben who gave the *Post* the range and courage to pursue such historic issues as Watergate. He supported his reporters with a tenacity that made them fearless and it is no accident that so many became authors of influential, best-selling books.

ROBERT L. BERNSTEIN, the chief executive of Random House for more than a quarter century, guided one of the nation's premier publishing houses. Bob was personally responsible for many books of political dissent and argument that challenged tyranny around the globe. He is also the founder and longtime chair of Human Rights Watch, one of the most respected human rights organizations in the world.

· · ·

For fifty years, the banner of Public Affairs Press was carried by its owner Morris B. Schnapper, who published Gandhi, Nasser, Toynbee, Truman, and about 1,500 other authors. In 1983, Schnapper was described by *The Washington Post* as "a redoubtable gadfly." His legacy will endure in the books to come.

Peter Osnos, *Founder and Editor-at-Large*